Waterfalls & Wildflowers
in the Southern Appalachians

Waterfalls & Wildflowers

in the Southern Appalachians

THIRTY GREAT HIKES

Timothy P. Spira

The University of North Carolina Press   CHAPEL HILL

*This book was published with the assistance of the Wells Fargo Fund
for Excellence of the University of North Carolina Press.*

Designed by Kimberly Bryant
Set in Utopia and Museo types by Rebecca Evans
Manufactured in the United States of America
The paper in this book meets the guidelines for permanence
and durability of the Committee on Production Guidelines for
Book Longevity of the Council on Library Resources. The University
of North Carolina Press has been a member of the Green Press
Initiative since 2003.

Cover illustrations: Pearson's Falls; sundrops (*Oenothera fruticosa*).
Courtesy of the author

Complete cataloging information can be obtained online at the
Library of Congress catalog website.
ISBN 978-1-4696-2264-4 (pbk.: alk. paper)
ISBN 978-1-4696-2265-1 (ebook)

There's something about a *waterfall* that digs deep in the psyche.

Maybe it's the sound.

Some say it's the way the falling water stirs the air.

Whatever the reason, I'm drawn to them.

So is everyone else.

—John Lane, *Chattooga* (2004)

Contents

Illustrations of basic plant structures appear at the back of the book, after the index.

I thank my spouse, Lisa Wagner, for her support, understanding, and valuable input during this project. Without her help, this book would not have been possible. George Ellison and Tom Wentworth provided helpful comments that improved the manuscript. I gratefully acknowledge the contributions of Dixie Damrel, Karen Patterson, William Standaert, Johnny Townsend, and Claiborne Woodall. I would also like to express my appreciation to Kathryn Stripling Byer, Thomas Rain Crowe, George Ellison, and Peter White for contributing original poems, to Elizabeth Ellison for the waterfall illustration, and to John Lane for allowing me to use an excerpt from his book, *Chattooga*. Special thanks to the staff at the University of North Carolina Press, especially senior executive editor Elaine Maisner, project editor Paul Betz (with the assistance of copyeditor Brendan Sutherland), design director Kim Bryant, and production manager Heidi Perov. I am indebted to Clemson University for supporting my work on this project. Finally, I would like to thank those who manage, maintain, and support the National Forests, National Parks, State Parks, and other public lands that make the southern Appalachian Mountains such a wonderful place.

Acknowledgments

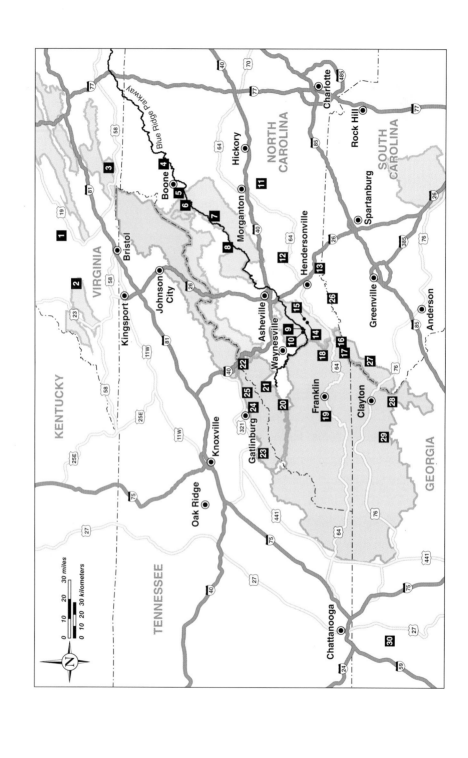

MAP LEGEND (FOR ALL MAPS)

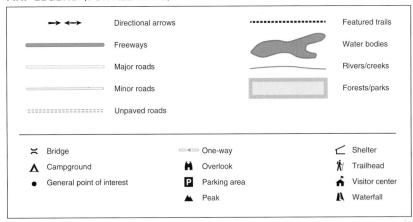

➜ ⟷	Directional arrows	▪▪▪▪▪▪▪▪▪▪▪▪▪▪▪▪▪	Featured trails
	Freeways		Water bodies
	Major roads		Rivers/creeks
	Minor roads		Forests/parks
═════════════════	Unpaved roads		

⋈ Bridge	⇔ One-way	⌐ Shelter
⋀ Campground	⛫ Overlook	🚶 Trailhead
● General point of interest	P Parking area	⌂ Visitor center
	▲ Peak	⬧ Waterfall

1 Big Falls	**16** Rainbow Falls
2 Falls on the Little Stony	**17** Whitewater Falls
3 Cabin Creek Falls	**18** Panthertown Valley
4 Cascades Trail	**19** Rufus Morgan Falls
5 Glen Burney Trail	**20** Deep Creek
6 Tanawha Trail	**21** Chasteen Creek Cascade
7 Linville Falls	**22** Big Creek
8 Crabtree Falls	**23** Abrams Falls
9 Skinny Dip Falls	**24** Rainbow Falls
10 Graveyard Fields	**25** Ramsey Cascades
11 High Shoals Falls	**26** Jones Gap Falls
12 Hickory Nut Falls	**27** Station Cove Falls
13 Pearson's Falls	**28** Panther Creek Falls
14 Moore Cove Falls	**29** Anna Ruby Falls
15 Twin Falls	**30** Pocket Falls

Locations of Waterfall Hikes

Waterfalls & Wildflowers
in the Southern Appalachians

PATTERNS

June 20, 2013 . . . Mid-morning
. . . Southwestern Virginia
From a ledge I watch as you
     move surefootedly from
rock to rock seeking the right
     angle in the right light
in the right frame of mind to
     capture on film the innate
disposition of yet another
     waterfall. Ghostly patterns
dissolve and then reappear as
     the tapestry of water
descends into the dark circle
     of its plunge pool.
The current spirals first
     clockwise then counter-
clockwise from bank to bank
     until a sluice carved
in stone by water and grit eons
     ago *suddenly*
diverts fallen water on its way
     again.

—George Ellison
Bryson City, North Carolina

PART I
Introduction

The southern Appalachians are well known for abundant waterfalls and diverse wildflowers. This book will guide you to scenic waterfalls and help you discover and enjoy wildflowers and other natural features along the way. Bring your enthusiasm and curiosity as you hike some of the best trails in the region for both waterfalls and wildflowers.

The guidebook is written for a wide audience, including casual visitors to the region, waterfall lovers, wildflower enthusiasts, hikers, naturalists, birders, and nature photographers.

It is organized into four sections. Part I lays the groundwork by providing background information on the southern Appalachians, their waterfalls and wildflowers, as well as safety tips. Brief descriptions of ten common plant communities in Part II will help you learn about wildflowers within the context of their natural communities, including rich cove forest, rocky streamside, spray cliff, and oak hickory forest.

A detailed guide to 30 waterfall hikes with good to excellent seasonal wildflower viewing comprises Part III. The hike narratives describe the waterfalls, wildflowers, plant communities, birds, and other natural features encountered along each trail. Most of the hikes are in western North Carolina (where waterfalls are most abundant), but hikes in southwestern Virginia, southeastern Tennessee, northwestern South Carolina, and northern Georgia are also included. All are day hikes, with round-trip distances ranging from less than one mile at Pearson's Falls to eight miles at Ramsey Cascades.

The profiles of 125 plants (each with an accompanying photo) in Part IV will help you identify common and conspicuous wildflowers. All are herbaceous (nonwoody) plants, except for 15 shrubs. Whether you're just learning about wildflowers or are already familiar with them, this book will enhance your knowledge and appreciation. Sections at the back of the book include a glossary, an index of wildflowers profiled, and line drawings of basic plant structures.

The highest mountains in eastern North America are found in the southern Appalachians. With more than 2,500 species of flowering plants, the region constitutes one of the most species-rich temperate deciduous forests in the world. Renowned for its wildflower displays, Great Smoky Mountains National Park has more species of flowering plants than any other park in the continental United States. A highly variable topography, coupled with a wide diversity of soils, climates, and geology, has fostered the enormous diversity of plant species that we see today, particularly in the southern Appalachians, where glaciers didn't scour the landscape.

The southern Appalachians have a remarkable number of waterfalls, including more than 1,000 in the mountains of western North Carolina alone. The high concentration of waterfalls in the region reflects the geology and high rainfall (upwards of 90 inches per year in some areas). A waterfall can be defined as a place where flowing water rapidly drops in elevation as it flows over a cliff or steep slope. Most waterfalls form where a stream encounters more resistant rock, but fault lines and earthquakes can cause rock masses to shift, altering the natural course of water flow and forming a waterfall.

From multiple cascades to tall free-falling water, each waterfall has its own unique character. But waterfalls are not static. A waterfall can be a gentle trickle of water one day. Then, after a heavy rainstorm, when rivers carry huge amounts of water, that same waterfall becomes a raging torrent of water. But, it's not only rainfall that determines the amount of water flowing, the total area drained by the stream (the size of the drainage basin) is also a factor.

Seasonal differences in foliage, subtle changes in light, and directional changes in the sun also change the appearance of waterfalls, providing a different perspective on successive visits. You may even spot a rainbow when sunlight passes through the mist of falling water. Each droplet of water acts as a tiny prism that disperses light into a full spectrum of colors reflected back to you.

Some waterfalls enchant you as water gently glides over bedrock. Others impress with their free-falling water and tumbling cascades, still others awe you with their sheer power. Something about watching falling water and hearing the roar of water striking the rocks and pool below is exhilarating, energizing, calming, and inspiring. Waterfalls make you feel good.

Using This Guidebook

PLANT COMMUNITY PROFILES (PART II)

The hike narratives take you through a number of plant communities, a term that refers to the kinds of plants that occur together in a particular place. In this section, I profile ten of the most prominent communities. Regional landscapes, including the hikes described in this book, often have a mosaic of plant communities present, reflecting differences in moisture availability, soil characteristics, geology, disturbance history, and other factors. Because adjoining communities often grade into one another, it can be difficult to tell where one plant community ends and another begins.

HIKE NARRATIVES (PART III)

At the beginning of each hike you'll find the following information.

Name of falls, trail, or area. Also included is the agency responsible for managing the property on which the trail is located.

Highlights. Lists some of the best features of the hike.

Flowering season. Typical period when you can expect to find some wildflowers in bloom.

Peak flowering. When the most wildflowers are likely to be in bloom. This may vary from year to year depending on the amount of rainfall and temperatures. Elevation also influences flowering times. While lower elevations may experience peak flowering in mid- to late March, spring may not come to the higher mountains until early May.

Trail length. Round trip distance is given, either out and back from the trailhead, or along a loop.

Trail rating. Based on adults in reasonably good physical condition. Ratings range from easy to strenuous depending on elevation change, distance, and terrain. You may want to read the full hike description when determining its suitability.

Elevation. Approximate trailhead elevation followed by either the high or low point of each hike. Trails with a number of ascents and descents are noted in the hike descriptions and their ratings are adjusted to reflect the added difficulty.

Nearest town. The closest town to the trailhead is given.

Contact. Phone number and website are listed for the agency responsible for managing the property on which the trail is located.

Directions. Driving instructions and GPS coordinates help get you to the trail-head. Be sure to have your own highway maps or other resources for additional reference.

Abbreviations for roads

I	Interstate
U.S.	National Highway
N.C.	Major State Road
S.R.	Secondary Road
F.R.	Forest (Service) Road

Overview. A brief summary introduces you to the hike.

The Hike. This section provides a detailed description of the hike, including information on waterfalls, wildflowers, plant communities, and other natural features, including birds and other animals. Common names for wildflowers may appear more than once in a hike description, since a species may be fading in one area but still blooming at higher elevations or in more moist or sheltered sites. Not every plant that grows along the trail is listed, leaving for you the fun of discovering and identifying other wildflowers in the area. Be aware that flooding, tree falls, and other factors can alter trails, river crossings, and the composition of wildflowers.

Maps. The maps included in this guidebook provide a general reference for the hikes described. If you plan to explore other nearby trails or do off-trail hiking, you'll want to bring along a more detailed map of the area.

Options. Opportunities to extend the hike (or explore nearby areas) are briefly described.

Species lists. Each hike includes a seasonal list of some of the more common, conspicuous, and unusual wildflowers along the trail.

WILDFLOWER PROFILES (PART IV)

Photos and descriptions of 125 species help you identify (and discover interesting features) of some of the more common and conspicuous wildflowers seen along the hikes described in this book. For added interest, some rare and unusual plants are also included. A glossary and line drawings of basic plant structures are included in the back of this book as a reference.

The wildflower profiles and the species lists (included in the community profiles and hike narratives) include both the common and scientific names of plants. While common names are widely used, they can be confusing as wildflowers frequently have multiple common names, depending on region, tradition, and source. A plant's scientific name is the most reliable because, no matter how widely distributed, each species has only one valid scientific name.

Scientific names consist of two parts: the genus name (capitalized) and a specific epithet (lowercase). Scientific names are italicized and generic names are sometimes abbreviated, as in *V. blanda*, where *V.* stands for *Viola*. If a particular species has recently been given a different scientific name, the previously used scientific name (called a synonym) is also listed in the species profile. The scientific names used in this guidebook generally conform to the terminology found in Alan S. Weakley's *Flora of the Southern and Mid-Atlantic States* (see reference on the next page).

If you want a more complete representation of the region's flora, consider obtaining a wildflower identification guide. Here are three of my favorites:

Horn, Dennis, David Duhl, Thomas E. Hemmerly, Tavia Cathcart, and Tennessee Native Plant Society. 2005. *Wildflowers of Tennessee, the Ohio Valley, and the Southern Appalachians.* Auburn, Wash.: Lone Pine. This guide includes descriptions of more than 1,250 species with color photographs.

Spira, Timothy P. 2011. *Wildflowers and Plant Communities of the Southern Appalachian Mountains and Piedmont: A Naturalist's Guide to the Carolinas, Virginia, Tennessee, and Georgia.* Chapel Hill: University of North Carolina Press. This book has wildflowers organized by plant community; includes photos, descriptions, and interesting information on 340 species and 21 natural plant communities.

Weakley, Alan S. 2012. *Flora of the Southern and Mid-Atlantic States.* This ebook is available online via the University of North Carolina Herbarium website; it's a comprehensive guide for more advanced wildflower enthusiasts.

For Your Safety

A well-prepared hiker carries the following: adequate water, food, extra clothing, waterproof matches, map, compass, flashlight, first-aid kit, and knife. I try to keep each of these items in my daypack, as it's better to have them and not need them than to need them and not have them.

Communicate your itinerary. Whether you're hiking alone or in a group, let someone know where you'll be hiking and when you expect to return.

Dress in layers, and always bring rain gear as weather conditions can change quickly in the mountains.

Reduce the risk of twisting an ankle by wearing good hiking shoes.

Stay on designated trails and away from cliff faces.

Be prepared to turn around if the trail is too difficult, the weather deteriorates, or daylight is waning.

Don't drink the water. No matter how clear (or pure) it looks, don't drink backcountry water, as it's likely to be contaminated by harmful bacteria and viruses. Instead, take water with you or bring a filtering device or purifier.

Stay out of fast-flowing streams as you can quickly lose control and be swept away.

Be safe around waterfalls. As beautiful as waterfalls are, they can be *extremely dangerous* if you put yourself in a bad situation. To reduce the risk of injury, stay on designated trails, observe all warning signs, and keep a close eye on children and pets. Use common sense and pay close attention to your surroundings. A good rule of thumb is to never put yourself in a position where you'll be seriously hurt if you fall. Don't get too close to the top of a waterfall, avoid climbing on waterfalls, and don't cross a stream anywhere near the top of a waterfall. Watch out for wet or algae-covered rocks, as slippery surfaces are the most common cause of injuries near waterfalls. Avoid diving into pools at the base of waterfalls as tree limbs and rocks may lie close to the surface.

Protecting Nature

Don't dig up wildflowers or pick flowers.

Stay on established trails (taking shortcuts not only destroys wildflowers, it also causes erosion and makes trails harder to follow).

Don't trample vegetation.

Avoid climbing on banks of waterfalls as the thin soils and plants they support are particularly vulnerable to disturbance.

Respect wildlife.

Take only photos and leave only footprints.

The magic of waterfalls and wildflowers can't be fully appreciated in words or photographs—they need to be seen and experienced. See you on the trail!

COMMUNITY
(FOREST AND THE TREES)
Maple, ash, and birch
Hemlock, basswood, beech
What is this assembled crew?
A fast grower, slow grower.
Shade lover, light lover.
Some feed birds for traveling seeds
But others send seeds freely on
   the wind.
The different trees
Have different personalities.
But are they the pieces of a
   symphony
Or just some random company?
Sit and listen, sit and watch, enjoy
   the forest's mystery.

—Peter White
Chapel Hill, North Carolina

PART II
Plant Community Profiles

Mid- to High Elevation Communities

HEATH BALD

Distinguishing Features
Heath balds differ from other high elevation communities in that the vegetation consists of a dense layer of shrubs with stunted trees and a sparse herbaceous layer.

Introduction
Heath balds are dense mostly evergreen shrublands that grow on exposed peaks, narrow sharp ridges, and steep slopes. Locals refer to them simply as "balds" or "slicks" for their smooth appearance when viewed from a distance. Up close, heath balds are anything but smooth as the vegetation typically consists of a tangled mass of branches that makes hiking off trails difficult if not impossible. A typical heath bald has only 10–20 species of flowering plants, most of which are shrubs in the heath (Ericaceae) family.

Heath balds form on landslide scars, grassy balds, and rock outcrops as well as on previously forested sites, where high winds, fires, or logging eliminated the trees but not the understory shrubs. Once established, heath balds often persist because dense shade, thick leaf litter, and shallow dry acidic soils make it difficult for trees to establish from seed. Some heath balds are still treeless after more than 100 years.

Vegetation
The vegetation ranges from dense impenetrable shrub thickets 3–12 feet tall to more open shrubland. High elevation balds are commonly dominated by Catawba rhododendron, an evergreen shrub that produces spectacular clusters of deep pink-to-purple flowers. Their flowering attracts thousands of visitors to the mountains

in late spring. Other common shrubs include mountain laurel, rosebay rhododendron, and highbush blueberry. Mountain laurel produces dense clusters of white-to-pinkish flowers in spring. Rosebay's mostly white flowers open in summer. The small flowers of highbush blueberry may not catch your eye, but its delicious sweet berries in summer will please your palate. The rare pinkshell azalea, a deciduous species, produces beautiful clusters of pink flowers on bare stems in late spring. Mountain sweet pepperbush, a multi-stemmed shrub with reddish brown peeling bark, produces elongate clusters of fragrant white flowers in summer. Stunted trees, including smooth serviceberry, fire cherry, and mountain ash, produce showy clusters of white flowers in spring and colorful fruits in summer.

Herbaceous plants are sparse under the dense shrubs and stunted trees. Among the showier herbs are galax, painted trillium, and wintergreen. Slender white flowering stalks of galax stand out against its round shiny leaves from mid-spring to early summer. The white flowers of painted trillium, with a splotch of red at the base of each petal, are a delight to see in spring as are the bright red berry-like fruits of wintergreen in fall to winter. Orange-yellow spaghetti-like strands wrapped around the leaves and stems of other plants are the leafless stems of Appalachian dodder, a parasitic flowering plant.

HEATH BALD: CHARACTERISTIC PLANTS

Trees

Fraser fir	*Abies fraseri*	NI
Smooth serviceberry	*Amelanchier laevis*	NI
Yellow birch	*Betula alleghaniensis*	NI
Red spruce	*Picea rubens*	NI
Fire cherry, Pin cherry	*Prunus pensylvanica*	NI
Mountain ash	*Sorbus americana*	NI

Shrubs and Woody Vines

ABUNDANT SPECIES

Mountain laurel	*Kalmia latifolia*	p. 236
Catawba rhododendron	*Rhododendron catawbiense*	p. 236
Rosebay rhododendron	*Rhododendron maximum*	p. 230

OCCASIONAL TO LOCALLY ABUNDANT SPECIES

Black chokeberry	*Aronia melanocarpa*	NI
Mountain sweet pepperbush	*Clethra acuminata*	NI
Southern bush honeysuckle	*Diervilla sessilifolia*	NI
Black huckleberry	*Gaylussacia baccata*	NI
Sand myrtle	*Kalmia buxifolia*	NI
Minniebush	*Menziesia pilosa*	NI
Mountain fetterbush	*Pieris floribunda*	NI
Flame azalea	*Rhododendron calendulaceum*	p. 267
Carolina rhododendron	*Rhododendron carolinianum*	NI
Allegheny blackberry	*Rubus alleghaniensis*	NI
Smooth blackberry	*Rubus canadensis*	NI
Common greenbrier	*Smilax rotundifolia*	NI
Highbush blueberry	*Vaccinium corymbosum*	NI

Highbush cranberry	*Vaccinium erythrocarpum*	NI
Upland highbush blueberry	*Vaccinium simulatum*	NI
Wild raisin	*Viburnum cassinoides*	NI

Herbs

OCCASIONAL TO LOCALLY ABUNDANT SPECIES

Appalachian dodder	*Cuscuta rostrata*	p. 232
Trailing arbutus	*Epigaea repens*	p. 207
Galax, Skunkweed	*Galax urceolata*	p. 224
Wintergreen	*Gaultheria procumbens*	p. 229
Indian cucumber root	*Medeola virginiana*	p. 264
Bracken fern	*Pteridium aquilinum*	NI
Painted trillium	*Trillium undulatum*	p. 219

Rare Plants

| Spreading avens | *Geum radiatum* | NI |
| Pinkshell azalea | *Rhododendron vaseyi* | NI |

NI = species not included in the wildflower profiles (Part IV)

NORTHERN HARDWOOD FOREST

Distinguishing Features
The dominant canopy trees in northern hardwood forest are American beech, yellow birch, and yellow buckeye. Other high elevation forest communities have Fraser fir, red spruce, or northern red oak as canopy dominants.

Introduction
Northern hardwood forest occurs on north-facing slopes, coves, and flats at elevations greater than about 4,000 feet. High rainfall, low temperatures, and northern exposures result in generally cool moist conditions. The relatively large trees typically form a dense canopy except on exposed high-elevation sites where the canopy is more open and the trees are stunted.

Nearly all of the trees found in this community are broad-leaved trees that drop their leaves in autumn and remain leafless until the following spring. In winter, the leafless trees impart a stark, almost lifeless appearance to the forest. Spring is a time of renewal as buds burst open and leaves and flowers emerge. Summer is green and lush, and autumn brings a brilliant display of colors as the leaves change from green to various shades of yellow, orange, red, and brown.

Vegetation
Moisture-loving trees such as American beech, yellow birch, yellow buckeye, and sugar maple are the primary canopy trees. Red spruce often occurs at higher elevations while cucumber magnolia occurs sporadically at lower elevations. Clusters of disturbance-dependent species such as yellow birch, fire cherry, and black locust are good indicators of past logging or fires. Common understory trees include striped maple, mountain maple, and smooth serviceberry. Wind-pollinated trees such as American beech, yellow birch, and mountain maple disperse enormous

amounts of pollen from relatively inconspicuous flowers in early spring, before the trees leaf out. In contrast, yellow buckeye, smooth serviceberry, and cucumber tree have relatively showy flowers that attract insect pollinators.

The shrub layer varies from sparse to moderately dense. One of the more conspicuous shrubs is witch hobble, a sprawling deciduous species with large paired leaves, flat-topped flower clusters, and berry-like fruits that change color from green to red to purplish black as they ripen in late summer. Wild hydrangea is a low-growing, rounded shrub with peeling bark and small white flowers in flat-topped or rounded clusters. The most prominent vine is pipevine, a climbing vine with large heart-shaped leaves and small pipe-shaped flowers.

The herbaceous layer is often dense and quite diverse, particularly on moist sheltered sites with deep soils. Among the showier herbs are wake robin, blue cohosh, black cohosh, white snakeroot, and large-flowered bellwort. Plant cover can be lush along streams and seepage areas with species such as cutleaf coneflower, umbrella leaf, wood nettle, and flowering raspberry. Ruby-throated hummingbirds are attracted to seeps when good nectar-producing plants such as crimson bee balm, cardinal flower, and jewelweed are in bloom. Seeps also provide good habitat for salamanders, including moist leaf litter to burrow under.

Nearly all of the herbaceous plants in mountain forests are long-lived perennials that store nutrients overwinter in underground structures (e.g., rhizomes, bulbs, or rootstalks) that supply the resources needed for resprouting in spring. Jewelweeds are an interesting exception as they are short-lived (annual) plants that regenerate from tiny seeds in spring and develop into mature plants up to 6 feet tall by late summer. Fringed phacelia is a winter annual—its seeds germinate in fall, it overwinters as a small rosette, and then flowers, fruits, and dies in spring as the canopy leafs out and the forest floor becomes shaded.

A variant of northern hardwood forest (beech gap forest) occurs in gaps and ridgetops at elevations greater than 4,500 feet where trees are exposed to drying winds, frequent low temperatures, and ice storms. Scattered downed trees and numerous broken branches on the forest floor reflect frequent high wind and ice damage. The extreme climate results in trees (mostly American beech) that are dwarfed with a distinctly gnarled appearance. Despite their small size, trees in beech gap forests can be quite old (more than 100 years). The understory and shrub layers are sparse, but the herbaceous layer can be quite dense, including a meadow-like groundcover dominated by Pennsylvania sedge. The showy flowers of white snakeroot and black cohosh add color in summer and fall.

NORTHERN HARDWOOD FOREST: CHARACTERISTIC PLANTS

Trees

ABUNDANT SPECIES

Yellow buckeye	*Aesculus flava*	NI
Yellow birch	*Betula alleghaniensis*	NI
American beech	*Fagus grandifolia*	NI

OCCASIONAL TO LOCALLY ABUNDANT SPECIES

Striped maple	*Acer pensylvanicum*	NI
Sugar maple	*Acer saccharum*	NI
Mountain maple	*Acer spicatum*	NI

Smooth serviceberry	*Amelanchier laevis*	NI
White ash	*Fraxinus americana*	NI
Cucumber tree	*Magnolia acuminata*	NI
Red spruce	*Picea rubens*	NI
White basswood	*Tilia americana*	NI

Shrubs

OCCASIONAL TO LOCALLY ABUNDANT SPECIES

Pipevine, Dutchman's pipe	*Aristolochia macrophylla*	p. 244
Alternate leaf dogwood	*Cornus alternifolia*	NI
Wild hydrangea	*Hydrangea arborescens*	p. 225
Catawba rhododendron	*Rhododendron catawbiense*	p. 236
Appalachian gooseberry	*Ribes rotundifolium*	NI
Allegheny blackberry	*Rubus allegheniensis*	NI
Flowering raspberry	*Rubus odoratus*	NI
Red elderberry	*Sambucus racemosa*	NI
Witch hobble, Hobblebush	*Viburnum lantanoides*	NI

Herbs

ABUNDANT SPECIES

White snakeroot	*Ageratina altissima*	p. 232
Hayscented fern	*Dennstaedtia punctilobula*	NI
Wood nettle	*Laportea canadensis*	p. 265
Plumed Solomon's seal	*Maianthemum racemosum*	p. 216
Canada violet	*Viola canadensis*	p. 220

OCCASIONAL TO LOCALLY ABUNDANT SPECIES

Black cohosh	*Actaea racemosa*	p. 226
Jack-in-the-pulpit	*Arisaema triphyllum*	p. 241
Goat's beard	*Aruncus dioicus*	NI
Pennsylvania sedge	*Carex pensylvanica*	NI
Blue cohosh	*Caulophyllum thalictroides*	p. 242
Carolina spring beauty	*Claytonia caroliniana*	p. 234
Umbrella leaf	*Diphylleia cymosa*	p. 215
Beechdrops	*Epifagus virginiana*	p. 233
Dimpled trout lily	*Erythronium umbilicatum*	p. 253
Yellow jewelweed	*Impatiens pallida*	NI
Crimson bee balm	*Monarda didyma*	p. 269
Fringed phacelia	*Phacelia fimbriata*	p. 211
Cutleaf coneflower	*Rudbeckia laciniata*	p. 260
Curtis's goldenrod	*Solidago curtisii*	p. 261
Giant chickweed	*Stellaria pubera*	p. 214
Wake robin, Stinking Willie	*Trillium erectum*	p. 243
Large-flowered bellwort	*Uvularia grandiflora*	NI

Invasive Exotic Plants

| Oriental bittersweet | *Celastrus orbiculatus* | NI |

Rare Plants

| White monkshood | *Aconitum reclinatum* | NI |
| Spotted coralroot | *Corallorhiza maculata* | NI |

NI = species not included in the wildflower profiles (Part IV)

Mid- to Low Elevation Moist to Wet Communities

RICH COVE FOREST

Distinguishing Features

Rich cove forests occur on sheltered sites such as broad ravines, narrow valleys, lower slopes, and on broad flats adjacent to streams. Moist fertile soils and a favorable microclimate result in an unusually diverse mixture of moisture-loving trees and a lush, species-rich herbaceous layer. Acidic cove forests, which I recognize as a separate vegetation type, also occur on moist sheltered sites, but because the soils are more acidic (and nutrient-poor), acidic cove forest has fewer tree species, a dense heath shrub layer, and a relatively low diversity of herbaceous species. Northern hardwood forests share many of the same species as rich cove forests but occur at higher elevations (greater than 4,000 feet).

Introduction

The term cove refers to the upper portions of mountain valleys and slopes that have been carved by small creeks and streams over millennia. Steep slopes and a dense canopy of tall deciduous trees moderate temperature and wind, and intercept the sun so that deep shade is present much of the year. The terrain can be rugged with steep slopes, scattered boulders, and fallen logs. Intermittent creeks, seeps, and springs dot the landscape.

The deep dark soils are commonly more nutrient-rich and less acidic than surrounding areas due to the presence of base-rich rocks (such as amphibolite, limestone, and marble) that release calcium (or magnesium) into the soil as they weather. A fertile soil, coupled with a relatively cool, moist environment, result in conditions that favor an unusually rich diversity of plants. Particularly striking is the diversity of spring wildflowers. Thousands of wildflowers can form a rich tapestry of whites, blues, yellows, and reds within a single cove.

Sheltered from major environmental changes such as glaciation or ocean inundation, rich cove forests have persisted for millions of years in the southern Appalachians. This antiquity, along with moist fertile soils, a favorable climate, and a diversity of microhabitats, has resulted in tremendous plant diversity. Nowhere else in eastern North America will you find so many different kinds of trees with such a lush and species rich herbaceous layer as in rich cove forests.

Vegetation

A variety of deciduous trees form a dense canopy that deeply shades the forest floor for much of the year. Common canopy trees include white basswood, yellow buckeye, sugar maple, and tulip tree. Rooted in moist fertile soils, the canopy trees grow taller and wider than in most forests. A rich diversity of understory trees includes smaller individuals of the canopy species as well as typical subcanopy trees such as Fraser magnolia, Carolina silverbell, and flowering dogwood. A generally sparse shrub layer includes sweet shrub, spicebush, and wild hydrangea. Heath shrubs such as rosebay rhododendron are often present but are not abundant in rich cove forests.

A key feature of this community is a lush herbaceous layer that often forms a nearly continuous carpet of plants. In spring, look for wildflowers such as Carolina spring beauty, bloodroot, acute-lobed hepatica, rue anemone, foamflower, and various species of trillium. Species that bloom in late spring or summer include black cohosh, orange (and yellow) jewelweed, and wood nettle. Wildflowers are particularly abundant on lower slopes and flats where soil nutrients, organic matter, and moisture accumulate, forming a rich compost-like soil.

RICH COVE FOREST: CHARACTERISTIC PLANTS

Trees

OCCASIONAL TO LOCALLY ABUNDANT SPECIES

Striped maple	*Acer pensylvanicum*	NI
Sugar maple	*Acer saccharum*	NI
Yellow buckeye	*Aesculus flava*	NI
Sweet birch	*Betula lenta*	NI
Ironwood, Musclewood	*Carpinus caroliniana*	NI
Yellowwood	*Cladrastis kentukea*	NI
Flowering dogwood	*Cornus florida*	NI
American beech	*Fagus grandifolia*	NI
White ash	*Fraxinus americana*	NI
Carolina silverbell	*Halesia tetraptera*	NI
Tulip tree, Yellow poplar	*Liriodendron tulipifera*	NI
Cucumber tree	*Magnolia acuminata*	NI
Fraser magnolia	*Magnolia fraseri*	NI
Hop hornbeam	*Ostrya virginiana*	NI
Black cherry	*Prunus serotina*	NI
White basswood	*Tilia americana*	NI

Shrubs and Woody Vines

OCCASIONAL TO LOCALLY ABUNDANT SPECIES

Pipevine, Dutchman's pipe	*Aristolochia macrophylla*	p. 244
Pawpaw	*Asimina triloba*	NI
Sweet shrub	*Calycanthus floridus*	p. 241
Wild hydrangea	*Hydrangea arborescens*	p. 225
Spicebush	*Lindera benzoin*	p. 263

Herbs

OCCASIONAL TO LOCALLY ABUNDANT SPECIES

Doll's eyes, White baneberry	*Actaea pachypoda*	p. 213
Black cohosh	*Actaea racemosa*	p. 226
Maidenhair fern	*Adiantum pedatum*	NI
Ramps, Wild leek	*Allium tricoccum*	NI
Acute-lobed hepatica	*Anemone acutiloba*	p. 207
Wood anemone	*Anemone quinquefolia*	p. 209
Jack-in-the-pulpit	*Arisaema triphyllum*	p. 241
Wild ginger	*Asarum canadense*	p. 242
Blue cohosh	*Caulophyllum thalictroides*	p. 242
Carolina spring beauty	*Claytonia caroliniana*	p. 234
Speckled wood lily	*Clintonia umbellulata*	p. 222
Dutchman's britches	*Dicentra cucullaria*	p. 208
Showy orchis	*Galearis spectabilis*	p. 234
Wild geranium	*Geranium maculatum*	p. 235
Orange jewelweed	*Impatiens capensis*	p. 268
Wood nettle	*Laportea canadensis*	p. 265
Plumed Solomon's seal	*Maianthemum racemosum*	p. 216
Mayapple	*Podophyllum peltatum*	p. 208
Solomon's seal	*Polygonatum biflorum*	p. 217
Bloodroot	*Sanguinaria canadensis*	p. 209
Rue anemone	*Thalictrum thalictroides*	p. 211
Foamflower	*Tiarella cordifolia*	p. 218
Large-flowered trillium	*Trillium grandiflorum*	p. 214
Vasey's trillium	*Trillium vaseyi*	p. 244
Canada violet	*Viola canadensis*	p. 220

Invasive Exotic Plants

Garlic mustard	*Alliaria petiolata*	NI
Japanese stiltgrass	*Microstegium vimineum*	NI

Rare Plants

Whorled horsebalm	*Collinsonia verticillata*	NI
Yellow lady's slipper	*Cypripedium parviflorum*	NI
Green violet	*Hybanthus concolor*	NI
Goldenseal	*Hydrastis canadensis*	NI
American ginseng	*Panax quinquefolius*	NI

NI = species not included in the wildflower profiles (Part IV)

ACIDIC COVE FOREST

Distinguishing Features
Acidic cove forest is similar to rich cove forest as it occurs on moist sheltered sites but has more acidic, less fertile soils with a dense layer of heath shrubs and a much lower diversity of trees and herbaceous plants.

Introduction
Acidic cove forest is a widespread community at mid- to low elevations in the mountains on steep ravines, lower slopes and ridges within coves, and narrow rocky gorges on acidic, nutrient-poor soils. The terrain often includes steep slopes, boulders, and fallen logs as well as seeps, springs, and ephemeral streams. Underlying sandstone, quartzite, or other acidic bedrock give soils a low pH, often less than 4.5, compared to the higher soil pH (about 6.0) usually associated with rich cove forest. Mesophytic (moisture-loving) trees, a dense evergreen shrub layer, and a relatively small group of mostly evergreen herbaceous species characterize this community.

Vegetation
Acidic cove forest typically has a dense canopy of a relatively small number of mesophytic trees, including tulip tree, sweet birch, yellow birch, and red maple. Other deciduous trees more typical of rich cove forest occur as scattered individuals, including American beech, white basswood, and white ash. Two important conifers are eastern hemlock and eastern white pine.

Eastern hemlock is currently being devastated by the hemlock woolly adelgid, an aphid-like insect that sucks sap from twigs, causing needle loss and tree death within a few years of infestation. Adelgid infested trees can be recognized by the appearance of tiny "cotton balls" at the base of needles along with a thinning crown due to needle loss. This tiny insect (inadvertently introduced from Asia) has left a trail of dead hemlocks in ravines and valleys, along streams and slopes of cove forests, and in steep rocky gorges in the southern Appalachians and beyond.

A relatively open subcanopy includes species such as Fraser magnolia, Carolina silverbell, and American holly. In spring, look for Fraser magnolia's large creamy white flowers (with a pleasant fruity fragrance) along with the showy white bell-shaped flowers of Carolina silverbell. From fall through winter, the bright red to orange fruits of American holly stand out among its shiny evergreen leaves.

A well-developed shrub layer often forms a dense thicket that makes travel difficult. Rosebay rhododendron is the most common shrub on mesic sites while mountain laurel is usually more abundant on drier sites. Historically a species of river valleys, rosebay rhododendron moved upslope and greatly increased its coverage following heavy logging, the loss of American chestnut due to chestnut blight, and fire suppression in the twentieth century. Rosebay thickets alter the environment by creating deep shade, reducing availability of water and nutrients, and forming a deep leaf litter layer. Collectively, these changes inhibit the growth of herbaceous plants and other shrubs and limit tree regeneration.

The generally sparse herbaceous layer includes evergreen species such as partridge berry, galax, and large flower heartleaf. Along trailside margins, look for Indian cucumber root, Robin's plantain, and halberdleaf yellow violet. Ferns such as New York fern, hayscented fern, and Christmas fern sometimes form dense glades on the forest floor. Oconee bells, a rare species restricted to gorges of the Blue Ridge Escarpment in the Carolinas and Georgia, grows on moist slopes and along creek banks usually beneath rosebay rhododendron or mountain laurel.

ACIDIC COVE FOREST: CHARACTERISTIC PLANTS

Trees

ABUNDANT SPECIES		
Red maple	*Acer rubrum*	NI
Sweet birch	*Betula lenta*	NI
Tulip tree, Yellow poplar	*Liriodendron tulipifera*	NI
Eastern hemlock, Canada hemlock	*Tsuga canadensis*	NI
OCCASIONAL TO LOCALLY ABUNDANT SPECIES		
Yellow birch	*Betula alleghaniensis*	NI
American beech	*Fagus grandifolia*	NI
Carolina silverbell	*Halesia tetraptera*	NI
American holly	*Ilex opaca*	NI
Cucumber tree	*Magnolia acuminata*	NI
Fraser magnolia	*Magnolia fraseri*	NI
Eastern white pine	*Pinus strobus*	NI
Northern red oak	*Quercus rubra*	NI

Shrubs and Woody Vines

ABUNDANT SPECIES		
Mountain laurel	*Kalmia latifolia*	p. 236
Mountain doghobble	*Leucothoe fontanesiana*	p. 213
Rosebay rhododendron	*Rhododendron maximum*	p. 230

Climbing hydrangea	*Decumaria barbara*	NI
Strawberry bush, Hearts-a-bustin'	*Euonymus americanus*	p. 264
Catawba rhododendron	*Rhododendron catawbiense*	p. 236
Mapleleaf viburnum	*Viburnum acerifolium*	NI

Herbs

ABUNDANT SPECIES

Galax, Skunkweed	*Galax urceolata*	p. 224
Partridge berry	*Mitchella repens*	p. 223
Christmas fern	*Polystichum acrostichoides*	NI
New York fern	*Thelypteris noveboracensis*	NI
Halberdleaf yellow violet	*Viola hastata*	p. 254

OCCASIONAL TO LOCALLY ABUNDANT SPECIES

Jack-in-the-pulpit	*Arisaema triphyllum*	p. 241
Trailing arbutus	*Epigaea repens*	p. 207
Robin's plantain	*Erigeron pulchellus*	p. 216
Large flower heartleaf	*Hexastylis shuttleworthii*	p. 245
Indian cucumber root	*Medeola virginiana*	p. 264

Invasive Exotic Plants

Chinese privet	*Ligustrum sinense*	NI

Rare Plants

Fraser's sedge	*Cymophyllus fraserianus*	NI
Appalachian twayblade	*Listera smallii*	NI
Fraser's loosestrife	*Lysimachia fraseri*	NI
Oconee bells	*Shortia galacifolia*	NI

NI = species not included in the wildflower profiles (Part IV)

ALLUVIAL FOREST

Distinguishing Features
Alluvial forests are easily recognized by their location along stream and river flood-plains. They share many of the same species as cove forests, but are subject to periodic flooding and have characteristic floodplain species such as sycamore.

Introduction
Alluvial forests are intermittently flooded by water overflowing the banks of rivers and streams after heavy rains. Also known as floodplain or bottomland forests, they vary in size from broad river valleys to narrow strips of streamside vegetation. Most mountain alluvial forests have narrow floodplains. The periodic input of nutrients in flood-deposited sediment enhances soil fertility. Floods can also disturb the vegetation by washing away plants and soil. More powerful, catastrophic floods occur less frequently but can be very destructive to stream channels and vegetation, sometimes eroding or completely washing away small patches of forest.

Floodplains and their rivers are in a continually dynamic state between deposition of substrate and loss of substrate. Sandbars and mudflats form on the inside curves of rivers as periodic flooding deposits alluvial material. Loss of substrate results from erosion during heavy flooding, the construction of upstream dams, and other forms of human disturbance.

The tendency of streamside trees to lean toward the river has both positive and negative consequences. Leaning trees gain access to canopy-free space with greater light levels that potentially increase growth rates, but because more of their trunks are immersed in fast running water during heavy floods, they are more vulnerable to being uprooted and washed away. Prolonged flooding can also stress or kill flood-plain trees. Most floodplain trees can tolerate short periods of flooding, but few species can tolerate prolonged flooding during the growing season.

Beavers affect alluvial forests by girdling and felling trees for food and construction of dams and lodges, but their greatest impact comes when large numbers of trees die due to prolonged flooding caused by their activities. Persistent flooding and the resulting loss of trees can change an alluvial forest into a marsh containing wetland shrubs and herbs. By building dams and creating ponds, beavers significantly alter the vegetation and provide habitat for a number of animals, including fish, waterfowl, reptiles, and amphibians.

Vegetation

Mountain alluvial forests have a well-developed canopy, an open-to-dense understory, and a species-rich herbaceous layer. The stream bank dominant is often sycamore. Large old sycamores, some more than 100 years old, can be found hugging the riverbank. Other common canopy trees include sweet birch, yellow birch, red maple, and tulip tree. The wider floodplains associated with larger rivers have a greater diversity and abundance of bottomland species, including river birch, sweetgum, and green ash. In contrast, the narrower floodplains typically found along smaller rivers and streams have vegetation more similar to cove forests with fewer bottomland plants. Common understory species include ironwood, rosebay rhododendron, and tag alder. The herbaceous layer can be both lush and species rich, but exotic invasives such as Japanese stiltgrass can be a problem.

ALLUVIAL FOREST: CHARACTERISTIC PLANTS

Trees

ABUNDANT		
Red maple	*Acer rubrum*	NI
Yellow birch	*Betula alleghaniensis*	NI
Sweet birch	*Betula lenta*	NI
Ironwood, Musclewood	*Carpinus caroliniana*	NI
Tulip tree, Yellow poplar	*Liriodendron tulipifera*	NI
Sycamore	*Platanus occidentalis*	NI
OCCASIONAL TO LOCALLY ABUNDANT SPECIES		
Box elder	*Acer negundo*	NI
Yellow buckeye	*Aesculus sylvatica*	NI
River birch	*Betula nigra*	NI
Hackberry, Sugarberry	*Celtis laevigata*	NI
Green ash	*Fraxinus pennsylvanica*	NI
Carolina silverbell	*Halesia tetraptera*	NI
Black walnut	*Juglans nigra*	NI
Sweetgum	*Liquidambar styraciflua*	NI
Cucumber tree	*Magnolia acuminata*	NI
White oak	*Quercus alba*	NI
Northern red oak	*Quercus rubra*	NI
Eastern hemlock, Canada hemlock	*Tsuga canadensis*	NI

Shrubs and Woody Vines

ABUNDANT

Tag alder	*Alnus serrulata*	NI
Mountain doghobble	*Leucothoe fontanesiana*	p. 213
Rosebay rhododendron	*Rhododendron maximum*	p. 230

OCCASIONAL TO LOCALLY ABUNDANT SPECIES

Giant cane, River cane	*Arundinaria gigantea*	NI
Pawpaw	*Asimina triloba*	NI
Silky dogwood	*Cornus amomum*	NI
Strawberry bush, Hearts-a-bustin'	*Euonymus americanus*	p. 264
Witch hazel	*Hamamelis virginiana*	p. 262
Spicebush	*Lindera benzoin*	p. 263
Virginia creeper	*Parthenocissus quinquefolia*	NI
Black willow	*Salix nigra*	NI
Poison ivy	*Toxicodendron radicans*	p. 223
Yellowroot	*Xanthorhiza simplicissima*	p. 240

Herbs

Jack-in-the-pulpit	*Arisaema triphyllum*	p. 241
Wild ginger	*Asarum canadense*	p. 242
Fairywand, Devil's bit	*Chamaelirium luteum*	p. 210
Virginia spring beauty	*Claytonia virginica*	NI
Dimpled trout lily	*Erythronium umbilicatum*	p. 253
Wood nettle	*Laportea canadensis*	p. 265
Cardinal flower	*Lobelia cardinalis*	p. 269
Great blue lobelia	*Lobelia siphilitica*	p. 251
Cinnamon fern	*Osmunda cinnamomea*	NI
Golden ragwort	*Packera aurea*	p. 257
Woodland phlox	*Phlox divaricata*	p. 248
Christmas fern	*Polystichum acrostichoides*	NI
New York fern	*Thelypteris noveboracensis*	NI
Common wingstem	*Verbesina alternifolia*	p. 262
New York ironweed	*Vernonia noveboracensis*	p. 246

Invasive Exotic Plants

Chinese privet	*Ligustrum sinense*	NI
Japanese honeysuckle	*Lonicera japonica*	NI
Japanese stiltgrass	*Microstegium vimineum*	NI

NI = species not included in the wildflower profiles (Part IV)

ROCKY STREAMSIDE

Distinguishing Features
The rocky streamside community occurs along rivers and streams that are too rocky, wet, or frequently flooded for trees to reach maturity. It differs from alluvial forest in that it lacks a tree canopy.

Introduction
The enormous energy of moving water in mountain rivers erodes and downcuts the landscape, forming relatively narrow valleys with small floodplains. Stream courses are fairly constant through time and are usually underlain by rock. Rocky streamside habitats vary from rock outcrops to piled cobbles and boulders, to gravel bars in and adjacent to rivers, and streams that are too rocky or wet for trees to persist.

After heavy rains, the rivers swell and overflow their banks and the tremendous force of fast flowing water transports and deposits large numbers of cobbles, stones, and even boulders downstream. You can actually hear large cobbles and boulders clunking as they tumble down the river in severe floods. When the floodwaters recede, a new or altered cobble bar has appeared. Floods also disturb the vegetation by washing away plants and the soil substrate. Small patches of forest can be eroded or completely washed away in severe floods. In winter, ice scouring can sheer off plants, including young trees on the river's edge.

The plants that grow along rocky streamsides must cope with a shifting substrate with highly fluctuating water levels. Flooding can occur at any time of year, resulting in soil flooding or water logging to total submergence of the vegetation. Rocky streamside habitats are dramatically altered by power-generating and flood-control dams, as well as by changes in hydrology and increased sedimentation resulting from logging, uncontrolled development, and other factors.

Vegetation

The vegetation is highly variable. Lower areas along river margins are more fre-quently flooded, have less stable substrates, and are sparsely vegetated. Annuals and short-lived perennials such as orange jewelweed, Appalachian bluet, and mountain dwarf dandelion often occur in the most exposed sites because they are most likely to successfully establish, grow vegetatively, and produce seeds before being washed away.

Large slabs of rock along rivers are mostly bare of plants except for cracks and fissures where soil can collect. On high-energy stretches of rivers where cobbles and boulders accumulate, a dominant species is twisted sedge, a tenaciously rooted perennial with a densely clumped growth form that is particularly well adapted to fast-water environments. Its dense fibrous roots and rhizomes trap soil and build up the substrate, thereby enabling other plants to colonize streamside habitats. Two conspicuous ferns with large upright fronds are cinnamon fern and royal fern.

In the more stable (elevated) zones along river margins, flooding occurs less frequently and moderate to dense shrub thickets are often present. Common shrubs include tag alder, black willow, mountain doghobble, and yellowroot. Rhododen-drons are common, including evergreen species such as rosebay rhododendron and deciduous species such as wild azalea, sweet azalea, and swamp azalea. Small saplings of trees such as sycamore sometimes occur but rarely reach maturity.

ROCKY STREAMSIDE: CHARACTERISTIC PLANTS

Trees

River birch	*Betula nigra*	NI
Sycamore	*Platanus occidentalis*	NI

Shrubs

ABUNDANT SPECIES

Tag alder	*Alnus serrulata*	NI
Giant cane, River cane	*Arundinaria gigantea*	NI
Buttonbush	*Cephalanthus occidentalis*	NI
Silky dogwood	*Cornus amomum*	NI
Virginia willow	*Itea virginica*	NI
Black willow	*Salix nigra*	NI
Common elderberry	*Sambucus canadensis*	p. 221
Yellowroot	*Xanthorhiza simplicissima*	p. 240

OCCASIONAL TO LOCALLY ABUNDANT SPECIES

Sweet shrub	*Calycanthus floridus*	p. 241
Mountain sweet pepperbush	*Clethra acuminata*	NI
Mountain laurel	*Kalmia latifolia*	p. 236
Mountain doghobble	*Leucothoe fontanesiana*	p. 213
Sweet azalea	*Rhododendron arborescens*	NI
Rosebay rhododendron	*Rhododendron maximum*	p. 230
Wild azalea, Pinxterflower	*Rhododendron periclymenoides*	NI
Swamp azalea, Clammy azalea	*Rhododendron viscosum*	NI

Herbs

ABUNDANT SPECIES

Twisted sedge	*Carex torta*	NI
Appalachian bluet	*Houstonia serpyllifolia*	p. 248
Orange jewelweed	*Impatiens capensis*	p. 268
American water willow	*Justicia americana*	NI

OCCASIONAL TO LOCALLY ABUNDANT SPECIES

Tall bellflower	*Campanulastrum americanum*	NI
White turtlehead	*Chelone glabra*	NI
Joe Pye weed	*Eutrochium fistulosum*	p. 239
Yellow jewelweed	*Impatiens pallida*	NI
Mountain dwarf dandelion	*Krigia montana*	p. 258
Cardinal flower	*Lobelia cardinalis*	p. 269
Cinnamon fern	*Osmunda cinnamomea*	NI
Royal fern	*Osmunda regalis*	NI
Obedient plant	*Physostegia virginiana*	NI
Riverweed	*Podostemum ceratophyllum*	NI
Pink smartweed	*Polygonum pensylvanicum*	NI
Cutleaf coneflower	*Rudbeckia laciniata*	p. 260
Little bluestem	*Schizachyrium scoparium*	NI
Indiangrass	*Sorghastrum nutans*	NI
New York ironweed	*Vernonia noveboracensis*	p. 246

Invasive Exotic Plants

Japanese stiltgrass	*Microstegium vimineum*	NI
Johnson grass	*Sorghum halepense*	NI

NI = species not included in the wildflower profiles (Part IV)

SPRAY CLIFF

Distinguishing Features
Spray cliffs occur on vertical to gently sloping rock faces that are kept moist by misting and splashing from waterfalls.

Introduction
Spray cliffs usually occur in ravines and gorges where steep slopes admit relatively little sunlight, trap humidity from waterfalls' spray, and block drying winds, resulting in a cool moist microclimate. The numerous ledges, crevices, and other protected microhabitats associated with waterfalls further moderate temperatures and contribute to the rich diversity of plants found here, including a number of rare and unusual species.

Take care when exploring this community as steep slopes and slippery rocks create a potentially dangerous environment. For your own safety, stay on established trails and observe all warning signs. Avoid climbing to the top of waterfalls or clambering over rocks or crossing a stream anywhere near the top of a waterfall, as a slight misstep could result in serious injury or even death.

Vegetation

Spray cliffs have a distinctive flora, featuring many species of bryophytes (mosses and liverworts), ferns, and flowering plants. Because of the nearly continuous spray from waterfalls, and because most other plants can't grow on bare rock substrates, mosses and liverworts are especially abundant. In the Whitewater River gorge alone, more than 285 species of moss have been identified. This represents nearly one-fourth of the total number of mosses known from the United States and Canada. Many of the mosses and liverworts, and some of the ferns, are largely restricted to the spray cliff zone; others are tropical disjuncts, living far north of their normal geographic range, reflecting long distance spore dispersal by wind.

Unlike mosses, flowering plants are largely restricted to sites where shallow pockets of soil accumulate, including crevices, shelves, and ledges. A few stunted shrubs, such as rosebay rhododendron and mountain laurel, may be present but trees are absent. Adjoining slopes with deeper soils often harbor trees that provide shade, thereby contributing to the relatively cool summer temperatures associated with spray cliffs. Cold air drainage further cools the air.

Plant cover in the spray cliff zone is highly variable. Moss mats, ferns, and flowering plants can densely cover spray cliffs. Sometimes plants are loosely distributed among the rocks, while other spray cliffs appear nearly devoid of vegetation. An important factor influencing plant cover is the extent and regularity of the spray, which is determined by the size of the stream. Other factors influencing plant cover include the type of rock present, the direction of slope (e.g., north versus south facing), amount of shading, and the distribution and depth of soil pockets. Periodic flooding, rock falls, and erosion can dislodge mats of vegetation, as can trampling by visitors.

Major floods, especially those associated with hurricanes, can clear the rocks of vegetation as well as deposit downed trees, boulders, and other kinds of debris. Logs carried over the falls in high water, as well as wind-toppled trees from adjoining slopes, often lie at the base of falls, much like driftwood washed up on beaches.

For your own safety (and that of the fragile plants that occupy this community), avoid clambering over the rocks in the spray cliff zone.

SPRAY CLIFF: CHARACTERISTIC PLANTS

Shrubs

OCCASIONAL TO LOCALLY ABUNDANT SPECIES

Wild hydrangea	*Hydrangea arborescens*	p. 225
Mountain laurel	*Kalmia latifolia*	p. 236
Rosebay rhododendron	*Rhododendron maximum*	p. 230
Yellowroot	*Xanthorhiza simplicissima*	p. 240

Herbs

OCCASIONAL TO LOCALLY ABUNDANT SPECIES

Maidenhair fern	*Adiantum pedatum*	NI
Mountain spleenwort	*Asplenium montanum*	NI
Maidenhair spleenwort	*Asplenium trichomanes*	NI
Pink turtlehead	*Chelone lyonii*	p. 239
Umbrella leaf	*Diphylleia cymosa*	p. 215
White wood aster	*Eurybia divaricata*	p. 231
Galax, skunkweed	*Galax urceolata*	p. 224
Cave alumroot	*Heuchera parviflora*	NI
Rock alumroot	*Heuchera villosa*	p. 230
Appalachian bluet	*Houstonia serpyllifolia*	p. 248
Cliff saxifrage	*Hydatica petiolaris*	p. 220
American water pennywort	*Hydrocotyle americana*	NI
Orange jewelweed	*Impatiens capensis*	p. 268
Yellow jewelweed	*Impatiens pallida*	NI
Wood nettle	*Laportea canadensis*	p. 265
Liverwort	*Marchantia* species	NI
Brook lettuce	*Micranthes micranthidifolia*	p. 217
Sundrops	*Oenothera fruticosa*	p. 257
Mountain wood sorrel	*Oxalis montana*	p. 237
Riverweed	*Podostemum ceratophyllum*	NI
Rock polypody	*Polypodium virginianum*	NI
Sphagnum	*Sphagnum* species	NI
Mountain meadowrue	*Thalictrum clavatum*	p. 226

Invasive Exotic Plants

Japanese stiltgrass	*Microstegium vimineum*	NI

Rare Plants

Brook saxifrage	*Boykinia aconitifolia*	NI
Fraser's sedge	*Cymophyllus fraseriana*	NI
Rock clubmoss	*Huperzia porophila*	NI
Appalachian shoestring fern	*Vittaria appalachiana*	NI

NI = species not included in the wildflower profiles (Part IV)

Mid- to Low Elevation Dry Communities

CHESTNUT OAK FOREST

Distinguishing Features
Chestnut oak forest is distinguished from all other mountain forest types by the dominance of chestnut oak or scarlet oak.

Introduction
Chestnut oak forest generally occurs on dry slopes and ridges at elevations from 3,000 to 4,500 feet. Thin, rocky soils and south- to southwest-facing slopes result in dry conditions that favor slow growing, drought tolerant trees such as chestnut oak and scarlet oak. An abundance of heath shrubs is a good indicator of this community's acidic, nutrient-poor soils. Dry slopes, flammable shrubs, and the accumulation of a thick leaf litter layer result in periodic fires, which favor oak regeneration. Wind-thrown trees are common because root depth is limited by thin soils underlain by rock. On drier sites, chestnut oak forest transitions to pine-oak-heath, which has more pines and a denser layer of heath shrubs.

Vegetation

A dense canopy of moderately tall well-shaped trees occurs on more favorable sites, whereas stunted trees with gnarled shapes and a more open canopy are typical on drier sites. The dominant canopy tree is chestnut oak, a slow-growing but long-lived tree. Scarlet oak replaces chestnut oak as the canopy dominant on dry ridgetops and upper slopes because it requires less moisture for growth and is more drought tolerant than chestnut oak. Other canopy trees include black oak, northern red oak, pignut hickory, mockernut hickory, and eastern white pine.

In the understory, look for red maple, black gum, and sassafras, each of which has separate male and female trees. Prior to the chestnut blight in the early twentieth century, American chestnut was a dominant or codominant canopy species in this forest type. Today, it is an understory species that persists via root sprouts. Slowly decomposing chestnut logs and old dead stumps can still be seen on the forest floor.

On drier sites, chestnut oak forest has a more open tree canopy with a nearly continuous shrub layer, including tall evergreen heath shrubs such as mountain laurel, rosebay rhododendron, and gorge rhododendron, as well as low-growing deciduous heath shrubs such as lowbush blueberry and bear huckleberry. Mountain laurel, flame azalea, gorge rhododendron, and rosebay rhododendron produce spectacular flower displays in spring or summer.

Where shrubs are less dense, herbaceous plants increase in number. Trailing arbutus, wintergreen, and pipsissewa are prostrate plants with thick leathery leaves and a slightly woody base. Galax forms dense patches of round shiny leaves with tiny white flowers on tall slender stalks. It sometimes smells like skunk spray or dog feces, which is why it's also called skunkweed. Vegetative stems of Indian cucumber root have a single whorl of leaves; in contrast, flowering stems have two whorls. As the fruits ripen in late summer, the basal portion of their associated leaves turn scarlet. The contrasting colors of the fruits and leaves help Indian cucumber root attract fruit-eating birds that eat the pulp and disperse the seeds.

CHESTNUT OAK FOREST: CHARACTERISTIC PLANTS

Trees

ABUNDANT SPECIES

Scarlet oak	*Quercus coccinea*	NI
Chestnut oak	*Quercus montana*	NI

OCCASIONAL TO LOCALLY ABUNDANT SPECIES

Red maple	*Acer rubrum*	NI
Pignut hickory	*Carya glabra*	NI
Mockernut hickory	*Carya tomentosa*	NI
American chestnut	*Castanea dentata*	NI
Tulip tree, Yellow poplar	*Liriodendron tulipifera*	NI
Black gum	*Nyssa sylvatica*	NI
Sourwood	*Oxydendrum arboreum*	NI
Eastern white pine	*Pinus strobus*	NI
White oak	*Quercus alba*	NI
Northern red oak	*Quercus rubra*	NI
Black oak	*Quercus velutina*	NI
Sassafras	*Sassafras albidum*	NI

Shrubs and Woody Vines

ABUNDANT SPECIES

Bear huckleberry	*Gaylussacia ursina*	NI
Mountain laurel	*Kalmia latifolia*	p. 236
Rosebay rhododendron	*Rhododendron maximum*	p. 230
Lowbush blueberry	*Vaccinium pallidum*	NI

OCCASIONAL TO LOCALLY ABUNDANT SPECIES

Hill cane	*Arundinaria appalachiana*	NI
Mountain sweet pepperbush	*Clethra acuminata*	NI
Beaked hazelnut	*Corylus cornuta*	NI
Buffalo nut	*Pyrularia pubera*	NI
Flame azalea	*Rhododendron calendulaceum*	p. 267
Gorge rhododendron, Punctatum	*Rhododendron minus*	p. 237
Common greenbrier	*Smilax rotundifolia*	NI
Deerberry	*Vaccinium stamineum*	NI

Herbs

OCCASIONAL TO LOCALLY ABUNDANT SPECIES

Fly poison	*Amianthium muscitoxicum*	NI
Appalachian oak leach	*Aureolaria laevigata*	NI
Pipsissewa, Striped wintergreen	*Chimaphila maculata*	p. 222
Hayscented fern	*Dennstaedtia punctilobula*	NI
Trailing arbutus	*Epigaea repens*	p. 207
Galax, Skunkweed	*Galax urceolata*	p. 224
Wintergreen	*Gaultheria procumbens*	p. 229
Rattlesnake orchid	*Goodyera pubescens*	p. 229
Dwarf iris	*Iris verna*	NI
Plumed Solomon's seal	*Maianthemum racemosum*	p. 216
Indian cucumber root	*Medeola virginiana*	p. 264
Pinesap	*Monotropa hypopitys*	NI
Lousewort, Wood betony	*Pedicularis canadensis*	p. 255
Solomon's seal	*Polygonatum biflorum*	p. 217

Rare Plants

Large witch alder	*Fothergilla major*	NI
Appalachian golden banner	*Thermopsis mollis*	NI

NI = species not included in the wildflower profiles (Part IV)

OAK HICKORY FOREST

Distinguishing Features
A mixture of oaks, hickories, and other hardwoods characterize this community. White oak is often the dominant canopy tree.

Introduction
Oak hickory forest is found throughout the mountain region at elevations from about 2,000 to 5,000 feet. It differs from other mountain oak forests in that it has a mixture of oaks, hickories, and hardwoods including tulip tree, red maple, and black gum. Oak hickory forest in the piedmont is similar but lacks mountain species such as Fraser magnolia, American chestnut, flame azalea, mountain laurel, and bear huckleberry.

While oak hickory forest typically occurs on fairly dry sites, it can also be found on moist fertile sites. Often associated with acidic soils, oak hickory forest also occurs on calcium- or magnesium-rich soils that are nearly basic. Differences among sites in soil type, moisture level, nutrient status, and disturbance history result in a forest type that is quite variable. On relatively dry open slopes, oak hickory forest is particularly susceptible to disturbance by fires and high winds.

Vegetation
The canopy includes a mixture of oaks, hickories, and other hardwoods. The three most common oaks are white, northern red, and chestnut oak. White oak is typically most common because it tolerates a wide range of soil types, moisture levels, and exposures. Northern red oak dominates on higher, cooler sites whereas chestnut oak is most common on hotter, drier sites at lower elevations. Mockernut and

pignut hickory are the two most common hickories. Tulip tree, eastern white pine, and black locust are opportunistic species that increase in abundance following disturbance.

Prior to the chestnut blight in the 1930s, American chestnut was a dominant canopy tree in mountain oak hickory forests. Today, it persists as root sprouts in the forest understory, occasionally reaching sufficient size to flower and produce fruits before being killed back by the chestnut blight fungus.

Other common understory trees include sourwood, flowering dogwood, red maple, black gum, downy serviceberry, and Fraser magnolia. Mountain laurel, rosebay rhododendron, and bear huckleberry often form a dense layer of heath shrubs. Other common shrubs include flame azalea, lowbush blueberry, mapleleaf viburnum, sweet shrub, and witch hazel.

The herbaceous layer is sparse to moderate in coverage with species such as Indian cucumber root, Solomon's seal, plumed Solomon's seal, wild yam, pipsissewa, and bearcorn. Ferns are common, including New York fern, hayscented fern, and Christmas fern. On more basic soils, heath shrubs are less common and the abundance and diversity of herbaceous wildflowers increases. Common species include bloodroot, mayapple, wideleaf spiderwort, Canada horsebalm, Jack-in-the-pulpit, and both blue and black cohosh.

OAK HICKORY FOREST: CHARACTERISTIC PLANTS

Trees

OCCASIONAL TO LOCALLY ABUNDANT SPECIES

Red maple	*Acer rubrum*	NI
Downy serviceberry	*Amelanchier arborea*	NI
Pignut hickory	*Carya glabra*	NI
Mockernut hickory	*Carya tomentosa*	NI
American chestnut	*Castanea dentata*	NI
Flowering dogwood	*Cornus florida*	NI
Tulip tree, Yellow poplar	*Liriodendron tulipifera*	NI
Cucumber tree	*Magnolia acuminata*	NI
Fraser magnolia	*Magnolia fraseri*	NI
Black gum	*Nyssa sylvatica*	NI
Sourwood	*Oxydendrum arboreum*	NI
Eastern white pine	*Pinus strobus*	NI
White oak	*Quercus alba*	NI
Chestnut oak	*Quercus montana*	NI
Northern red oak	*Quercus rubra*	NI
Black locust	*Robinia pseudoacacia*	NI
Sassafras	*Sassafras albidum*	NI

Shrubs and Woody Vines

OCCASIONAL TO LOCALLY ABUNDANT SPECIES

Hill cane	*Arundinaria appalachiana*	NI
Bear huckleberry	*Gaylussacia ursina*	NI
Witch hazel	*Hamamelis virginiana*	p. 262
Mountain laurel	*Kalmia latifolia*	p. 236
Buffalo nut	*Pyrularia pubera*	NI
Flame azalea	*Rhododendron calendulaceum*	p. 267
Rosebay rhododendron	*Rhododendron maximum*	p. 230
Whiteleaf greenbrier	*Smilax glauca*	NI
Poison ivy	*Toxicodendron radicans*	p. 223
Lowbush blueberry	*Vaccinium pallidum*	NI
Mapleleaf viburnum	*Viburnum acerifolium*	NI

Herbs

OCCASIONAL TO LOCALLY ABUNDANT SPECIES

Hog peanut	*Amphicarpaea bracteata*	p. 238
Appalachian oak leach	*Aureolaria laevigata*	NI
Pipsissewa, Striped wintergreen	*Chimaphila maculata*	p. 222
Canada horsebalm	*Collinsonia canadensis*	p. 261
Bearcorn, Squawroot	*Conopholis americana*	p. 255
Pink lady's slipper	*Cypripedium acaule*	p. 235
Hayscented fern	*Dennstaedtia punctilobula*	NI
Wild yam	*Dioscorea villosa*	NI
Rattlesnake orchid	*Goodyera pubescens*	p. 229
Plumed Solomon's seal	*Maianthemum racemosum*	p. 216
Indian cucumber root	*Medeola virginiana*	p. 264
Indian pipe, Ghost flower	*Monotropa uniflora*	p. 231
Grassleaf golden aster	*Pityopsis graminifolia*	p. 259
Mayapple	*Podophyllum peltatum*	p. 208
Solomon's seal	*Polygonatum biflorum*	p. 217
Christmas fern	*Polystichum acrostichoides*	NI
Curtis's goldenrod	*Solidago curtisii*	p. 261
New York fern	*Thelypteris noveboracensis*	NI
Cranefly orchid	*Tipularia discolor*	p. 246
Wideleaf spiderwort	*Tradescantia subaspera*	p. 250

RARE SPECIES

Ashy hydrangea	*Hydrangea cinerea*	NI
Sweet pinesap	*Monotropsis odorata*	NI

NI = species not included in the wildflower profiles (Part IV)

PINE-OAK-HEATH

Distinguishing Features
A dense layer of heath shrubs beneath a relatively open canopy of pines and dry-site oaks characterize the pine-oak-heath community.

Introduction
This widespread community occurs on exposed ridges and south- to southwest-facing slopes at elevations from about 1,500 feet to over 4,000 feet. A somewhat stunted canopy of pines and drought-tolerant oaks and a dense layer of heath shrubs dominate the vegetation. The herbaceous layer is sparse and overall plant diversity is low on the dry, nutrient-poor acidic soils that characterize this community.

Sites occupied by pine-oak-heath are especially prone to fire. This is because ridges and upper slopes are exposed to lightning and high winds, conditions are often dry, and a thick leaf litter layer and dense shrubs provide abundant fuel. Plant species cope with fire in various ways. The trees most likely to survive fire are large trees with thick bark, as bark provides insulation from the heat of fire. Small and medium-sized trees are often killed, as are thin-barked species. Following topkill by fire, many trees, shrubs, and herbaceous plants resprout from dormant buds on roots and rhizomes. Other species regenerate primarily by seeds, benefitting from the increased light, reduced competition, and increased soil nutrients that follow a burn.

Beginning in the 1930s, federal and state agencies implemented a massive program of fire suppression throughout the southern Appalachians. Stands of pine-oak-heath that historically experienced fire about every 10–15 years rarely burned. As a result, pine regeneration was greatly reduced, and hardwoods such as chestnut oak and scarlet oak increased in size, overtopping pines and eventually shading them out. As the canopy pines die and are not replaced, succession to an oak-dominant forest occurs. To reverse this trend, land managers are currently using controlled burns to maintain pine-dominant woodlands, including the pine-oak-heath community.

Vegetation

The vegetation varies with elevation, exposure, and soil depth. The two most common oaks are scarlet oak and chestnut oak. The dominant pines are Virginia pine and shortleaf pine at the lowest elevations, pitch pine at intermediate elevations, and table mountain pine at the highest elevations. Common subcanopy trees include black gum, sourwood, red maple, and sassafras. Sprouts of American chestnut can also be seen in the understory.

Heath shrubs, including deciduous species such as bear huckleberry, lowbush blueberry, and deerberry, along with evergreen species such as mountain laurel, rosebay rhododendron, and Catawba rhododendron occur in the shrub layer. Once established, these species often form dense thickets via vegetative spread. Vines such as common greenbrier and whiteleaf greenbrier also spread vegetatively, sometimes forming dense tangles of thorny stems that are nearly impenetrable, almost like green barbed wire.

The herbaceous layer is best developed in areas where the shrubs are absent or less dense. Characteristic species include evergreen clump-forming species such as trailing arbutus, galax, and wintergreen. Deciduous species with showy flowers include pink lady's slipper, grassleaf golden aster, and whorled coreopsis. You may also see the triangular fronds of bracken fern.

PINE-OAK-HEATH: CHARACTERISTIC PLANTS

Trees

ABUNDANT SPECIES		
Table mountain pine	*Pinus pungens*	NI
Pitch pine	*Pinus rigida*	NI
Scarlet oak	*Quercus coccinea*	NI
Chestnut oak	*Quercus montana*	NI
OCCASIONAL TO LOCALLY ABUNDANT SPECIES		
Red maple	*Acer rubrum*	NI
American chestnut	*Castanea dentata*	NI
Chinquapin	*Castanea pumila*	NI
Black gum	*Nyssa sylvatica*	NI
Sourwood	*Oxydendrum arboreum*	NI
Shortleaf pine	*Pinus echinata*	NI
Virginia pine	*Pinus virginiana*	NI
Sassafras	*Sassafras albidum*	NI
Horse sugar	*Symplocos tinctoria*	NI
Carolina hemlock	*Tsuga caroliniana*	NI

Shrubs and Woody Vines

ABUNDANT SPECIES		
Bear huckleberry	*Gaylussacia ursina*	NI
Mountain laurel	*Kalmia latifolia*	p. 236
Lowbush blueberry	*Vaccinium pallidum*	NI

OCCASIONAL TO LOCALLY ABUNDANT SPECIES		
Catawba rhododendron	*Rhododendron catawbiense*	p. 236
Rosebay rhododendron	*Rhododendron maximum*	p. 230
Whiteleaf greenbrier	*Smilax glauca*	NI
Common greenbrier	*Smilax rotundifolia*	NI
Deerberry	*Vaccinium stamineum*	NI

Herbs

OCCASIONAL TO LOCALLY ABUNDANT SPECIES		
Appalachian oak leach	*Aureolaria laevigata*	NI
Pipsissewa, Striped wintergreen	*Chimaphila maculata*	p. 222
Whorled coreopsis	*Coreopsis major*	p. 259
Pink lady's slipper	*Cypripedium acaule*	NI
Trailing arbutus	*Epigaea repens*	p. 207
Galax, Skunkweed	*Galax urceolata*	p. 224
Wintergreen	*Gaultheria procumbens*	p. 229
Carolina lily	*Lilium michauxii*	NI
Grassleaf golden aster	*Pityopsis graminifolia*	p. 259
Gaywings	*Polygala paucifolia*	NI
Bracken fern	*Pteridium aquilinum*	NI
Goat's rue	*Tephrosia virginiana*	NI
Turkeybeard, Beargrass	*Xerophyllum asphodeloides*	NI

NI = species not included in the wildflower profiles (Part IV)

WATER FALLS
Soft spraying solitude of hush
in chicanery of crash and
whisp almost as whisper, screamed, sensual
from the voice of rock. . . . this hill side skip
of smooth stone soothing opening eyes:
the braille of water weaving wetness. . . .
    into the elegy of air.
Skinny Dip Falls

—Thomas Rain Crowe
Tuckasegee, North Carolina

PART III

Hike Narratives

Virginia

1 / Big Falls

PINNACLE NATURAL AREA PRESERVE

Highlights	Streamside hike with abundant wildflowers and a cascading waterfall
Flowering season	March through early October
Peak flowering	April–May
Trail length	2.5 miles out and back
Trail rating	Easy
Elevation	1,770–1,670 feet
Nearest town	Lebanon, Russell County, Va.
Contact	276-676-5673; www.dcr.virginia.gov
Directions	From Abingdon, follow U.S. 19 north for 19 miles to Lebanon. In Lebanon, take 19 Business (north toward Cleveland) for 1 mile and turn left onto Route 82 West. Drive 1 mile on Route 82 and turn right onto Route 640 (River Mountain Road). Follow Route 640 for 4 miles and turn left on Route 721. Follow the gravel road 0.8 mile to the parking area for the Pinnacle Natural Area Preserve. GPS: N36 57.215 W82 03.291
Overview	This delightful hike along a designated scenic river begins on a suspension bridge and ends at a river-wide waterfall. Along the way, you'll hike through rich cove forests with spectacular spring wildflowers, including infrequently seen species such as dwarf larkspur, twinflower, and yellow lady's slipper. The preserve is

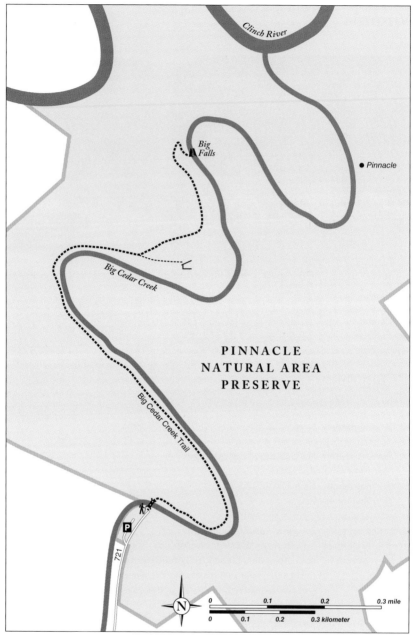

Big Falls, Pinnacle Natural Area Preserve

named for The Pinnacle, a dolomitic spire that towers nearly 400 feet over Big Cedar Creek, a short distance downstream from the falls. Facilities include picnic tables near the parking area and a day-use shelter with pit toilets 1.0 mile up the trail. From the parking area, cross the creek via a 75-foot-long suspension bridge to reach the Big Cedar Creek Trail on the far side.

The Hike

Just before the wooden steps for the suspension bridge, look to your left for a dense stand of pawpaw, a tall shrub with 1–2 inch wide purple flowers that bloom before the 6–12 inch long leaves emerge. If you're hiking in summer, look for the striking yellow flower heads and tall leafy stems of cup plant near the pawpaws. Northern water snakes (which resemble copperheads but are nonvenomous) can sometimes be seen basking in the sun on riverbanks, on downed trees, or in overhanging vegetation along streams. On my first hike on this trail, the mating calls of a newly emerged brood of 17-year cicadas pierced the hot afternoon air.

Immediately after crossing the suspension bridge, you enter a rich cove forest and the spring wildflower show takes off. Early blooming species include yellow trout lily, acute-lobed hepatica, and bloodroot, along with common blue violet, longspur violet, and spicebush. Later in spring, Robin's plantain, woodland phlox, green and gold, fourleaf milkweed, and Seneca snakeroot add to the color palette.

The trail soon levels off and intersects a concrete pad at 0.12 mile that extends across the river. The bright yellow flower heads of golden ragwort provide a splash of color in the rocky streamside community. Other spring wildflowers include Robin's plantain, giant chickweed, wild geranium, and buttercups. Hikers in late summer through early fall can expect to find colorful wildflower displays, including great blue lobelia, tall ironwood, cutleaf coneflower, and common wingstem. Keep an eye out for poison ivy as well.

Notice the series of riffles in the river. The river is well stocked with trout and you'll likely see a few people fishing. You might also spot a pair of mallard ducks bobbing in the water. A local birding club spotted 43 species of birds along this trail one spring morning, including red-eyed vireo, wood thrush, indigo bunting, and Louisiana waterthrush.

Bypass the Grapevine Hill spur trail at 0.4 mile, and continue to follow the old roadbed downstream. Common trees in the narrow alluvial forest along the river include sycamore, box elder, and pawpaw. Yellow buckeye is also common but on slightly higher ground. Look for the vibrant purplish-pink flowers of eastern redbud in early spring. The yellow flowers of witch hazel, in contrast, don't bloom until autumn.

A number of introduced species grow along the old roadbed including common dandelion, common chickweed, garlic mustard, Queen Anne's lace, and chicory. Also present are weedy native species such as lyreleaf sage and common ragweed.

You may notice a variety of butterflies along the trail, including giant swallowtails, eastern tiger swallowtails, pipevine swallowtails, and zebra swallowtails; they may be visiting flowers for nectar, laying eggs on host plants, or sipping moisture (and obtaining salts) from mud puddles.

At 0.7 mile, the river bends sharply to the right and the trail begins a gradual climb. The wooded slopes in this rich cove forest are chock full of spring wildflowers, including dwarf larkspur (with dark blue, white, and bicolored flower forms), twinleaf, and wild ginger. If you're hiking in summer or early fall, you may notice tall bellflower, bearsfoot, and white snakeroot. The low growing shrub with soft wood, peeling bark, and white flowers in rounded clusters is wild hydrangea.

As the trail descends to the river, look for rue anemone, bloodroot, and Solomon's seal in early spring. You might also notice the large heart-shaped leaves of pipevine clambering up the trunks of trees. The flowers of wild yam, a small vine with heart-shaped leaves, produce 3-winged fruits that hang like ornaments from twining stems in late summer through fall. The first birth control pills were made by chemically modifying extracts from the roots of this plant in the 1960s.

Just before a clearing with picnic tables and pit toilets at 1.0 mile, the Big Cedar Creek Trail veers left and heads upslope. As the trail climbs, the vegetation changes from a rich cove forest dominated by deciduous trees to an evergreen woodland dominated by Virginia pine, eastern red cedar, and northern white cedar.

Continue on the main trail, bypassing the Grapevine Hill spur trail on the left. The trail soon tops out. As it gradually descends toward the river, the vegetation reverts to rich cove forest with a medley of spring wildflowers, including wild ginger, perfoliate bellwort, lousewort, rue anemone, woodland phlox, large-flowered trillium, and blue cohosh. You may even see a yellow lady's slipper or two in spring.

Near the base of the slope at 1.2 miles, take the short spur trail to the right for a close-up view of Big Falls. The rich cove forest on the right side of the trail is a good area for spring wildflowers, including acute-lobed hepatica, bloodroot, twinleaf, and puttyroot. In late summer through early fall, look for robust wildflowers with showy flowers, including whiteflower leafcup, common wingstem, orange and yellow jewelweed, and great blue lobelia. Weedy species such as common ragweed, giant ragweed, and crown vetch also grow here, taking advantage of the disturbance caused by periodic flooding.

The river-wide cascade, about 10 feet tall, plunges over multiple layers of erosion-resistant sandstone, thrust on edge by the mountain building process. When the water levels are high, Big Falls is a powerful sight. Scouring associated with flooding keeps plant cover sparse in the spray cliff zone. The small beach that skirts the large pool at the base of the falls is a pleasant place to relax and have a snack before retracing your steps back to the trailhead.

Options. Continue on the Big Cedar Creek Trail to the Pinnacle Trail. This 0.25-mile loop with interesting wildflower displays provides a good view of the dolomite spire known as The Pinnacle.

1 / BIG FALLS: WHAT TO LOOK FOR

Spring

Acute-lobed hepatica	*Anemone acutiloba*	p. 207
Puttyroot, Adam and Eve	*Aplectrum hyemale*	NI
Jack-in-the-pulpit	*Arisaema triphyllum*	p. 241
Wild ginger	*Asarum canadense*	p. 242
Cutleaf toothwort	*Cardamine concatenata*	p. 210
Blue cohosh	*Caulophyllum thalictroides*	p. 242
Fairywand, Devil's bit	*Chamaelirium luteum*	p. 210

Bearcorn, Squawroot	*Conopholis americana*	p. 255
Yellow lady's slipper	*Cypripedium parviflorum*	NI
Dwarf larkspur	*Delphinium tricorne*	NI
Robin's plantain	*Erigeron pulchellus*	p. 216
Yellow trout lily	*Erythronium americanum*	NI
Wild geranium	*Geranium maculatum*	p. 235
Little brown jugs	*Hexastylis arifolia*	NI
Dwarf crested iris	*Iris cristata*	p. 247
Twinleaf	*Jeffersonia diphylla*	NI
Plumed Solomon's seal	*Maianthemum racemosum*	p. 216
Purple phacelia	*Phacelia bipinnatifida*	p. 243
Woodland phlox	*Phlox divaricata*	p. 248
Solomon's seal	*Polygonatum biflorum*	p. 217
Yellow mandarin	*Prosartes lanuginosa*	p. 263
Bloodroot	*Sanguinaria canadensis*	p. 209
Giant chickweed	*Stellaria pubera*	p. 214
Rue anemone	*Thalictrum thalictroides*	p. 211
Foamflower	*Tiarella cordifolia*	p. 218
Large-flowered trillium	*Trillium grandiflorum*	p. 214
Perfoliate bellwort	*Uvularia perfoliata*	p. 256
Longspur violet	*Viola rostrata*	NI
Common blue violet	*Viola sororia*	p. 247

Spring–Summer

Thimbleweed	*Anemone virginiana*	NI
Pipevine, Dutchman's pipe	*Aristolochia macrophylla*	p. 244
Fourleaf milkweed	*Asclepias quadrifolia*	NI
Green and gold	*Chrysogonum virginianum*	NI
Wild comfrey	*Cynoglossum virginianum*	NI
Queen Anne's lace	*Daucus carota*	NI
Wild yam	*Dioscorea villosa*	NI
Common alumroot	*Heuchera americana*	NI
Wild hydrangea	*Hydrangea arborescens*	p. 225
Broadleaf waterleaf	*Hydrophyllum canadense*	NI
Moonseed	*Menispermum canadense*	NI
Golden ragwort	*Packera aurea*	p. 257
Roundleaf ragwort	*Packera obovata*	NI
Lousewort, Wood betony	*Pedicularis canadensis*	p. 255
Seneca snakeroot	*Polygala senega*	NI
Wine raspberry	*Rubus phoenicolasius*	NI
Lyreleaf sage	*Salvia lyrata*	NI
Hairy skullcap	*Scutellaria elliptica*	NI
Poison ivy	*Toxicodendron radicans*	p. 223

Summer

Spikenard	*Aralia racemosa*	p. 265
Crown vetch	*Coronilla varia*	NI
Beggar's ticks	*Desmodium nudiflorum*	p. 238
Wood nettle	*Laportea canadensis*	p. 265
Basil bee balm	*Monarda clinopodia*	p. 227
Hoary mountain mint	*Pycnanthemum incanum*	NI
Cup plant	*Silphium perfoliatum*	NI

White snakeroot	*Ageratina altissima*	p. 232
Common ragweed	*Ambrosia artemisiifolia*	p. 266
Giant ragweed	*Ambrosia trifida*	NI
Hog peanut	*Amphicarpaea bracteata*	p. 238
Appalachian oak leach	*Aureolaria laevigata*	NI
Tall bellflower	*Campanulastrum americanum*	NI
Chicory	*Cichorium intybus*	NI
Canada horsebalm	*Collinsonia canadensis*	p. 261
Leafy elephant's foot	*Elephantopus carolinianus*	NI
White wood aster	*Eurybia divaricata*	p. 231
Sweet Joe Pye weed	*Eutrochium purpureum*	NI
Thinleaf sunflower	*Helianthus decapetalus*	NI
Woodland sunflower	*Helianthus divaricatus*	NI
Rock alumroot	*Heuchera villosa*	p. 230
Orange jewelweed	*Impatiens capensis*	p. 268
Yellow jewelweed	*Impatiens pallida*	NI
Downy lobelia	*Lobelia puberula*	NI
Great blue lobelia	*Lobelia siphilitica*	p. 251
Whiteflower leafcup	*Polymnia canadensis*	NI
Tall rattlesnake root	*Prenanthes altissima*	NI
Gall-of-the-earth	*Prenanthes trifoliata*	NI
Cutleaf coneflower	*Rudbeckia laciniata*	p. 260
Bearsfoot, Yellow leafcup	*Smallanthus uvedalius*	p. 260
Goldenrod	*Solidago* species	NI
Heartleaf aster	*Symphyotrichum cordifolium*	p. 251
Common wingstem	*Verbesina alternifolia*	p. 262
Tall ironweed	*Vernonia gigantea*	NI

Fall

Witch hazel	*Hamamelis virginiana*	p. 262

NI = species not included in the wildflower profiles (Part IV)

2 / Falls on the Little Stony

JEFFERSON NATIONAL FOREST

Highlights	A scenic river gorge with three waterfalls
Flowering season	Late March through early October
Peak flowering	April–May
Trail length	1.2 miles out and back
Trail rating	Easy
Elevation	2,270–2,190 feet
Nearest town	Coeburn, Wise County, Va.
Contact	Clinch River Ranger District; 276-328-2931; www.fs.usda.gov
Directions	From Dungannon, take Va. 72 north for 9.0 miles, and turn left on Route 644 (Corder Town Road). Follow Corder Town Road for 1.1 miles, and turn left onto F.R. 700. Follow F.R. 700 for 1.3 miles, then take a slight left onto F.R. 701. Drive 0.8 mile on F.R. 701 to the parking area on the left. GPS: N36 52.168 W82 27.811
Overview	If you like short hikes with lots of waterfalls, then you'll love this three-waterfall hike on the Little Stony National Recreation Trail. Like most of the southern Appalachians, this area was logged in the early 1900s. The current trail follows the old narrow-gauge railroad bed that was used to haul out the cut timber. Today, the Little Stony gorge is vegetated by a relatively lush acidic cove forest. On my hikes through this gorge, I've seen a variety of wildflowers, a black bear, great blue herons, Louisiana waterthrushes, and numerous salamanders. Who knows what surprises await you?

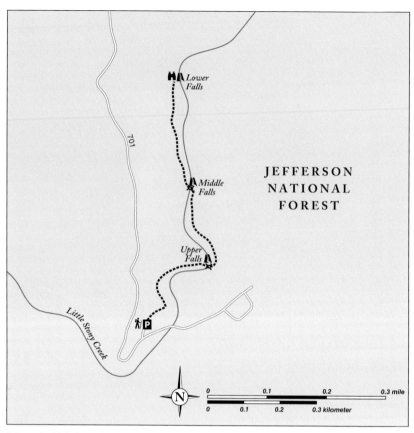

Falls on the Little Stony, Jefferson National Forest

The Hike

The trail begins at the lower end of the parking area adjacent to the kiosk. Notice the charred tree trunks on the slope above the parking area. The Forest Service conducted a prescribed burn in early spring 2013 to reduce the fuel load (thereby reducing the risk of a catastrophic canopy fire) and to enhance food availability for wildlife by promoting the growth of shrubs and herbaceous plants.

As you start down the trail, look for wildflowers such as wood anemone, Indian cucumber root, Solomon's seal, and plumed Solomon's seal, along with Queen Anne's lace, lyreleaf sage, whorled coreopsis, and common cinquefoil. You may also notice dense carpets of New York fern near the trailhead. Overhead are trees such as northern red oak, chestnut oak, Fraser magnolia, red maple, striped maple, and sassafras. Bird enthusiasts may notice migrants including thrushes, warblers, and tanagers along the trail in fall and spring.

After descending a short series of steps, go left at the T-junction and you'll soon see Little Stony Creek on your right. Clumps of galax, wintergreen, heartleaf, and trailing arbutus, all of which have thick evergreen leaves, grow along the trail. Spring flowering species include lousewort, pink lady's slipper, rattlesnake orchid, sessileleaf bellwort, yellow star grass, and speckled wood lily. You might also notice white, blue, and yellow-flowered violets in spring. From late summer through early fall look for grassleaf golden aster, white wood aster, white snakeroot, and goldenrod in this acidic cove forest.

Cross Little Stony Creek via a footbridge at 0.2 mile and take in the view of Upper Falls as it tumbles fast and strong over an overhanging ledge. Just past the footbridge, you'll get a better view of the falls, including the large amphitheater-like cliffs and the wooden bridge in the background. For a closer look, take the stone path down to the base of the falls where the force of the falling water has carved out a deep plunge pool. Don't be surprised to see a hiker or two taking a dip in the cold water on a hot summer day.

As the trail descends into Little Stony gorge, the air becomes cooler, soil moisture increases, and plant cover increases. Trees in this acidic cove forest include two birches (sweet and yellow), two maples (red and striped), and three magnolias (Fraser, cucumber, and umbrella leaf). The neat rows of shallow holes commonly seen in the bark of trees is the work of yellow-bellied sapsuckers. Winter residents in our region, yellow-bellied sapsuckers lap up the sugary sap that leaks into the holes from the tree (along with any insects that get caught there). Sapsuckers drill holes in a wide variety of trees but particularly like birches and maples.

Rosebay rhododendron, mountain laurel, witch hazel, and mountain sweet pepperbush grow in the forest understory. On the forest floor, look for galax, trailing arbutus, and partridge berry, along with scattered plants of rattlesnake orchid, cranefly orchid, and pipsissewa.

As you continue, look for a rock spire, more than 75 feet tall, on your right. At 0.3 mile, the trail reaches a second footbridge over Little Stony Creek, directly above Middle Falls, which drops just 12 feet. Rosebay rhododendron lines the margin of the falls with sweet birch as the canopy dominant. Once common, most eastern hemlocks in this gorge are either dead or dying due to infestations of woolly adelgids. The gangly shrub with peeling brown bark is mountain sweet pepperbush.

The rocky streamside here and elsewhere along Little Stony Creek is a good place to spot Louisiana waterthrushes. They nest in crevices along the stream bank and feed on aquatic invertebrates. Birders may also see or hear Swainson's warblers in the rhododendron thickets along the stream. Don't be surprised to see a great blue heron along the stream.

In late spring, look for the large creamy white flowers of Fraser magnolia just downstream from the bridge. As you continue into the gorge, keep an eye out for scattered clumps of painted trillium—its white flowers (with reddish markings at the base) bloom in late spring and its red fruits light up the forest floor in July–August. Like many woodland herbs, ants disperse trillium seeds.

As you approach the viewing platform for Lower Falls, the gorge becomes deeper and the vegetation lusher. Here, the acidic cove forest includes wild hydrangea, rosebay rhododendron, and mountain sweet pepperbush under a canopy of yellow birch and tulip tree. Both ferns and mosses are abundant in this area, as are late summer–early fall flowering species such as white wood aster and white snakeroot.

The viewing platform at 0.6 mile provides an excellent view of the falls. The nearly vertical waterfall stretches across the river, creating a curtain of water that cascades and free falls 30 feet over numerous narrow ledges into a large plunge pool at the base. Rosebay rhododendron is common along the margin of the falls. Canopy trees include sweet birch, tulip tree, and several large eastern hemlocks whose canopy foliage is thinning due to adelgids.

On the slope directly behind the viewing platform is a dense patch of wood nettle. If you touch (or brush against) the stinging hairs that cover this plant, you'll feel a stinging sensation that lasts several minutes. The stinging hairs deter most insects and other animals from feeding on the plant.

After enjoying the falls, retrace your steps back to the trailhead.

Options. Continue down the trail another 2.3 miles to experience spectacular views within a gorge that becomes 400 feet deep and 1,700 feet wide. The trail ends at the Hanging Rock Picnic Area from where you can retrace your steps back to the trailhead for a total hiking distance of 5.6 miles.

2 / FALLS ON THE LITTLE STONY: WHAT TO LOOK FOR

Spring

Doll's eyes, White baneberry	*Actaea pachypoda*	p. 213
Wood anemone	*Anemone quinquefolia*	p. 209
Jack-in-the-pulpit	*Arisaema triphyllum*	p. 241
Bearcorn, Squawroot	*Conopholis americana*	p. 255
Pink lady's slipper	*Cypripedium acaule*	p. 235
Trailing arbutus	*Epigaea repens*	p. 207
Heartleaf	*Hexastylis* species	NI
Yellow star grass	*Hypoxis hirsuta*	NI
Lousewort, Wood betony	*Pedicularis canadensis*	p. 255
Dwarf cinquefoil	*Potentilla canadensis*	p. 253
Yellow mandarin	*Prosartes lanuginosa*	p. 263
Foamflower	*Tiarella cordifolia*	p. 218
Painted trillium	*Trillium undulatum*	p. 219
Sessileleaf bellwort	*Uvularia sessilifolia*	NI
Sweet white violet	*Viola blanda*	p. 219
Longspur violet	*Viola rostrata*	NI

Spring–Summer

Colicroot	*Aletris farinosa*	NI
Pipsissewa, Striped wintergreen	*Chimaphila maculata*	p. 222
Speckled wood lily	*Clintonia umbellulata*	p. 222
Galax, Skunkweed	*Galax urceolata*	p. 224
Rattlesnake hawkweed	*Hieracium venosum*	p. 256
Wild hydrangea	*Hydrangea arborescens*	p. 225
Mountain laurel	*Kalmia latifolia*	p. 236
Plumed Solomon's seal	*Maianthemum racemosum*	p. 216
Indian cucumber root	*Medeola virginiana*	p. 264
Partridge berry	*Mitchella repens*	p. 223
Solomon's seal	*Polygonatum biflorum*	p. 217
Lyreleaf sage	*Salvia lyrata*	NI

Summer

Mountain sweet pepperbush	*Clethra acuminata*	NI
Whorled coreopsis	*Coreopsis major*	p. 259
Queen Anne's lace	*Daucus carota*	NI
Wintergreen	*Gaultheria procumbens*	p. 229
Rattlesnake orchid	*Goodyera pubescens*	p. 229
Wood nettle	*Laportea canadensis*	p. 265
Rosebay rhododendron	*Rhododendron maximum*	p. 230
Cranefly orchid	*Tipularia discolor*	p. 246

Summer–Fall

Hog peanut	*Amphicarpaea bracteata*	p. 238
White wood aster	*Eurybia divaricata*	p. 231
Goldenrod	*Solidago* species	NI
Cardinal flower	*Lobelia cardinalis*	p. 269
Southern harebell	*Campanula divaricata*	p. 250
Downy lobelia	*Lobelia puberula*	NI
Grassleaf golden aster	*Pityopsis graminifolia*	p. 259
White snakeroot	*Ageratina altissima*	p. 232

Fall

Witch hazel	*Hamamelis virginiana*	p. 262

NI = species not included in the wildflower profiles (Part IV)

3 / Cabin Creek Falls

GRAYSON HIGHLANDS STATE PARK

Highlights	Mountain grandeur with a cascading stream
Flowering season	Mid-April through late September
Peak flowering	May–June
Trail length	1.8-mile loop trail
Trail rating	Moderate
Elevation	4,660–4,300 feet
Nearest town	Volney, Grayson County, Va.
Contact	276-579-7092; www.dcr.virginia.gov
Directions	The park is off U.S. 58, midway between Damascus and Independence. From the park entrance, drive 3.4 miles on Grayson Highland Lane (Route 362) and park on the right at the Massie Gap parking area. GPS: N36 38.020 W81 30.557
Overview	High-elevation peaks and ridges with open meadows, dense forests, and panoramic views make Grayson Highlands State Park and the adjoining Mount Rogers National Recreation Area a paradise for outdoor enthusiasts. The Cabin Creek loop trail takes you through grassy meadows, shrublands, northern hardwood forest, and acidic cove forest along a scenic stream with two waterfalls and numerous wildflowers. It's a relatively easy hike except for a short, steep, boggy section along Cabin Creek. Facilities at the park include a visitor center, restrooms, campground, and small store. A small entrance fee is charged for parking.

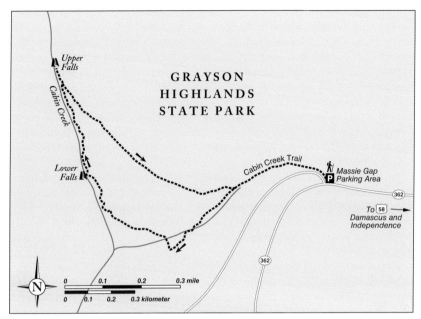

Cabin Creek Falls, Grayson Highlands State Park

The Hike

From the upper parking area at Massie Gap, walk into the open meadow-like area and go left (west) where well-marked signs indicate the start of the Cabin Creek Trail and yellow blazes help keep you on the trail. In the meadow, you'll see scattered trees including hawthorn, fire cherry, and red spruce, along with wildflowers such as common dandelion, dwarf cinquefoil, and heal all. In early May, the "clouds" of white in the meadow and nearby slopes are the blooms of smooth serviceberry. In late June to July, look for birds plucking its sweet juicy fruits, including eastern phoebes, brown thrashers, scarlet tanagers, and red-eyed vireos.

Once covered by a dense spruce-fir forest, Massie Gap was heavily logged in the early 1900s. A harsh climate, strong winds, and soil loss following logging has slowed the recovery process such that the current vegetation is a mosaic of meadows, scrubland, and regenerating forest. Spring comes late at this elevation—the wildflower show typically begins in late April to early May.

From the grassy meadow, the trail soon enters a dense shrubby area with highbush blueberry (produces edible fruits in mid-to-late summer), mountain laurel, minniebush, and flame azalea. In small openings between shrubs, look for spring wildflowers such as trailing arbutus, wild strawberry, common blue violet, painted trillium, and pink lady's slipper, along with later blooming species such as whorled loosestrife, roundleaf pyrola, yarrow, heal all, and goldenrod.

Cross the horse trail and pass through another area of mixed shrubs before entering a rosebay rhododendron tunnel. After passing a kiosk, go left at the fork (you'll come back to this junction on the return loop). Some of the boulders here and elsewhere on the trail are partially covered with smooth rock tripe, a large leathery lichen. In mid-to-late spring, look for yellow trout lily, wood anemone, and Canada mayflower.

As the trail wanders downslope, the vegetation transitions to northern hardwood forest with red spruce, yellow birch, sugar maple, striped maple, northern red oak, American beech, and Fraser magnolia, along with shrubs such as rosebay rhododendron, witch hobble, witch hazel, and flame azalea. Spring wildflowers include Appalachian bluet, wood anemone, painted trillium, and Canada mayflower. If you're hiking in late summer or early fall, look for mountain wood aster and white snakeroot. Keep an eye out for white turtlehead, crimson bee balm, and large purple fringed orchid in wet areas. On drier slopes, you may see Indian pipe, a parasitic flowering plant that has waxy white stems. Five different violets can be found along the trail—roundleaf yellow, yellow woodland, halberdleaf yellow, sweet white, and common blue violet.

In spring and fall, birding enthusiasts may see numerous migratory warblers, thrushes, and vireos. In summer, look for nesting songbirds typical of high elevation forests, including black-throated green, black-throated blue, and chestnut-sided warblers, as well as scarlet tanager, and rose-breasted grosbeaks. Other wildlife include black bear, bobcat, red fox, white-tailed deer, eastern chipmunk, ruffed grouse, and wild turkey.

At 0.6 mile, several bigtooth aspens, a rare tree in the southern Appalachians, can be seen just upslope from the trail (at the time of writing, a temporary sign pinpointed their location). Like quaking aspen, the triangular leaves of bigtooth aspen quiver in the slightest breeze and turn a brilliant shade of yellow in autumn.

The slope below the trail, just before reaching Cabin Creek at 0.65 mile, has good wildflower displays, including yellow trout lily, wood anemone, southern red trillium, Indian cucumber root, foamflower, umbrella leaf, and doll's eyes. If you're hiking in summer, you may notice tassel rue and Turk's cap lily.

As the trail follows Cabin Creek upstream, the vegetation transitions from northern hardwood forest to acidic cove forest. The clear, cold water that tumbles over rocks and boulders with scattered pools provides habitat for native brook trout (regulations require artificial lures, single hooks, and a 9-inch minimum). Dense thickets of rosebay rhododendron dominate the rocky streamside community—its showy clusters of pinkish-white flowers bloom in July. You may also see yellow trout lily, wood anemone, and southern red trillium in spring, and black cohosh, whorled aster, and white wood aster in late summer through early fall.

At 0.8 mile, the lower falls comes into view. Here the stream splits into several cascades that tumble 25 feet over boulders into a clear pool. Rosebay rhododendron and wild hydrangea grow along the rocky stream with yellow birch and red spruce overhead. Near the falls, the trail skirts a large seepage rock with mountain meadowrue, umbrella leaf, and Jack-in-the-pulpit.

The trail continues to climb alongside the stream, crossing a boggy area where cutleaf coneflower and crimson bee balm flower in late summer and fall. At the signed junction, continue straight on a short spur trail to an observation area for the upper falls at 1.1 miles. Here, you'll see a long narrow cascade along a boulder-strewn stream with rosebay rhododendron on the margin. Yellow birch is the dominant canopy tree (notice how some individuals appear to have established on boulders with the roots extending over the rock). Understory species include wild hydrangea, witch hobble, and pipevine. Along the spur trail, keen observers may notice the white bell-shaped flowers of American lily-of-the-valley in spring and the pink striped flowers and clover-like leaves of mountain wood sorrel in summer.

Return to the junction and turn left to continue on the loop trail. The vegetation soon reverts to northern hardwood forest with yellow buckeye, sugar maple, yellow birch, and red spruce as canopy dominants. Along the slope, you'll see grass-like sedges forming a dense turf, large mats of running cedar, and fern glades. This part of the trail was a railroad bed in the early 1900s that carried cut logs out of the forest. After the forest was logged, woody debris from the cut trees as well as organic matter on the soil surface easily caught fire, causing fires that swept through the area.

As you continue along the trail, keep an eye out for blue cohosh and giant chickweed in spring and the bright orange-to-red flowers of flame azalea in early summer. Hikers in late summer through early fall may see southern harebell, white snakeroot, and goldenrod. Less conspicuous is beechdrops, a root parasite on American beech that produces clusters of narrow pale brown stems up to 18 inches tall. Notice regenerating red spruce in the forest understory.

Along this part of the trail, I startled a wild turkey on one hike, which took flight through the trees. Keep an eye out for broad-winged hawks soaring above the canopy. Barred owls can sometimes be seen and heard during daylight hours. Listen for their distinctive "who cooks for you" call.

Just before the creek, at 1.7 miles, you'll come to the Y junction you encountered early in the hike. Go left here to return to the parking area at Massie Gap.

Options. The upper parking lot at Massie Gap is the starting point for several fantastic hikes, including to the top of Mount Rogers (see the trail guide pamphlet provided at the park entrance or stop by the visitor center for details). Wild ponies are a popular attraction along the Mount Rogers Trail. Be prepared for severe weather, including high winds, low temperatures, dense fog, and strong thunderstorms, as weather conditions on the mountain can change rapidly.

3 / CABIN CREEK FALLS: WHAT TO LOOK FOR

Spring

Doll's eyes, White baneberry	*Actaea pachypoda*	p. 213
Wood anemone	*Anemone quinquefolia*	p. 209
Jack-in-the-pulpit	*Arisaema triphyllum*	p. 241
Blue cohosh	*Caulophyllum thalictroides*	p. 242
Pink lady's slipper	*Cypripedium acaule*	p. 235
Trailing arbutus	*Epigaea repens*	p. 207
Yellow trout lily	*Erythronium americanum*	NI
Wild strawberry	*Fragaria virginiana*	p. 212
Solomon's seal	*Polygonatum biflorum*	p. 217
Dwarf cinquefoil	*Potentilla canadensis*	p. 253
Giant chickweed	*Stellaria pubera*	p. 214
Foamflower	*Tiarella cordifolia*	p. 218
Southern red trillium	*Trillium sulcatum*	NI
Painted trillium	*Trillium undulatum*	p. 219
Highbush blueberry	*Vaccinium corymbosum*	NI
Sweet white violet	*Viola blanda*	p. 219
Halberdleaf yellow violet	*Viola hastata*	p. 254
Yellow woodland violet	*Viola pubescens*	NI
Roundleaf yellow violet	*Viola rotundifolia*	NI
Common blue violet	*Viola sororia*	p. 247

Spring–Summer

Pipevine, Dutchman's pipe	*Aristolochia macrophylla*	p. 244
Pipsissewa, Striped wintergreen	*Chimaphila maculata*	p. 222
Speckled wood lily	*Clintonia umbellulata*	p. 222
American lily-of-the-valley	*Convallaria majuscula*	NI
Umbrella leaf	*Diphylleia cymosa*	p. 215
Fleabane	*Erigeron* species	NI
Appalachian bluet	*Houstonia serpyllifolia*	p. 248
Wild hydrangea	*Hydrangea arborescens*	p. 225
Mountain laurel	*Kalmia latifolia*	p. 236
Whorled loosestrife	*Lysimachia quadrifolia*	p. 258
Canada mayflower	*Maianthemum canadense*	p. 225
Indian cucumber root	*Medeola virginiana*	p. 264
Minniebush	*Menziesia pilosa*	NI
Basil bee balm	*Monarda clinopodia*	p. 227
Small's ragwort	*Packera anonyma*	NI
Roundleaf pyrola	*Pyrola americana*	NI
Flame azalea	*Rhododendron calendulaceum*	p. 267
Common dandelion	*Taraxacum officinale*	NI
Mountain meadowrue	*Thalictrum clavatum*	p. 226
Witch hobble, Hobblebush	*Viburnum lantanoides*	NI

Summer

Black cohosh	*Actaea racemosa*	p. 226
Rattlesnake orchid	*Goodyera pubescens*	p. 229
Wood nettle	*Laportea canadensis*	p. 265
Turk's cap lily	*Lilium superbum*	p. 268
Mountain wood sorrel	*Oxalis montana*	p. 237
Large purple fringed orchid	*Platanthera grandiflora*	NI
Rosebay rhododendron	*Rhododendron maximum*	p. 230
Tassel rue	*Trautvetteria caroliniensis*	p. 228

Summer–Fall

Yarrow	*Achillea millefolium*	p. 221
White snakeroot	*Ageratina altissima*	p. 232
Appalachian oak leach	*Aureolaria laevigata*	NI
Southern harebell	*Campanula divaricata*	p. 250
White turtlehead	*Chelone glabra*	NI
Appalachian dodder	*Cuscuta rostrata*	p. 232
Mountain wood aster	*Eurybia chlorolepis*	NI
Crimson bee balm	*Monarda didyma*	p. 269
Indian pipe, Ghost flower	*Monotropa uniflora*	p. 231
Whorled aster	*Oclemena acuminata*	NI
Heal all	*Prunella vulgaris*	p. 249
Cutleaf coneflower	*Rudbeckia laciniata*	p. 260
Goldenrod	*Solidago* species	NI

Fall

Beechdrops	*Epifagus virginiana*	p. 233
Witch hazel	*Hamamelis virginiana*	p. 262

NI = species not included in the wildflower profiles (Part IV)

North Carolina

4 / Cascades Trail

E. B. JEFFRESS PARK, BLUE RIDGE PARKWAY

Highlights	A long cascading waterfall and numerous wildflowers
Flowering season	Late April through September
Peak flowering	No distinct peak
Trail length	1.2-mile loop trail
Trail rating	Mostly easy but with some steep steps
Elevation	3,580–3,385 feet
Nearest town	Boone, Watauga County, N.C.
Contact	828-271-4779; www.nps.gov/blri
Directions	At mile 271.9 on the Blue Ridge Parkway, turn into E. B. Jeffress Park (located 4.4 miles north of U.S. 421 and 11 miles south of S.R. 16) and park in the large parking lot near the Cascades Overlook. GPS: N36 14.742 W81 27.467

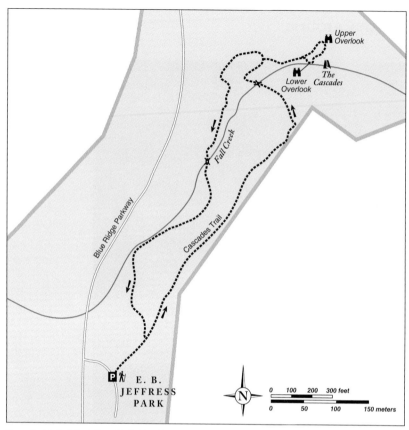

Cascades Trail, E. B. Jeffress Park, Blue Ridge Parkway

Overview E. B. Jeffress Park lies on the edge of the Blue Ridge Escarpment nearly 2,000 feet above the adjoining piedmont. The main attraction of the park is the Cascades Trail, a 1.2-mile loop that begins in an oak hickory forest before descending to an upper and lower overlook of Fall Creek plunging nearly 100 feet over a rock cliff. On the return loop, the trail follows a stream through an acidic cove forest. Scenic views of the surrounding mountains and piedmont are best when the trees are leafless (from November to early May). Interpretive signs help you identify some of the common trees and shrubs along the trail. It's also a good birding area for spring migrants and summer residents. Facilities at this popular stop along the Blue Ridge Parkway include picnic tables, water, and restrooms.

The Hike

The Cascades Trail begins on a paved path in front of the restroom building near the entrance to the parking area. Trees in this oak hickory forest include northern red oak, white oak, chestnut oak, white ash, sassafras, eastern white pine, black locust, and hickory. Near the trailhead, look for the bright yellow flower heads of golden ragwort, the pale yellow dangling flowers of sessileleaf bellwort, and the arched stems of Solomon's seal in spring. You might also notice clumps of bearcorn, a parasitic flowering plant whose yellowish brown stems resemble small ears of corn popping up through the leaf litter.

As you hike along the ridge, look for the flowers of pink lady's slipper and fire pink in spring, flame azalea in June, and rosebay rhododendron in July. In late summer and fall, the ridge trail is dotted with members of the sunflower family, including white snakeroot, white wood aster, and Curtis's goldenrod.

Bird enthusiasts may notice white-breasted nuthatch, dark-eyed junco, eastern towhee, eastern wood-pewee, wood thrush, downy woodpecker, ovenbird, scarlet tanager, American redstart, and various warblers, including the elusive cerulean warbler.

The trail descends gradually at 0.25 mile and soon crosses Fall Creek via a wooden footbridge, where yellow jewelweed, mountain angelica, and basil bee balm bloom in summer. Here, the habitat is cooler and moister than the ridge, and the vegetation transitions to an acidic cove forest with rosebay rhododendron and mountain doghobble forming a dense shrub layer along the creek.

Continue on the trail to a series of stone stairs leading down to the upper overlook, where bloodroot, common cinquefoil, wild strawberry, and plumed Solomon's seal flower in spring. The upper overlook at 0.4 mile provides a birds-eye view of the falls cascading nearly 100 feet down a cliff. For most of the way, the slope is gentle enough that the water slides down (rather than falls over) the rock face. Peak over the wall to see if fire pink, sundrops, orange jewelweed, pink turtlehead, or wild hydrangea are blooming and listen for the buzz of ruby-throated hummingbirds as they dart from flower to flower seeking nectar. The surrounding mountains are part of the Blue Ridge, which runs from Virginia south to Georgia.

For a closer view of the falls, continue down another set of stone steps to the lower overlook at 0.45 mile. Spring hikers may see various violets, wake robin, Solomon's seal, plumed Solomon's seal, Jack-in-the-pulpit, and mountain doghobble. Yellow jewelweed, common wingstem, Canada horsebalm, and white wood aster flower in summer to early fall.

The lower overlook provides good views of the waterfall cascading, free falling, and sliding along numerous ledges until it drops out of sight. Look for wildflowers such as brook lettuce, mountain meadowrue, sundrops, orange jewelweed, mountain angelica, and pink turtlehead in the spray cliff zone. Fall Creek continues its journey down the Blue Ridge Escarpment to the Yadkin River, which eventually flows into the Atlantic Ocean.

After enjoying the sights, hike back up the stone steps. Where the trail forks at 0.5 mile, veer right on the signed return trail. This portion of the trail parallels the creek through an acidic cove forest, supporting many of the wildflowers already mentioned.

At the second footbridge (0.6 mile), look for the dainty blue flowers of Appalachian bluet in late spring, and the two-lipped flowers of heal all and pink turtlehead in summer to fall. Rosebay rhododendron is common along the creek. As you continue along the trail, be on the lookout for pink lady's slipper and Jack-in-the-pulpit in spring, galax in summer, and soapwort gentian in fall.

As the trail veers away from the creek and begins climbing toward the ridge, look for painted trillium, Indian cucumber root, Jack-in-the-pulpit, and various violets in mid-to-late spring. Fall hikers may spot the yellow flowers of witch hazel, a common shrub along this part of the trail. If the temperature and humidity are just right, you may hear a popping sound as the fruits of witch hazel split open, shooting the small seeds up to 15 feet from the parent plant.

At the T-junction (1.0 mile), turn right and follow the ridge trail back to the trailhead. As you hike through this oak hickory forest, notice the abundant woody debris on the forest floor. Ridgetops such as this one are frequently exposed to high winds that break off branches and sometimes topple large trees, creating gaps in the canopy that allow more light to reach the forest floor, which in turn provides good habitat for wildflowers.

Options. You may want to explore the oak hickory forest and historic structures along the Tompkins Knob Trail. This easy 1.2-mile round-trip trail begins at the far (south) end of the parking area for E. B. Jeffress Park and ends at the Tompkins Knob parking area (milepost 272.5).

4 / CASCADES TRAIL: WHAT TO LOOK FOR

Spring

Jack-in-the-pulpit	*Arisaema triphyllum*	p. 241
Bearcorn, Squawroot	*Conopholis americana*	p. 255
Pink lady's slipper	*Cypripedium acaule*	p. 235
Trailing arbutus	*Epigaea repens*	p. 207
Wild strawberry	*Fragaria virginiana*	p. 212
Mountain laurel	*Kalmia latifolia*	p. 236
Mountain doghobble	*Leucothoe fontanesiana*	p. 213
Plumed Solomon's seal	*Maianthemum racemosum*	p. 216
Brook lettuce	*Micranthes micranthidifolia*	p. 217
Golden ragwort	*Packera aurea*	p. 257
Solomon's seal	*Polygonatum biflorum*	p. 217
Common cinquefoil	*Potentilla simplex*	NI
Bloodroot	*Sanguinaria canadensis*	p. 209
Wake robin, Stinking Willie	*Trillium erectum*	p. 243
Painted trillium	*Trillium undulatum*	p. 219
Sessileleaf bellwort	*Uvularia sessilifolia*	NI
Sweet white violet	*Viola blanda*	p. 219
Halberdleaf yellow violet	*Viola hastata*	p. 254
Roundleaf yellow violet	*Viola rotundifolia*	NI
Common blue violet	*Viola sororia*	p. 247

Spring–Summer

Goatsbeard	*Aruncus dioicus*	NI
Pipsissewa, Striped wintergreen	*Chimaphila maculata*	p. 222
Galax, Skunkweed	*Galax urceolata*	p. 224
Bowman's root	*Gillenia trifoliata*	NI
Indian cucumber root	*Medeola virginiana*	p. 264
Flame azalea	*Rhododendron calendulaceum*	p. 267
Fire pink	*Silene virginica*	p. 267
Mountain meadowrue	*Thalictrum clavatum*	p. 226

Summary

Summer		
Thimbleweed	*Anemone virginiana*	NI
Mountain angelica	*Angelica triquinata*	p. 266
Leather flower	*Clematis viorna*	NI
Wild hydrangea	*Hydrangea arborescens*	p. 225
Wood nettle	*Laportea canadensis*	p. 265
Whorled loosestrife	*Lysimachia quadrifolia*	p. 258
Basil bee balm	*Monarda clinopodia*	p. 227
Sundrops	*Oenothera fruticosa*	p. 257
Rosebay rhododendron	*Rhododendron maximum*	p. 230
Common elderberry	*Sambucus canadensis*	p. 221
Summer–Fall		
Pink turtlehead	*Chelone lyonii*	p. 239
Canada horsebalm	*Collinsonia canadensis*	p. 261
White wood aster	*Eurybia divaricata*	p. 231
Joe Pye weed	*Eutrochium fistulosum*	p. 239
Rock alumroot	*Heuchera villosa*	p. 230
Orange jewelweed	*Impatiens capensis*	p. 268
Yellow jewelweed	*Impatiens pallida*	NI
Long-bristled smartweed	*Polygonum caespitosum*	NI
Heal all	*Prunella vulgaris*	p. 249
Curtis's goldenrod	*Solidago curtisii*	p. 261
Common wingstem	*Verbesina alternifolia*	p. 262
Fall		
White snakeroot	*Ageratina altissima*	p. 232
Soapwort gentian	*Gentiana saponaria*	p. 252
Witch hazel	*Hamamelis virginiana*	p. 262

NI = species not included in the wildflower profiles (Part IV)

5 / Glen Burney Trail

BLOWING ROCK

Highlights	Three waterfalls and lots of wildflowers
Flowering season	April through mid-October
Peak flowering	Late April–May
Trail length	2.4 miles out and back
Trail rating	Moderate
Elevation	3,535–2,940 feet
Nearest town	Blowing Rock, Watauga County, N.C.
Contact	828-295-5222; www.blowingrock.com/areahiking.htm
Directions	From the intersection of U.S. 221 and 321 Business in central Blowing Rock, go south on Main Street (321 Business) for two blocks and turn right onto Laurel Lane. Continue straight through the four-way intersection and immediately turn left into the small parking lot. The trail begins on a gravel road at the lower end of the parking area. GPS: N36 07. 936 W81 40.835
Overview	This popular hike during the summer tourist season takes you through an acidic cove forest in a ravine that's a stone's throw from downtown Blowing Rock, a small resort town near Boone. Following a path first used by Native Americans, the trail makes an enjoyable hike for tourists staying in the Blowing Rock region as well as locals wanting to walk in the woods without having to leave town. The first quarter mile or so passes houses, fences, and the ruins of an old sewer treatment plant. Don't worry—things improve as the trail follows New Years Creek into a deep ravine with three waterfalls and a surprising array of wildflowers.

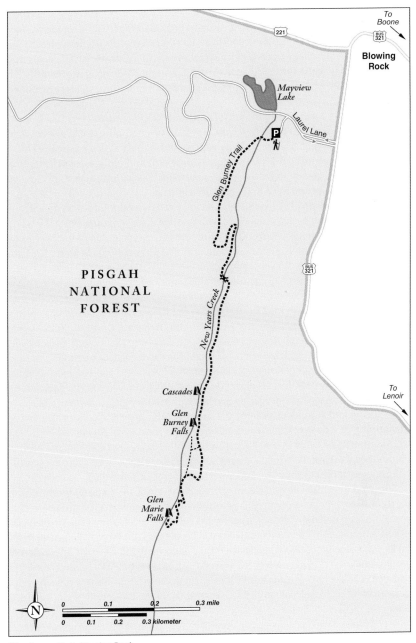

Glen Burney Trail, Blowing Rock

The Hike

Take a minute to review the trail information posted in the parking lot kiosk, then begin the hike at the far end of the parking area where a gravel road descends. At the trailhead, look for a dense patch of multiflora rose, an exotic invasive species that produces showy white flowers in late spring. Its bright red fruits mature in the fall and are eaten by birds that disperse the seeds. Both orange and yellow jewelweed also grow here.

After 25 yards, turn right off the gravel road and rock hop across New Years Creek. Follow the trail downstream where you may see common blue violet, sweet white violet, Solomon's seal, and heal all, as well as dense mats of two exotic species— ground ivy (with purplish blue two-lipped flowers) and Japanese pachysandra. The latter species covers an entire slope illustrating how an introduced species can reduce the diversity and abundance of native plants.

You'll soon pass an old sewer lift station followed by a huge house on the far side of the creek. The tall herbaceous plant with reddish stems growing along the wood fence is Japanese knotweed, another exotic invasive species. On a happier note, rosebay rhododendron is abundant here and elsewhere along the trail—look for its showy pinkish-white flowers in July.

Along a long flat stretch of the trail, you may notice Fraser magnolia in the over-story and golden ragwort, buttercup, and yellow horsebalm at your feet. As the trail winds down to the creek, look for the scarlet red flowers of fire pink in late spring, the showy white flower heads of basil bee balm in summer, and the fuzzy white flower heads of white snakeroot in fall.

The trail skirts the concrete ruins of a small 1920s-era sewer treatment plant at 0.4 mile that now harbors orange and yellow jewelweed and one of the wood ferns. Spring hikers may spot two chickweeds—giant chickweed (a native species) and common chickweed (an introduced species with smaller leaves and flowers).

In spring and summer, listen for the songs of migratory and resident birds and the tapping of woodpeckers. Woodpeckers detect insects (to forage on) by listening for chewing sounds in tree bark. Birding enthusiasts may also notice Carolina chickadees working the trunks of trees. In this case, it's the discerning eyes of the chickadees that spot insects tucked away in tiny cracks in the bark.

The trail continues downstream, crossing the creek on a sturdy footbridge at 0.5 mile. The river cutting into the mountain over the ages formed the ravine that you are hiking through. Canopy trees in this acidic cove forest include sweet birch, yellow birch, Fraser magnolia, and American beech. The large old eastern hemlocks that once graced this forest are either dead or dying from an infestation of woolly adelgids (sucking insects the size of an aphid that have decimated hemlocks through much of the eastern United States). Look for spring wildflowers such as Appalachian bluet, bloodroot, golden ragwort, and Jack-in-the-pulpit as you continue along the trail.

At 0.8 mile, you'll see a sign for the Cascades. Continue down the trail a short distance where there is a good view back toward the Cascades (with a large Fraser magnolia leaning across the river). Spring hikers may see large-flowered trillium, painted trillium, and dwarf crested iris, each of which has ant-dispersed seeds. In contrast, the berry-like fruits of Jack-in-the-pulpit and yellow mandarin are eaten by birds and rodents which disperse the seeds in their droppings.

At the signed fork in the trail, go right and follow the short spur trail (stone steps) to the wooden platform at the top of Glen Burney Falls (0.9 mile). In spring, look for golden ragwort, sessileleaf bellwort, and sweet white violet, whereas hikers in late summer to early fall may notice white snakeroot, Canada horsebalm, cutleaf coneflower, and orange and yellow jewelweed. The rocky streamside habitat is dominated by rosebay rhododendron.

Continue on the main trail for 25 yards, then turn right at the fork and follow a short spur trail to get a good view of Glen Burney Falls sliding down the rock face. Continue on the main trail to a T-junction and follow the short spur trail to the base of the falls at 1.2 miles. The spray cliff includes cliff saxifrage, cutleaf coneflower, and rosebay rhododendron. Near the base, you may notice brook lettuce, garlic mustard, and buttercup in spring and orange jewelweed, white snakeroot, and white wood aster in summer or fall. By midsummer, wood nettle covers much of the ground. If you feel a stinging sensation, you've likely brushed against a wood nettle plant. Crushed leaves of jewelweed will soothe your skin but probably won't be necessary as the stinging sensation normally subsides in a few minutes.

Retrace your steps to the T-junction and go right, following the trail to the top of Glen Marie Falls at 1.4 miles. Be careful—the rocks above the falls can be slippery. A steep descent on switchbacks, followed by a right turn on a spur trail takes you to the base of Glen Marie Falls at 1.6 miles. Here, you can view a cascade zigzagging nearly 60 feet down a rock face. Sweet birch and Fraser magnolia grow near the falls, as does rosebay rhododendron.

Boulders broken off the rock face are piled up at the base of the falls as are old tree trunks washed over the falls in floodwaters, the river equivalent of driftwood. The trail ends at the base of the falls, so you'll need to backtrack from here to the parking area.

Options. Broyhill Park provides a pleasant walk around Mayview Lake with a variety of plants, including some native species. Getting there is easy. From the upper end of the parking area for the Glen Burney Trail, walk 25 yards and you'll see the park entrance on your left.

5 / GLEN BURNEY TRAIL: WHAT TO LOOK FOR

Spring

Garlic mustard	*Alliaria petiolata*	NI
Jack-in-the-pulpit	*Arisaema triphyllum*	p. 241
Bearcorn, Squawroot	*Conopholis americana*	p. 255
Catchweed bedstraw	*Galium aparine*	NI
Appalachian bluet	*Houstonia serpyllifolia*	p. 248
Dwarf crested iris	*Iris cristata*	p. 247
Plumed Solomon's seal	*Maianthemum racemosum*	p. 216
Indian cucumber root	*Medeola virginiana*	p. 264
Japanese pachysandra	*Pachysandra terminalis*	NI
Purple phacelia	*Phacelia bipinnatifida*	p. 243
Solomon's seal	*Polygonatum biflorum*	p. 217
Yellow mandarin	*Prosartes lanuginosa*	p. 263
Bloodroot	*Sanguinaria canadensis*	p. 209
Common chickweed	*Stellaria media*	NI
Giant chickweed	*Stellaria pubera*	p. 214
Foamflower	*Tiarella cordifolia*	p. 218
Large-flowered trillium	*Trillium grandiflorum*	p. 214

Painted trillium	*Trillium undulatum*	p. 219
Sessileleaf bellwort	*Uvularia sessilifolia*	NI
Sweet white violet	*Viola blanda*	p. 219
Halberdleaf yellow violet	*Viola hastata*	p. 254
Roundleaf yellow violet	*Viola rotundifolia*	NI
Common blue violet	*Viola sororia*	p. 247

Spring–Summer

Speckled wood lily	*Clintonia umbellulata*	p. 222
Robin's plantain	*Erigeron pulchellus*	p. 216
Galax, Skunkweed	*Galax urceolata*	p. 224
Ground ivy	*Glechoma hederacea*	NI
Common alumroot	*Heuchera americana*	NI
Cliff saxifrage	*Hydatica petiolaris*	p. 220
Brook lettuce	*Micranthes micranthidifolia*	p. 217
Golden ragwort	*Packera aurea*	p. 257
Fire pink	*Silene virginica*	p. 267

Summer

Mountain angelica	*Angelica triquinata*	p. 266
Spikenard	*Aralia racemosa*	p. 265
Mountain sweet pepperbush	*Clethra acuminata*	NI
Rattlesnake orchid	*Goodyera pubescens*	p. 229
Wild hydrangea	*Hydrangea arborescens*	p. 225
Wood nettle	*Laportea canadensis*	p. 265
Basil bee balm	*Monarda clinopodia*	p. 227
Rosebay rhododendron	*Rhododendron maximum*	p. 230
Common elderberry	*Sambucus canadensis*	p. 221

Summer–Fall

Southern harebell	*Campanula divaricata*	p. 250
Canada horsebalm	*Collinsonia canadensis*	p. 261
Whorled wood aster	*Eurybia acuminatus*	NI
White wood aster	*Eurybia divaricata*	p. 231
Japanese knotweed	*Fallopia japonica*	NI
Orange jewelweed	*Impatiens capensis*	p. 268
Yellow jewelweed	*Impatiens pallida*	NI
Pokeweed	*Phytolacca americana*	p. 227
Heal all	*Prunella vulgaris*	p. 249
Cutleaf coneflower	*Rudbeckia laciniata*	p. 260
Curtis's goldenrod	*Solidago curtisii*	p. 261
Small false hellebore	*Veratrum parviflorum*	NI

Fall

| White snakeroot | *Ageratina altissima* | p. 232 |
| Witch hazel | *Hamamelis virginiana* | p. 262 |

NI = species not included in the wildflower profiles (Part IV)

6 / Tanawha Trail

BLUE RIDGE PARKWAY

Highlights	Stunning views, abundant wildflowers, exceptional fall colors
Flowering season	April through September
Peak flowering	May–June
Trail length	1.6 miles out and back
Trail rating	Moderate
Elevation	4,295–4,680 feet
Nearest town	Linville, Avery County, N.C.
Contact	828-271-4779; www.nps.gov/blri
Directions	The waterfall can be viewed and the hike begins at the Rough Ridge parking area on the Blue Ridge Parkway at milepost 302.9, located 1.5 miles north of the Linn Cove Viaduct Visitor Center on the Parkway. GPS: N 36 05.904 W 81 47.836

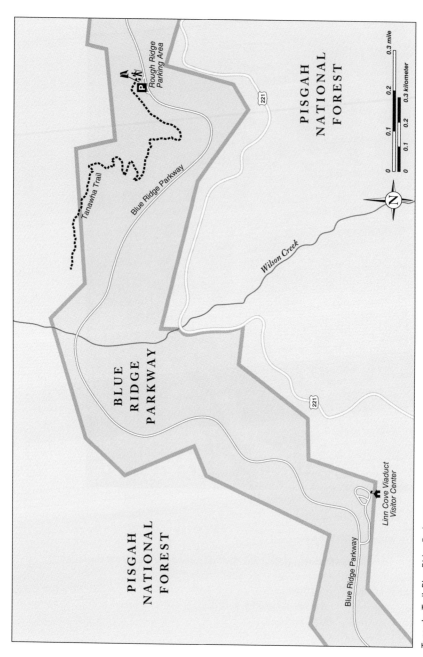

Tanawha Trail, Blue Ridge Parkway

Overview   This short ascending hike is on the Grandfather Mountain portion
of the Blue Ridge Parkway. At 5,964 feet, Grandfather is the highest
mountain along the Blue Ridge front, where it rises nearly 4,000
feet above the adjoining piedmont. Designated an International
Biosphere Preserve in 1992, Grandfather Mountain harbors more
than 30 species of rare or endangered plants and animals. From the
Rough Ridge parking area, you can view a sliding waterfall and gain
access to the section of the Tanawha Trail that follows the cliff-lined
crest of Rough Ridge through northern hardwood forest, heath
balds, and rock outcrops where panoramic views of the surrounding
mountains are among the best on the parkway, making this a very
popular hike.

The Hike

Among the hikes described in this book, this one's unique in that you can view the
waterfall from the parking area. After a good rain, water slides (rather than falls) over
the rock substrate. During dry periods, the water slows to a trickle. Growing on the
margin of the falls are rosebay rhododendron, umbrella leaf, and white snakeroot.
In a good year, the white-to-pale-pink flowers of rosebay rhododendron can be quite
colorful in July. The pink-flowered shrub that typically blooms in May is pinkshell
azalea, a rare plant whose natural distribution is limited to western North Carolina.

After viewing the falls, walk to your right (east) to the end of the parking area
where the trail begins. As the trail ascends, you may notice sweet white violet, common blue violet, and speckled wood lily in spring. At the junction, take the Tanawha
Trail left (toward Linn Cove). An arched footbridge provides a bird's eye view of the
small creek sliding down the rock face. You're standing in a northern hardwood
forest with yellow buckeye, yellow birch, red spruce, Fraser magnolia, and red maple
in the overstory. At this elevation, the trees don't begin leafing out until early May
which is about when the spring wildflowers get interesting.

The change in plant communities as you ascend provides habitat for a diversity
of birds, including Carolina chickadee, tufted titmouse, blue-headed and white-
eyed vireos, golden-crowned kinglet, Blackburnian warbler, and dark-eyed junco.

The next section of the trail weaves through dense shrubs, rock outcrops, stunted
trees, showy flowers, and unforgettable vistas. The steadily ascending trail is lined
with heath shrubs: first, rosebay rhododendron, then Catawba rhododendron
(similar to rosebay but with dense clusters of pink-to-purple flowers that typically
bloom in early June). Spring wildflowers include yellow trout lily, wood anemone,
dwarf iris, Canada mayflower, and painted trillium. If you detect a skunk spray odor
along the trail, it's probably coming from galax (also known as skunkweed). Birders
may notice dark-eyed juncos, ruffed grouse, and indigo buntings in this area.

At 0.2 mile, you'll reach a boardwalk with a distinctive stack rock formation on
the right. The shrubby vegetation all around you is a heath bald, including Catawba
rhododendron, mountain laurel, and highbush blueberry. Scattered among the
shrubs are stunted trees such as red spruce, mountain ash, smooth serviceberry,
fire cherry, and the regionally rare bigtooth aspen. Other rare species include sand
myrtle (a low-growing shrub with small shiny leaves and white-to-pink flowers),
turkeybeard (which has small needle-like leaves and an upright showy white inflorescence), and Heller's blazing star (which has dense showy lavender flowers

above a basal rosette of narrow leaves). Stay on the boardwalk to avoid trampling the fragile vegetation.

Enjoy the stunning views of Grandfather Mountain towering overhead, the piedmont below, nearby Linville Gorge, and the numerous ridges in the distance. The Blue Ridge Parkway (including the Linn Cove Viaduct) is clearly visible as it winds through the Blue Ridge Mountains.

Beyond the boardwalk, the often-soggy trail with rocky tread ascends another 0.3 mile to the crest. At the junction, take the short spur trail to the left and scramble up the rock promontory (called Ship Rock) at 0.6 mile. A mosaic of heath bald, rock outcrop, and northern hardwood forest surrounds you.

The Cherokee name for Grandfather Mountain is Tanawha, meaning great hawk or eagle, which aptly fits the soaring views that hikers experience on this trail. It also provides a great vantage point for watching the broad-winged hawk migration from September through mid-October and enjoying the spectacular fall colors.

Backtrack a few yards to the junction and go left, continuing on the Tanawha Trail as it descends a series of stone steps before skirting a huge boulder draped with smooth rock tripe, a large lichen that curls up and appears brittle when dry, but has a slimy rubbery appearance when wet. As the trail descends, the vegetation abruptly changes from heath bald to northern hardwood forest with yellow birch, yellow buckeye, and red spruce in the canopy, and rosebay rhododendron, Catawba rhododendron, pinkshell azalea, and wild hydrangea in the understory. Along the trail, you may notice spring wildflowers such as yellow trout lily, bluebead lily, painted trillium, wake robin, and Solomon's seal.

There are breeding populations of pileated, hairy, and downy woodpeckers in the forest, although you may be more likely to hear them than see them. You may also hear northern saw-whet owl in April and May.

The wildflower show really gets going at 0.8 mile on a relatively open (sunny) slope with shallow rocky soil kept moist by seepage flow. One of the best wildflower spots in the area, the parade of flowers extends from mid-spring through early fall. In spring, look for the dainty white flowers of fringed phacelia, the white (fading to pink) flowers of Canada violet, the yellowish-green to purple-green flowers of blue cohosh, the dangling yellow flowers of large-flowered bellwort, the tiny blue flowers of Quaker ladies, and the maroon flowers of wake robin.

Summer brings a new color palette including the bright red flowers of crimson bee balm, a tall pink-flowered phlox, the showy white flowers of tassel rue (and basal bee balm), the pale blue flowers of tall bellflower (and wideleaf spiderwort), and the yellows of Canada horsebalm, cutleaf coneflower, and other members of the sunflower family. Orange and yellow jewelweed adds to the wildflower mix, as does mountain angelica, false hellebore, and umbrella leaf. The open canopy in this northern hardwood forest is dominated by yellow buckeye, including several old trees whose tops have broken off.

Spend some time exploring this wildflower wonderland before turning around and retracing your steps to the parking area.

Options. If you'd like to extend the hike and explore more wildflowers, the Tanawha Trail continues another 1.8 miles to the Linn Cove Viaduct Visitor Center on the parkway. The 2.6-mile one-way hike from the Rough Ridge parking area to the visitor center is the most scenic section of the 13.5-mile Tanawha Trail and is one of the best hikes in the southern Appalachians.

Spring

Wood anemone	*Anemone quinquefolia*	p. 209
Blue cohosh	*Caulophyllum thalictroides*	p. 242
Yellow trout lily	*Erythronium americanum*	NI
Dwarf crested iris	*Iris cristata*	p. 247
Dwarf iris	*Iris verna*	NI
Fringed phacelia	*Phacelia fimbriata*	p. 211
Yellow mandarin	*Prosartes lanuginosa*	p. 263
Giant chickweed	*Stellaria pubera*	p. 214
Wake robin, Stinking Willie	*Trillium erectum*	p. 243
Painted trillium	*Trillium undulatum*	p. 219
Large-flowered bellwort	*Uvularia grandiflora*	NI
Sweet white violet	*Viola blanda*	p. 219
Common blue violet	*Viola sororia*	p. 247

Spring–Summer

Bluebead lily	*Clintonia borealis*	NI
Speckled wood lily	*Clintonia umbellulata*	p. 222
Umbrella leaf	*Diphylleia cymosa*	p. 215
Quaker ladies	*Houstonia caerulea*	NI
Sand myrtle	*Kalmia buxifolia*	NI
Mountain laurel	*Kalmia latifolia*	p. 236
Canada mayflower	*Maianthemum canadense*	p. 225
Solomon's seal	*Polygonatum biflorum*	p. 217
Catawba rhododendron	*Rhododendron catawbiense*	p. 236
Pinkshell azalea	*Rhododendron vaseyi*	NI
Canada violet	*Viola canadensis*	p. 220

Summer

Mountain angelica	*Angelica triquinata*	p. 266
Tall bellflower	*Campanulastrum americanum*	NI
Whorled coreopsis	*Coreopsis major*	p. 259
Appalachian dodder	*Cuscuta rostrata*	p. 232
Galax, Skunkweed	*Galax urceolata*	p. 224
Wild hydrangea	*Hydrangea arborescens*	p. 225
Wood nettle	*Laportea canadensis*	p. 265
Heller's blazing star	*Liatris helleri*	NI
Basil bee balm	*Monarda clinopodia*	p. 227
Rosebay rhododendron	*Rhododendron maximum*	p. 230
Tall meadowrue	*Thalictrum pubescens*	NI
Wideleaf spiderwort	*Tradescantia subaspera*	p. 250
Tassel rue	*Trautvetteria caroliniensis*	p. 228
False hellebore	*Veratrum viride*	NI
Turkeybeard, Beargrass	*Xerophyllum asphodeloides*	NI

Canada horsebalm	*Collinsonia canadensis*	p. 261
Whorled wood aster	*Eurybia acuminatus*	NI
Mountain wood aster	*Eurybia chlorolepis*	NI
Cliff saxifrage	*Hydatica petiolaris*	p. 220
Orange jewelweed	*Impatiens capensis*	p. 268
Yellow jewelweed	*Impatiens pallida*	NI
Crimson bee balm	*Monarda didyma*	p. 269
Cutleaf coneflower	*Rudbeckia laciniata*	p. 260

Fall

White snakeroot	*Ageratina altissima*	p. 232
Witch hazel	*Hamamelis virginiana*	p. 262
Sand myrtle	*Kalmia buxifolia*	NI
Curtis's goldenrod	*Solidago curtisii*	p. 261
Canada violet	*Viola canadensis*	p. 220

NI = species not included in the wildflower profiles (Part IV)

7 / Linville Falls

BLUE RIDGE PARKWAY

Highlights	Old-growth forest with a deep river gorge and powerful waterfall
Flowering season	April through September
Peak flowering	No distinct peak
Trail length	2 miles out and back
Trail rating	Mostly easy but with some steep steps
Elevation	3,225–3,390 feet
Nearest town	Linville Falls, Burke County, N.C.
Contact	828-271-4779; www.nps.gov/blri
Directions	From the junction of the Blue Ridge Parkway and U.S. 221 in the town of Linville Falls, drive north on the parkway 1.0 mile and turn right at the sign for the Linville Falls Visitor Center (milepost 316.5). Drive 1.4 miles to where the road ends at the visitor center. GPS: N35 57.257 W81 55.671
Overview	Linville Falls is the most popular waterfall hike along the Blue Ridge Parkway, for good reason. The Cherokee called the area Eeseeoh, meaning "river of many cliffs." Eons ago, the waterfall that visitors see today along the Linville River was 12 miles downstream from its current location. As the river plunged over a steep precipice with a hard rock layer on top, it cut into the softer rock beneath it. Once the softer rock was sufficiently undercut, the hard rock lip broke off. As this process was repeated over millions of years, the waterfall slowly migrated upstream, creating the gorge we see today. With steep rock walls rising well over 2,000 feet, Linville Gorge is one of the deepest

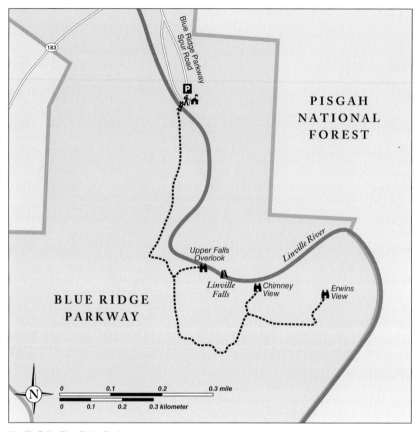

Linville Falls, Blue Ridge Parkway

and most rugged gorges in the eastern United States. Much of the gorge is old-growth acidic cove forest. Some of the scenes in the movie *The Last of the Mohicans* were filmed here. Facilities include a picnic area, restrooms, a small bookshop/visitor center, and campground.

The Hike

Easy-to-follow trails lead to good waterfall views on both sides of the river. Take the trail on the right (west) side for the best views and wildflower displays. To do so, walk through the breezeway at the visitor center and follow the paved path to the bridge over the Linville River. Canopy trees include yellow birch, eastern white pine, red maple, and yellow buckeye. A variety of birds, including osprey, green-backed heron, belted kingfisher, Louisiana waterthrush, and wood duck may be seen along the river. On the far side of the bridge, spring wildflowers include giant chickweed and three violets: common blue, sweet white, and halberdleaf yellow violet. Summer and fall hikers may notice yellow jewelweed, orange jewelweed, cutleaf coneflower, and white wood aster.

The undulating trail passes through acidic cove forest (where speckled wood lily, showy orchis, and yellow mandarin flower in spring) before skirting a grassy field where thimbleweed, heal all, and white snakeroot flower in summer to fall. Just past the field, growing on a moist slope below the trail is crimson bee balm. Look for ruby-throated hummingbirds visiting its bright red nectar-rich flowers in summer. Birding enthusiasts may also see ovenbird, northern parula, red-breasted nuthatch, scarlet tanager, rose-breasted grosbeak, and various warblers along the trail.

Just after the trail descends to the river, look for wood anemone and wild strawberry in spring. At 0.3 mile, the trail crosses a short bridge where multiflora rose (an invasive species), wild hydrangea, and mountain laurel flower in late spring to early summer. The trail ascends through an acidic cove forest with eastern hemlock, eastern white pine, yellow birch, and Fraser magnolia in the canopy, and dense thickets of rosebay rhododendron in the understory. Many of the large eastern hemlocks in this old-growth forest have been killed by woolly adelgids; healthy individuals have been treated with an insecticide.

Follow the signed spur trail to Upper Falls Overlook, where you can view a small waterfall (about 10 feet tall and 40 feet wide), a large pool, and a rocky streamside habitat that harbors shrubs such as ninebark, mountain doghobble, yellowroot, gorge rhododendron, and rosebay rhododendron. Nonwoody wildflowers include tassel rue, thimbleweed, whorled coreopsis, cutleaf coneflower, and orange jewelweed. Downstream, the river tumbles into a narrow curving flume (a powerful sight!) before spiraling out of view on its way to the lower falls.

Back on the main trail, follow the sign to Chimney View Overlook. You'll soon pass a small field on the right where buttercup, common dandelion, and forget-me-not grow, as do a few Jack-in-the-pulpits. The trail ascends more steeply through an old-growth acidic cove forest with eastern hemlock and eastern white pine in the canopy and galax, partridge berry, and large flower heartleaf on the forest floor.

After the trail tops out, and a short descent, veer left at the junction and follow a series of steps to the Chimney View Overlook at 0.9 mile. Here, you'll have stunning views of the lower waterfall as it drops nearly 60 feet into a large plunge pool surrounded on either side by the vertical cliffs that line the gorge. In spring, you may see the showy pink-to-white flowers of gorge rhododendron at the overlook and on the cliffs on the far side of the gorge. Watch for peregrine falcons and red crossbills, both of which are known to nest in the gorge.

Return to the main trail and go left toward Erwins View Overlook. Rosebay rhododendron, gorge rhododendron, and Catawba rhododendron line this section of the trail. In spring, look for painted trillium and pink lady's slipper.

Just before the stone wall, turn left on the short spur trail to Erwins View Overlook, where you'll enjoy sweeping views of the falls, the gorge, and surrounding mountains. At the time of writing, hundreds of standing dead eastern hemlock trees killed by hemlock woolly adelgids are visible in the gorge from the various overlooks. Growing on the steep cliffs (including alongside this overlook) is a second species of hemlock, the Carolina hemlock (its needles surround the twig whereas the needles of eastern hemlock tend to occur in a single plane). Restricted to the southern Appalachians, the Carolina hemlock is also being killed off by the hemlock woolly adelgid, an aphid-like insect that was inadvertently introduced from Asia. Eastern white pine and pitch pine also grow along this overlook and elsewhere in the gorge.

Back on the main trail, turn left and walk a few yards to where the trail ends at a stone wall (1.3 miles) for another great view of the gorge. Because of its remoteness and ruggedness, most of Linville Gorge (including the portion seen from this overlook) has been designated a wilderness area. It's one of the few places in the region where the forests have never been logged and trees three to four feet in diameter are common. Unfortunately, none of the trails at Linville Falls connect with the trails in the Linville Gorge Wilderness Area. Take a few minutes to enjoy the view before turning around and retracing your steps to the visitor center.

Options. You may want to explore the two moderately strenuous trails on the left (east) side of the Linville River—the Linville Gorge Trail (about 1.5 miles round trip) and the Plunge Basin Trail (about 1-mile round trip). Both begin at the visitor center and are well signed and easily followed. An easy (0.2-mile) hike to a small but scenic waterfall is the Duggers Creek Loop Trail—it begins opposite the visitor center. A sign indicating trails of the area and additional information is available at the small visitor center/bookshop.

7 / LINVILLE FALLS: WHAT TO LOOK FOR

Spring

Wood anemone	*Anemone quinquefolia*	p. 209
Jack-in-the-pulpit	*Arisaema triphyllum*	p. 241
Pipevine, Dutchman's pipe	*Aristolochia macrophylla*	p. 244
Pink lady's slipper	*Cypripedium acaule*	p. 235
Wild strawberry	*Fragaria virginiana*	p. 212
Showy orchis	*Galearis spectabilis*	p. 234
Large flower heartleaf	*Hexastylis shuttleworthii*	p. 245
Mountain doghobble	*Leucothoe fontanesiana*	p. 213
Indian cucumber root	*Medeola virginiana*	p. 264
Common cinquefoil	*Potentilla simplex*	NI
Yellow mandarin	*Prosartes lanuginosa*	p. 263
Gorge rhododendron, Punctatum	*Rhododendron minus*	p. 237
Giant chickweed	*Stellaria pubera*	p. 214
Painted trillium	*Trillium undulatum*	p. 219
Sweet white violet	*Viola blanda*	p. 219
Halberdleaf yellow violet	*Viola hastata*	p. 254
Common blue violet	*Viola sororia*	p. 247
Yellowroot	*Xanthorhiza simplicissima*	p. 240

Spring–Summer

Galax, Skunkweed	*Galax urceolata*	p. 224
Mountain laurel	*Kalmia latifolia*	p. 236
Partridge berry	*Mitchella repens*	p. 223
Catawba rhododendron	*Rhododendron catawbiense*	p. 236
Fire pink	*Silene virginica*	p. 267

Summer

Thimbleweed	*Anemone virginiana*	NI
Pipsissewa, Striped wintergreen	*Chimaphila maculata*	p. 222
Whorled coreopsis	*Coreopsis major*	p. 259
Wintergreen	*Gaultheria procumbens*	p. 229
Wild hydrangea	*Hydrangea arborescens*	p. 225
Wood nettle	*Laportea canadensis*	p. 265
Whorled loosestrife	*Lysimachia quadrifolia*	p. 258
Forget-me-not	*Myosotis laxa*	NI
Ninebark	*Physocarpus opulifolius*	NI
Flame azalea	*Rhododendron calendulaceum*	p. 267
Rosebay rhododendron	*Rhododendron maximum*	p. 230
Broadleaf arrowhead	*Sagittaria latifolia*	NI
Common elderberry	*Sambucus canadensis*	p. 221
Cranefly orchid	*Tipularia discolor*	p. 246
Tassel rue	*Trautvetteria caroliniensis*	p. 228

Summer–Fall

Canada horsebalm	*Collinsonia canadensis*	p. 261
White wood aster	*Eurybia divaricata*	p. 231
Joe Pye weed	*Eutrochium fistulosum*	p. 239
Orange jewelweed	*Impatiens capensis*	p. 268
Yellow jewelweed	*Impatiens pallida*	NI
Crimson bee balm	*Monarda didyma*	p. 269
Pokeweed	*Phytolacca americana*	p. 227
Heal all	*Prunella vulgaris*	p. 249
Cutleaf coneflower	*Rudbeckia laciniata*	p. 260
New York ironweed	*Vernonia noveboracensis*	p. 246

Fall

White snakeroot	*Ageratina altissima*	p. 232
Common ragweed	*Ambrosia artemisiifolia*	p. 266
Witch hazel	*Hamamelis virginiana*	p. 262
Curtis's goldenrod	*Solidago curtisii*	p. 261

NI = species not included in the wildflower profiles (Part IV)

8 / Crabtree Falls

BLUE RIDGE PARKWAY

Highlights	A picture-perfect waterfall, lush forests, abundant wildflowers
Flowering season	April through September
Peak flowering	Late April through May
Trail length	2.2 miles out and back
Trail rating	Moderate
Elevation	3,760–3,280 feet
Nearest town	Little Switzerland, McDowell and Mitchell Counties, N.C.
Contact	828-271-4779; www.nps.gov/blri
Directions	At milepost 339.5 on the Blue Ridge Parkway turn into the Crabtree Falls Recreation Area located about 8.6 miles south of N.C. 226 in Little Switzerland and 4.6 miles north of N.C. 80 at Buck Gap. Park in the front portion of the paved parking lot to the right of the snack bar and gift shop where there is a sign to the falls. GPS: N35 48.758 W82 08.598
Overview	This popular trail along the Blue Ridge Parkway meanders through mature oak hickory forest, acidic and rich cove forests, and open fields with tall trees and colorful wildflowers before reaching one of the most picturesque waterfalls in the region. The falls forms a wide

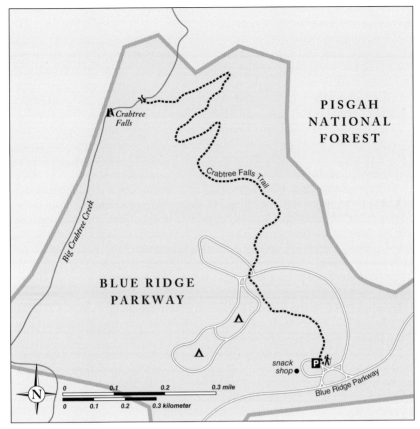

Crabtree Falls, Blue Ridge Parkway

veil as it cascades over numerous narrow rock ledges on its 70-foot drop. A bridge with a built-in bench spans the creek at the base of the falls, providing great views. Facilities include a snack shop and gift store with restrooms, picnic area, and campground.

The Hike

Before heading down the Crabtree Falls Trail, take a minute to explore the wildflowers at the trailhead, including spring-blooming species such as giant chickweed, golden ragwort, and common blue violet. If you're hiking in summer, look for the scarlet red flowers of fire pink and the tall narrow stalks and white tassel-like flowers of black cohosh. As the trail descends, it skirts an amphitheater, then enters a large open meadow with abundant wildflowers from spring through fall, many of which don't occur in other places on this mostly forested trail (including three summer-flowering milkweeds). Birding enthusiasts may spot eastern meadowlark, indigo bunting, and various sparrows in the open field.

At the junction (0.2 mile), turn right and look for large-flowered trillium in spring, and basil bee balm and Turk's cap lily in summer. Various swallowtail butterflies, including spicebush, pipevine, and eastern tiger sip nectar and pollinate the orange-red flowers of Turk's cap lily.

Cross the paved road at the campground and head straight across to a small parking area where you'll see an information sign for Crabtree Falls at 0.3 mile. The trail immediately descends through a thicket of rosebay rhododendron with mats of Canada mayflower hugging the ground. You'll soon enter an oak hickory forest with large canopy trees, including white oak, northern red oak, mockernut hickory, tulip tree, cucumber magnolia, and white basswood.

Birding enthusiasts may spot a variety of birds along the trail, including scarlet tanager, Acadian flycatcher, yellow-billed cuckoo, red-headed woodpecker, and various warblers. Barred owls also occur in the forest and can sometimes be seen and heard during daylight hours.

At the T-junction (0.5 mile), turn right and continue downhill through an area rich in spring wildflowers, including bloodroot, mayapple, blue cohosh, showy orchis, and yellow mandarin. You may also see bearcorn, a parasitic flowering plant that resembles small ears of corn popping up through the leaf litter. If you're hiking in late summer or early fall, keep an eye out for heartleaf skullcap, yellow horsebalm, and pink turtlehead. The climbing vine with large heart-shaped leaves is pipevine.

The vegetation soon changes to an acidic cove forest with a dense understory of rosebay rhododendron and mountain laurel. Fall hikers may spot a few clumps of soapwort gentian. As you walk down a series of stone steps, listen for the sound of the falls and look for spring blooming species such as American lily-of-the-valley, dwarf crested iris, and speckled wood lily.

Cross a footbridge at 0.8 mile and head down two more sets of stone steps where black cohosh blooms from mid-to-late summer. In seepage areas, look for the large leaves of umbrella leaf and the tiny white flowers of mountain meadowrue. Seeps provide habitat for a variety of salamanders, including moist decomposing leaves for burrowing.

False goatsbeard is scattered along the slope; you may also see a clump or two of Indian pipe, a small parasitic flowering plant with fleshy white stems. From here to the falls, the increasingly rocky trail traverses a rich cove forest that is chock-full of spring wildflowers, including Carolina spring beauty, foamflower, wake robin, wild ginger, yellow mandarin, and Jack-in-the-pulpit.

A sturdy footbridge (with a built-in bench) at 1.1 miles provides an excellent viewing platform for Crabtree Falls. The silky white water cascades down hundreds of narrow ledges of amphibolite (a dark metamorphic rock) into a small pool at the base. At the top of the falls, the amphibolite is covered by a ledge of gneiss that serves as a resistant cap, protecting the amphibolite from erosion by the falls. Bluets and mountain meadowrue grow in the spray cliff zone. Cutleaf toothwort, plumed Solomon's seal, wood nettle, orange jewelweed, and white wood aster grow along the rocky streamside, along with rosebay rhododendron, mountain doghobble, and wild hydrangea. Cold air drainage lowers the air temperature at the base of the falls, allowing higher-elevation species such as yellow birch, mountain maple, and mountain wood sorrel to grow here.

From the Blue Ridge Mountains, Big Crabtree Creek flows westward toward the Mississippi Basin, eventually draining into the Gulf of Mexico. But just across the Parkway, on the other side of the continental divide, Armstrong Creek, whose course is shorter, steeper, and straighter, flows in the opposite direction, toward the Atlantic Ocean.

After enjoying the waterfall, backtrack to the parking area on the same trail (or see below to continue on the loop trail).

Options. Complete the loop by climbing the stairs on the far side of the footbridge and continuing on the trail for 2.0 miles to the parking area. The most difficult part of the full loop trail is just past the falls, as you hike up a ridge via several steep switchbacks. Toward the end of the loop, bypass the two spur trails to the right (they go to the campground) by staying on the main trail until you come to the T-junction, from where you can retrace your steps to the parking area.

8 / CRABTREE FALLS: WHAT TO LOOK FOR

Spring

Wild ginger	*Asarum canadense*	p. 242
Cutleaf toothwort	*Cardamine concatenata*	p. 210
Blue cohosh	*Caulophyllum thalictroides*	p. 242
Carolina spring beauty	*Claytonia caroliniana*	p. 234
Bearcorn, Squawroot	*Conopholis americana*	p. 255
American lily-of-the-valley	*Convallaria majuscula*	NI
Pink lady's slipper	*Cypripedium acaule*	p. 235
Squirrel corn	*Dicentra canadensis*	NI
Umbrella leaf	*Diphylleia cymosa*	p. 215
Robin's plantain	*Erigeron pulchellus*	p. 216
Showy orchis	*Galearis spectabilis*	p. 234
Dwarf crested iris	*Iris cristata*	p. 247
Mountain doghobble	*Leucothoe fontanesiana*	p. 213
Canada mayflower	*Maianthemum canadense*	p. 225
Plumed Solomon's seal	*Maianthemum racemosum*	p. 216
Indian cucumber root	*Medeola virginiana*	p. 264
Lousewort, Wood betony	*Pedicularis canadensis*	p. 255
Mayapple	*Podophyllum peltatum*	p. 208
Solomon's seal	*Polygonatum biflorum*	p. 217
Yellow mandarin	*Prosartes lanuginosa*	p. 263
Bloodroot	*Sanguinaria canadensis*	p. 209
Giant chickweed	*Stellaria pubera*	p. 214
Foamflower	*Tiarella cordifolia*	p. 218
Catesby's trillium	*Trillium catesbaei*	p. 212
Wake robin, Stinking Willie	*Trillium erectum*	p. 243
Large-flowered trillium	*Trillium grandiflorum*	p. 214
Painted trillium	*Trillium undulatum*	p. 219
Perfoliate bellwort	*Uvularia perfoliata*	p. 256
Roundleaf yellow violet	*Viola rotundifolia*	NI

Spring–Summer

Jack-in-the-pulpit	*Arisaema triphyllum*	p. 241
Pipevine, Dutchman's pipe	*Aristolochia macrophylla*	p. 244
Speckled wood lily	*Clintonia umbellulata*	p. 222
Galax, Skunkweed	*Galax urceolata*	p. 224
Golden ragwort	*Packera aurea*	p. 257
Lyreleaf sage	*Salvia lyrata*	NI
Fire pink	*Silene virginica*	p. 267
Canada violet	*Viola canadensis*	p. 220

Summer

Yarrow	*Achillea millefolium*	p. 221
Poke milkweed	*Asclepias exaltata*	p. 228
Common milkweed	*Asclepias syriaca*	NI
Butterfly weed	*Asclepias tuberosa*	NI
False goatsbeard	*Astilbe biternata*	p. 224
Common fleabane	*Erigeron philadelphicus*	NI
Rattlesnake orchid	*Goodyera pubescens*	p. 229
Wild hydrangea	*Hydrangea arborescens*	p. 225
Mountain laurel	*Kalmia latifolia*	p. 236
Wood nettle	*Laportea canadensis*	p. 265
Turk's cap lily	*Lilium superbum*	p. 268
Whorled loosestrife	*Lysimachia quadrifolia*	p. 258
Basil bee balm	*Monarda clinopodia*	p. 227
Mountain wood sorrel	*Oxalis montana*	p. 237
Wild sweet William	*Phlox maculata*	NI
Hoary mountain mint	*Pycnanthemum incanum*	NI
Flame azalea	*Rhododendron calendulaceum*	p. 267
Rosebay rhododendron	*Rhododendron maximum*	p. 230
Heartleaf skullcap	*Scutellaria ovata*	NI
Tall meadowrue	*Thalictrum pubescens*	NI
Wideleaf spiderwort	*Tradescantia subaspera*	p. 250

Summer–Fall

Mountain black cohosh	*Actaea podocarpa*	NI
Pink turtlehead	*Chelone lyonii*	p. 239
Oxeye daisy	*Chrysanthemum leucanthemum*	NI
Canada horsebalm	*Collinsonia canadensis*	p. 261
Queen Anne's lace	*Daucus carota*	NI
Flowering spurge	*Euphorbia corollata*	NI
White wood aster	*Eurybia divaricata*	p. 231
Rock alumroot	*Heuchera villosa*	p. 230
Orange jewelweed	*Impatiens capensis*	p. 268
Indian pipe, Ghost flower	*Monotropa uniflora*	p. 231
Heal all	*Prunella vulgaris*	p. 249
Black-eyed Susan	*Rudbeckia hirta*	NI

Fall

White snakeroot	*Ageratina altissima*	p. 232
Tall thistle	*Cirsium altissimum*	NI
Beechdrops	*Epifagus virginiana*	p. 233
Soapwort gentian	*Gentiana saponaria*	p. 252
Witch hazel	*Hamamelis virginiana*	p. 262
Curtis's goldenrod	*Solidago curtisii*	p. 261
Common wingstem	*Verbesina alternifolia*	p. 262
Canada violet	*Viola canadensis*	p. 220

NI = species not included in the wildflower profiles (Part IV)

9 / Skinny Dip Falls

BLUE RIDGE PARKWAY

Highlights	Short cascading waterfall, picturesque pools, and numerous wildflowers
Flowering season	April through mid-October
Peak flowering	May–June
Trail length	0.8 mile out and back
Trail rating	Easy (with a few rough spots)
Elevation	4,400–4,500 feet
Nearest town	Brevard, Transylvania County, N.C.
Contact	Pisgah Ranger District; 828-877-3265; www.fs.usda.gov/nfsnc
Directions	Park at the Looking Glass Rock Overlook at milepost 417 on the Blue Ridge Parkway. The overlook is located 5.1 miles south of the junction of the parkway and U.S. 276 and 8.1 miles north of the junction of the parkway and N.C. 215. GPS: N35 19.339 W82 49.686
Overview	This short, relatively easy hike through a northern hardwood forest takes you to a small cascading waterfall that plunges into a charming pool on the Yellowstone Prong of the Big East Fork of the Pigeon

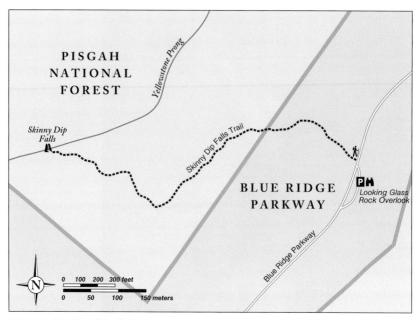

Skinny Dip Falls, Blue Ridge Parkway

River. There are numerous spring wildflowers, including two trilliums (painted trillium and wake robin), two native azaleas (flame azalea and pinkshell azalea), and four spring ephemerals (dimpled trout lily, Carolina spring beauty, Dutchman's britches, and wood anemone). Among the trees are four maples (sugar, mountain, striped, and red). In summer, you may want to get an early start to avoid the crowds. If you're planning to take a dip in the pools, be sure to bring along swim attire, as it's unlikely anyone will be demonstrating how the falls got its name.

The Hike

Before heading down the trail, take time to enjoy the view of Looking Glass Rock, a massive dome-shaped outcrop that was named for its winter appearance. When water freezes on the face of the rock, the rock reflects sunlight, much like a giant mirror. The trail begins across the parkway on the northern side of the overlook. As you enter the northern hardwood forest, look for cucumber magnolia, black cherry, and witch hazel and keep an eye out for spring wildflowers, including dense mats of dimpled trout lily and scattered clumps of painted trillium and Indian cucumber root. Pinkshell azalea, a rare shrub restricted to the mountains of western North Carolina, blooms in May while the orange-to-red flowers of flame azalea light up the forest in early summer. Galax is common along the trail, forming dense mats of shiny round leaves with tall slender white flower stalks in early summer.

Follow the trail up the steps to a four-way trail intersection. Here, the Mountains-to-Sea (MTS) Trail goes right and straight ahead. Go straight on the MTS Trail where you'll soon see several large Fraser magnolia trees with multiple trunks. Less conspicuous are the root sprouts of American chestnut. If you're hiking in fall, striped gentian may be in flower.

The rocky root-exposed trail gradually descends and crosses a small ephemeral tributary where the maroon (sometimes white) flowers of wake robin bloom in spring. In late summer and fall, look for pink turtlehead in the moist substrate. As you climb up a short hill, you'll walk under a dense thicket of rosebay rhododendron. You may also notice the large, heart-shaped leaves of pipevine clambering up the trunks of trees. Small flies are fooled into visiting and pollinating the strongly bent, pipe-shaped flowers by a floral odor that mimics fungi, carrion, or feces, depending on the particular species of pipevine.

The trail soon drops into a small valley where the canopy trees in this northern hardwood forest include yellow birch, yellow buckeye, American beech, and sugar maple, with scattered red spruce. The trunks of many of these trees are densely covered with grayish-green lichens. This is a good area for wildflowers, including spring ephemerals such as dimpled trout lily, Carolina spring beauty, wood anemone, and Dutchman's britches. Spring flowering species that persist into early summer include mayapple, Canada mayflower, Solomon's seal, blue cohosh, and yellow mandarin. Summer hikers may spot the diminutive mountain wood sorrel with its clover-like leaves and pink-veined flowers.

As you cross a small wooden footbridge over a side stream, listen for the sound of the falls in the distance and look for the flowers of wood nettle, black cohosh, pink turtlehead, and white snakeroot in summer to early fall. You may also notice ruby-throated hummingbirds visiting the nectar-rich flowers of crimson bee balm and both orange and yellow jewelweed. Overhead are several large yellow buckeye trees with wide trunks, tall crowns, and palmately compound leaves.

In addition to hummingbirds, birders may spot a variety of birds in northern hardwood forests, including Blackburnian warblers, winter wrens, dark-eyed juncos, rose-breasted grosbeaks, and blue-headed vireos.

The trail ascends slightly to a scenic overlook of Skinny Dip Falls at 0.4 mile. The 30-foot falls consists of three short cascading tiers, the last of which drops into a pool with clear cold water. After enjoying the view, take the steps down to a wooden footbridge across the Yellowstone Prong for a closer look. The spray cliff includes wood nettle, sweet white violet, umbrella leaf, and various ferns and mosses. You'll see lots of rosebay rhododendron with scattered wild hydrangea, mountain wood aster, and white snakeroot along the rocky streamside. Take time to relax and enjoy the scenery at this turnaround point.

9 / SKINNY DIP FALLS: WHAT TO LOOK FOR

Spring

Wood anemone	*Anemone quinquefolia*	p. 209
Jack-in-the-pulpit	*Arisaema triphyllum*	p. 241
Blue cohosh	*Caulophyllum thalictroides*	p. 242
Carolina spring beauty	*Claytonia caroliniana*	p. 234
Bearcorn, Squawroot	*Conopholis americana*	p. 255
Dutchman's britches	*Dicentra cucullaria*	p. 208
Dimpled trout lily	*Erythronium umbilicatum*	p. 253
Mayapple	*Podophyllum peltatum*	p. 208
Solomon's seal	*Polygonatum biflorum*	p. 217

Dwarf cinquefoil	*Potentilla canadensis*	p. 253
Yellow mandarin	*Prosartes lanuginosa*	p. 263
Pinkshell azalea	*Rhododendron vaseyi*	NI
Foamflower	*Tiarella cordifolia*	p. 218
Wake robin, Stinking Willie	*Trillium erectum*	p. 243
Painted trillium	*Trillium undulatum*	p. 219
Sweet white violet	*Viola blanda*	p. 219
Roundleaf yellow violet	*Viola rotundifolia*	NI

Spring–Summer

Pipevine, Dutchman's pipe	*Aristolochia macrophylla*	p. 244
Umbrella leaf	*Diphylleia cymosa*	p. 215
Galax, Skunkweed	*Galax urceolata*	p. 224
Mountain laurel	*Kalmia latifolia*	p. 236
Canada mayflower	*Maianthemum canadense*	p. 225
Indian cucumber root	*Medeola virginiana*	p. 264
Flame azalea	*Rhododendron calendulaceum*	p. 267
Common dandelion	*Taraxacum officinale*	NI
False hellebore	*Veratrum viride*	NI

Summer

Black cohosh	*Actaea racemosa*	p. 226
Rattlesnake orchid	*Goodyera pubescens*	p. 229
Wild hydrangea	*Hydrangea arborescens*	p. 225
Wood nettle	*Laportea canadensis*	p. 265
Whorled loosestrife	*Lysimachia quadrifolia*	p. 258
Mountain wood sorrel	*Oxalis montana*	p. 237
Rosebay rhododendron	*Rhododendron maximum*	p. 230

Summer–Fall

Pink turtlehead	*Chelone lyonii*	p. 239
Orange jewelweed	*Impatiens capensis*	p. 268
Yellow jewelweed	*Impatiens pallida*	NI
Crimson bee balm	*Monarda didyma*	p. 269
Whorled aster	*Oclemena acuminata*	NI

Fall

White snakeroot	*Ageratina altissima*	p. 232
Beechdrops	*Epifagus virginiana*	p. 233
Mountain wood aster	*Eurybia chlorolepis*	NI
Striped gentian	*Gentiana decora*	NI
Witch hazel	*Hamamelis virginiana*	p. 262
Long-bristled smartweed	*Polygonum caespitosum*	NI
Curtis's goldenrod	*Solidago curtisii*	p. 261
Heartleaf aster	*Symphyotrichum cordifolium*	p. 251

NI = species not included in the wildflower profiles (Part IV)

10 / Graveyard Fields

BLUE RIDGE PARKWAY AND PISGAH NATIONAL FOREST

Highlights Scenic landscape, cascading waterfalls, colorful wildflowers

Flowering season May through early October

Peak flowering No distinct peak

Trail length 3.2-mile partial loop trail

Trail rating Mostly easy

Elevation 5,120–5,320 feet

Nearest town Brevard, Transylvania County, N.C.

Contact Pisgah Ranger District; 828-877-3265; www.fs.usda.gov/nfsnc

Directions Park at the Graveyard Fields Overlook at milepost 418.8 on the Blue Ridge Parkway. The overlook is located 6.9 miles south of the junction of the parkway and U.S. 276 and 6.3 miles north of the junction of the parkway and N.C. 215. The trailhead is located on the northeast side of the parking lot. GPS: N35 19.226 W82 50.818

Overview Graveyard Fields is a high-elevation valley that lacks the dense forests that blanket much of the region. Because tree-covered slopes are so pervasive in the mountains, the open meadow-like vistas seen here are especially appealing. Adding to the charm

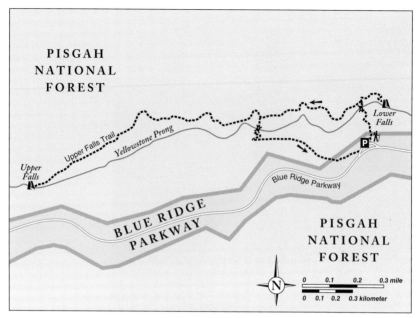

Graveyard Fields, Blue Ridge Parkway and Pisgah National Forest

is a scenic river, the Yellowstone Prong, running through the valley, forming picturesque waterfalls. Looming on the horizon to the west is Graveyard Ridge. The tapestry of colors across the landscape changes seasonally; in early May, before the trees leaf out, the reddish hues are the stem tips, flowers, and winged fruits of red maple; the "clouds" of white are smooth serviceberry trees in flower, and the dark green conical crowns are red spruce, an evergreen species. In late summer, the meadow-like areas are filled with the yellow flowers of goldenrod and the reddish leaves of blueberries. The colors of autumn are too complex to be described here—better to see them for yourself.

The name Graveyard Fields originated after a huge fire in 1925 destroyed the forest leaving behind dead trunks and stumps that from a distance resembled a tombstone-studded graveyard. The intense fire burned the soil's organic matter and subsequent erosion washed away more of the topsoil, dramatically slowing tree regeneration, resulting in the unusual mix of meadows, shrublands, bogs, and recovering forest that we see today.

The stunning scenery, waterfalls, and abundant wildflowers make this one of the most popular hiking spots along the Blue Ridge Parkway. It's a trail to visit in all seasons as wildflowers can be enjoyed from May through early October, blueberries and blackberries are ripe for picking in late summer, and the fall leaf colors are among the best on the parkway. Basic restroom facilities are available adjacent to the parking area.

The Hike

Walk down the stone steps at the trailhead and follow the paved path through a tunnel of Catawba rhododendron. Imagine trying to walk through this maze of twisted stems without benefit of a trail! It makes you appreciate the folks who build and maintain these trails. Among the few wildflowers growing beneath the densely packed rhododendrons is painted trillium—look for its white flowers (with a splotch of red) in May and its bright red fruits in August.

Cross the footbridge over the Yellowstone Prong and turn right at the T-junction. A long set of wooden steps leads you down to the base of Lower Falls (0.3 mile) where you can enjoy the cascade as it drops nearly 60 feet over a large rock face into a deep pool. While the spray cliff is mostly devoid of plants, a variety of showy wildflowers occur in the rocky streamside habitat, including Catawba rhododendron, whose deep pink-to-purple flowers put on a show in June. Bushy St. John's wort and southern bush honeysuckle also grow here and elsewhere along the trail. Look for their bright yellow flowers in summer.

Retrace your steps to the T-junction at 0.4 mile and veer left (following the sign) to Upper Falls. Passing through open meadows and shrublands with scattered trees, the trail meanders through Graveyard Fields. Shrubs and trees are gradually colonizing the meadows. Eventually much of the area will likely revert back to northern hardwood forest or spruce-fir forest (don't worry, the meadows will still be here on your next visit).

Trees colonizing the area include fire cherry, smooth serviceberry, and mountain holly (all of which have fleshy fruits with seeds that are widely dispersed by birds). Red maple and yellow birch are also common but have wind-dispersed seeds.

In late summer, feast on blueberries, blackberries, and gooseberries along the trail. You'll be competing with other frugivores (fruit-eating animals) such as black bears, white-tailed deer, and a surprising variety of birds, including gray catbirds, brown thrashers, mockingbirds, song sparrows, rose-breasted grosbeaks, indigo buntings, northern cardinals, scarlet tanagers, cedar waxwings, blue jays, crows, and downy and hairy woodpeckers.

At the junction (0.6 mile), bypass the Graveyard Ridge Connector Trail; instead, veer left and continue to follow the Upper Falls Trail. At the fork (0.8 mile), go right (the one to the left is the one you'll want to take on the return to make this a partial loop trail). As you pass through the valley, you'll cross small boardwalks, several small tributaries, and pass through rhododendron tunnels. You may also see lots of wildflowers, including clumps of painted trillium in spring, a nice patch of Turk's cap lily in summer, and mountain wood aster in late summer and fall.

Various swallowtail butterflies visit (and pollinate) the nectar-rich flowers of Turk's cap lily, including spicebush, pipevine, and eastern tiger swallowtails. White-tailed deer feed on the shoots of Turk's cap lily, halting growth and hindering seed production. Rodents are even more damaging, as they consume the bulbs, killing the plant.

At the far end of the valley (1.4 miles), the narrow rocky path begins a gradual climb to Upper Falls. Suddenly, the trees are larger and denser. You've stepped into a fairly mature northern hardwood forest, with yellow birch, northern red oak, red maple, and smooth serviceberry.

At 1.7 miles, you'll come to a small fork among some boulders (you'll likely hear the falls)—take the short spur trail to the left which leads down to the creek; cross it and carefully scramble up the rock face on the far side of the stream to view the falls.

If you miss the spur trail, continue on the rocky path another 200 feet or so to reach the base of the falls. Upper Falls cascades and slides down a steep rock face about 50 feet. Given the small size of the parent stream, the falls are a pretty impressive sight. Various plants grow in nooks and crannies where small amounts of soil have collected on the rock face adjacent to the falls, including Catawba rhododendron, pink turtlehead, tassel rue, and Appalachian bluet.

On the return route, continue on the main trail for about one mile before turning right at a fork which soon (within 50 yards) crosses the Yellowstone Prong via a footbridge. The trail continues through rhododendron tunnels and over a long footbridge through a boggy area (with sundrops, kidneyleaf grass of Parnassus, and sphagnum moss) before a set of stone steps leads to the southwest end of the parking area.

10 / GRAVEYARD FIELDS: WHAT TO LOOK FOR

Spring

Dimpled trout lily	*Erythronium umbilicatum*	p. 253
Lousewort, Wood betony	*Pedicularis canadensis*	p. 255
Fetterbush	*Pieris floribunda*	NI
Common cinquefoil	*Potentilla simplex*	NI
Pinkshell azalea	*Rhododendron vaseyi*	NI
Painted trillium	*Trillium undulatum*	p. 219
Blueberry	*Vaccinium* species	NI
Sweet white violet	*Viola blanda*	p. 219
Common blue violet	*Viola sororia*	p. 247

Spring–Summer

Wild strawberry	*Fragaria virginiana*	p. 212
Galax, Skunkweed	*Galax urceolata*	p. 224
Quaker ladies	*Houstonia caerulea*	NI
Appalachian bluet	*Houstonia serpyllifolia*	p. 248
Canada mayflower	*Maianthemum canadense*	p. 225
Indian cucumber root	*Medeola virginiana*	p. 264
Common dandelion	*Taraxacum officinale*	NI

Summer

Yarrow	*Achillea millefolium*	p. 221
Southern bush honeysuckle	*Diervilla sessilifolia*	NI
Common fleabane	*Erigeron philadelphicus*	NI
Granite dome St. John's wort	*Hypericum buckleyi*	NI
Bushy St. John's wort	*Hypericum densiflorum*	NI
Mountain St. John's wort	*Hypericum graveolens*	NI
Mountain laurel	*Kalmia latifolia*	p. 236
Turk's cap lily	*Lilium superbum*	p. 268
Carolina rhododendron	*Rhododendron carolinianum*	NI
Catawba rhododendron	*Rhododendron catawbiense*	p. 236
Smooth blackberry	*Rubus canadensis*	NI
Tassel rue	*Trautvetteria caroliniensis*	p. 228
Wild raisin	*Viburnum cassinoides*	NI

Summer–Fall

Mountain angelica	*Angelica triquinata*	p. 266
Pink turtlehead	*Chelone lyonii*	p. 239
Mountain wood aster	*Eurybia chlorolepis*	NI
Joe Pye weed	*Eutrochium fistulosum*	p. 239
Orange jewelweed	*Impatiens capensis*	p. 268
Yellow jewelweed	*Impatiens pallida*	NI
Indian pipe, Ghost flower	*Monotropa uniflora*	p. 231
Whorled aster	*Oclemena acuminata*	NI
Sundrops	*Oenothera fruticosa*	p. 257
Kidneyleaf grass of Parnassus	*Parnassia asarifolia*	p. 233
Heal all	*Prunella vulgaris*	p. 249
Goldenrod	*Solidago* species	NI

Fall

White snakeroot	*Ageratina altissima*	p. 232
Striped gentian	*Gentiana decora*	NI

NI = species not included in the wildflower profiles (Part IV)

11 / High Shoals Falls

SOUTH MOUNTAINS STATE PARK

Highlights	Scenic creek, good wildflower displays, and an 80-foot waterfall
Flowering season	Mid-March through early October
Peak flowering	April
Trail length	2.5-mile loop trail
Trail rating	Moderate
Elevation	1,330–1,930 feet
Nearest town	Connelly Springs, Burke County, N.C.
Contact	828-433-4772; www.ncparks.gov
Directions	From I-40 in Morganton, take exit 105 and go south on N.C. 18 for 10.8 miles before turning right onto Sugar Loaf Road (S.R. 1913). Continue on Sugar Loaf Road for 4.3 miles to a T-intersection (Old N.C. 18). Turn left and go 2.7 miles before turning right onto Ward's Gap Road (S.R. 1901). Continue for 1.3 miles to a fork, and bear right onto South Mountains Park Avenue (S.R. 1904). Proceed past the gate and visitor center for 2.3 miles to where the road ends at the large paved Jacob Fork Parking Area. The trailhead is located on the upper end of the parking lot. GPS: N35 36.134 W81 37.770

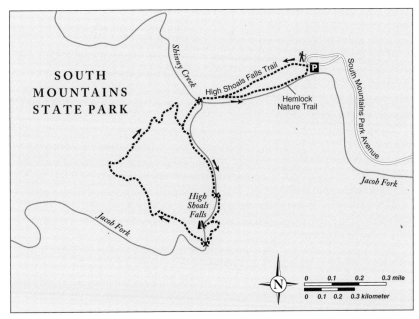

High Shoals Falls, South Mountains State Park

Overview Carved out of the Blue Ridge Mountains by erosion, the South
Mountains are an isolated rugged mountain range with elevations
up to 3,000 feet in the transition zone between the mountains and
piedmont of western North Carolina. The highlight of a visit to the
region is the trail to High Shoals Falls in South Mountains State Park,
where you'll hike through an acidic cove forest along the Jacob Fork
stream to the base of an 80-foot waterfall, with scenic views of the
falls, cascading stream, and river gorge. The moderate 2.5-mile hike
climbs to the top of the falls before looping around and passing
through forests dominated by oaks, pines, and hemlocks. Numerous
wildflowers line the trail, especially in spring. You'll find picnic areas,
restrooms, and interpretive signs along the trail. The park visitor
center is informative.

The Hike

This well-marked loop trail through mostly acidic cove forest begins along the paved
path to the right of the picnic area. Veer left on the gravel roadbed, pass the restroom
on the left, and look for spring wildflowers, including Robin's plantain, mayapple,
common blue violet, and bloodroot. In early spring, you may also notice the maroon
bell-shaped flowers of pawpaw, a small tree that flowers before its leaves emerge.
Bearsfoot, leafy elephants head, and Asiatic dayflower bloom in early summer
through fall. Less common are the bright red flowers of cardinal flower.

The trail crosses Shinny Creek via a wooden footbridge at 0.4 mile and soon
enters a large grassy clearing (the Shinny Creek Picnic Area) where the white blooms
of flowering dogwood and purplish-pink flowers of redbud add a splash of color in
early spring. In summer, the color palette includes the white flowers of basil bee

balm, the blue-violet flowers of heal all and wild petunia, and the showy yellow flower heads of bearsfoot and yellow crownbeard. Look for goldfinches feeding on the seeds of the latter two species in late summer and fall.

At the far end of the picnic area, continue straight (the trail on the right is the one you'll use on the return loop). The trail soon descends a steep flight of stairs to the Jacob Fork. This clear cold stream provides good habitat for native brook trout along with introduced rainbow and brown trout. Minnows, darters, and other small fish can also be seen.

The trail along the river is a good area for spring wildflowers, including wake robin, giant chickweed, Jack-in-the-pulpit, showy orchis, and foamflower. Rosebay rhododendron abounds along the boulder-strewn stream while the trunks of sycamore, yellow birch, and tulip tree reach high into the canopy of this alluvial forest. Birders may spot Swainson's warbler, Louisiana waterthrush, and yellow-throated warbler.

A long wooden bridge spans the gorge at 0.8 mile, providing good views of the cascading river. If the leaves aren't too dense, you can catch a glimpse of High Shoals Falls at the head of the cove.

As you pick up the trail on the far end of the bridge, you may notice spring-flowering acute-lobed hepatica, wake robin, foamflower, and mountain doghobble. As the trail climbs steeply toward the viewing platform at the base of the falls, look for black cohosh, white snakeroot, wild hydrangea, and rosebay rhododendron.

From the viewing platform at 0.9 mile, you're rewarded with scenic views of the waterfall, cascading stream, and the acidic cove forest that covers most of the gorge. Look for rock alumroot, orange jewelweed, white turtlehead, and white wood aster in the spray cliff zone. Growing among the rocks adjacent to the platform are spring flowering wood anemone, wake robin, and Jack-in-the-pulpit. The latter species is unusual in that individuals switch gender from year to year with smaller plants typically male (pollen producing) and larger individuals female (fruit producing). Because fruits require more resources than pollen, it makes sense that larger plants of Jack-in-the-pulpit are female.

To continue on the loop trail, take the steep staircase leading to the top of the waterfall (the hardest part of the hike). Notice the dense groundcover of poison ivy and Virginia creeper alongside the trail. You can tell them apart by their leaves; poison ivy has three leaflets per leaf, Virginia creeper has five or more leaflets per leaf.

As you approach the ridge at 1.0 mile, the soil gets thinner and drier and the vegetation changes from an acidic cove forest to a chestnut oak forest. Gorge rhododendron is abundant in this area. In a good year, its pink-to-white blooms light up the forest in late April to early May.

Take a few minutes to enjoy the small but scenic waterfall that drops into a large pool. The flowing water soon plunges over the cliff forming High Shoals Falls.

After crossing the river on a footbridge, you enter a forest dominated by eastern white pine. It's an unusual pine in that the branches are produced in whorls. Because one whorl is produced per year, you can estimate the age of an individual by counting the number of whorls of branches on the main trunk.

As the trail (an old road bed) ascends, look for mats of partridge berry and trailing arbutus along with Robin's plantain and halberdleaf yellow violet. The red fruits of partridge berry can be seen most any time of year as they persist on the plant long after they're produced.

At the T-junction, veer right, following the trail as it climbs steadily through a mixed pine-hardwood forest with flowering dogwood and redbud in the understory, and whorled coreopsis and leafy elephant's foot on the forest floor. Numerous birds, including fall migrants, consume the high-fat-content red fruits of flowering dogwood and disperse its seeds.

The trail tops out at a second T-junction at 1.5 miles; turn right and begin a long descent. If you're hiking in spring, look for foamflower, dwarf crested iris, cucumber root, and green and gold. You may also hear the taps of pileated woodpeckers reverberating through the forest. As you drop into a sheltered ravine, the vegetation reverts to an acidic cove forest with understory species such as rosebay rhododendron, witch hazel, and Carolina silverbell, along with the saplings of numerous trees.

The trail bottoms out at the Shinny Creek Picnic Area at 2.0 miles. Cross the creek on a footbridge and follow the gravel roadbed about 200 yards before veering right onto the Hemlock Nature Trail, which parallels Shinny Creek. The eastern hemlocks that once dominated this acidic cove forest have been decimated by hemlock woolly adelgids (the state park is trying to save as many as possible). Birders may spot Louisiana waterthrush, hooded warbler, and blue-headed vireo near the stream. The interpretive signs along the trail are interesting. The best spot for wildflowers is at the end of the nature trail (just before the parking area) where bloodroot, mayapple, foamflower, wood anemone, giant chickweed, dwarf crested iris, and wild geranium flower in spring.

11 / HIGH SHOALS FALLS: WHAT TO LOOK FOR

Spring

Acute-lobed hepatica	*Anemone acutiloba*	p. 207
Wood anemone	*Anemone quinquefolia*	p. 209
Jack-in-the-pulpit	*Arisaema triphyllum*	p. 241
Pink lady's slipper	*Cypripedium acaule*	p. 235
Trailing arbutus	*Epigaea repens*	p. 207
Robin's plantain	*Erigeron pulchellus*	p. 216
Strawberry bush, Hearts-a-bustin'	*Euonymus americanus*	p. 264
Showy orchis	*Galearis spectabilis*	p. 234
Wild geranium	*Geranium maculatum*	p. 235
Large flower heartleaf	*Hexastylis shuttleworthii*	p. 245
Dwarf crested iris	*Iris cristata*	p. 247
Mountain laurel	*Kalmia latifolia*	p. 236
Mountain doghobble	*Leucothoe fontanesiana*	p. 213
Indian cucumber root	*Medeola virginiana*	p. 264
Large yellow wood sorrel	*Oxalis grandis*	NI
Mayapple	*Podophyllum peltatum*	p. 208
Solomon's seal	*Polygonatum biflorum*	p. 217
Gorge rhododendron, Punctatum	*Rhododendron minus*	p. 237
Lyreleaf sage	*Salvia lyrata*	NI
Bloodroot	*Sanguinaria canadensis*	p. 209
Hairy skullcap	*Scutellaria elliptica*	NI
Giant chickweed	*Stellaria pubera*	p. 214
Foamflower	*Tiarella cordifolia*	p. 218
Poison ivy	*Toxicodendron radicans*	p. 223
Wake robin, Stinking Willie	*Trillium erectum*	p. 243
Halberdleaf yellow violet	*Viola hastata*	p. 254
Common blue violet	*Viola sororia*	p. 247
Yellowroot	*Xanthorhiza simplicissima*	p. 240

Spring–Summer

Green and gold	*Chrysogonum virginianum*	NI
Galax, Skunkweed	*Galax urceolata*	p. 224
Rattlesnake hawkweed	*Hieracium venosum*	p. 256
Partridge berry	*Mitchella repens*	p. 223
Virginia creeper	*Parthenocissus quinquefolia*	NI

Summer

Black cohosh	*Actaea racemosa*	p. 226
Spikenard	*Aralia racemosa*	p. 265
Yellow false foxglove	*Aureolaria flava*	NI
Butterfly pea	*Clitoria mariana*	NI
Whorled coreopsis	*Coreopsis major*	p. 259
Beggar's ticks	*Desmodium nudiflorum*	p. 238
Wild hydrangea	*Hydrangea arborescens*	p. 225
Downy lobelia	*Lobelia puberula*	NI
Basil bee balm	*Monarda clinopodia*	p. 227
Rosebay rhododendron	*Rhododendron maximum*	p. 230
Wild petunia	*Ruellia caroliniensis*	NI
Starry campion	*Silene stellata*	NI
Cranefly orchid	*Tipularia discolor*	p. 246

Summer–Fall

Hog peanut	*Amphicarpaea bracteata*	p. 238
Southern harebell	*Campanula divaricata*	p. 250
White turtlehead	*Chelone glabra*	NI
Canada horsebalm	*Collinsonia canadensis*	p. 261
Asiatic dayflower	*Commelina communis*	p. 249
Leafy elephant's foot	*Elephantopus carolinianus*	NI
Flowering spurge	*Euphorbia corollata*	NI
White wood aster	*Eurybia divaricata*	p. 231
Rock alumroot	*Heuchera villosa*	p. 230
Orange jewelweed	*Impatiens capensis*	p. 268
Cardinal flower	*Lobelia cardinalis*	p. 269
Jumpseed	*Polygonum virginianum*	NI
Heal all	*Prunella vulgaris*	p. 249
Bearsfoot, Yellow leafcup	*Smallanthus uvedalius*	p. 260
Yellow crownbeard	*Verbesena occidentalis*	NI

Fall

White snakeroot	*Ageratina altissima*	p. 232
Witch hazel	*Hamamelis virginiana*	p. 262

NI = species not included in the wildflower profiles (Part IV)

12 / Hickory Nut Falls

CHIMNEY ROCK STATE PARK

Highlights	Sheer cliffs with a 400-foot waterfall and abundant spring wildflowers
Flowering season	March through mid-October
Peak flowering	April
Trail length	2.5 miles out and back
Trail rating	Moderate
Elevation	1,475–2,105 feet
Nearest town	Chimney Rock, Rutherford County, N.C.
Contact	800-277-9611; www.chimneyrockpark.com
Directions	Chimney Rock State Park is located 25 miles southeast of Asheville, N.C. on U.S. 64/74A between Bat Cave and Lake Lure. Look for the stone gate entrance in the small village of Chimney Rock, cross the bridge, and follow the paved road to the ticket booth. After paying the admission fee, continue on the paved road to the lower parking area. A large sign indicates the trailhead for the Four Seasons Trail. GPS: N35 25.847 W82 14.594

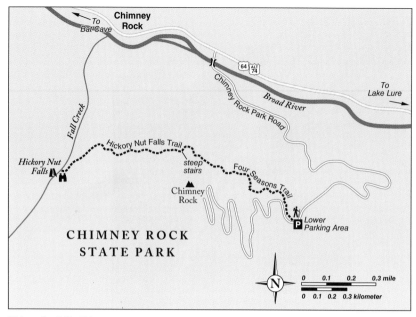

Hickory Nut Falls, Chimney Rock State Park

Overview   Nestled in Hickory Nut Gorge, a valley cut into the Blue Ridge
Escarpment, Chimney Rock State Park is one of North Carolina's
newest state parks. Its most famous landmark is the park's namesake,
a spectacular granite monolith known as Chimney Rock, providing
panoramic views of Lake Lure, the surrounding mountains, and
nearby piedmont. The park's other main attraction is Hickory Nut
Falls, one of the tallest waterfalls east of the Mississippi River,
featured in the movie *The Last of the Mohicans*. This moderate
hike with abundant spring wildflowers takes you through several
communities (oak hickory forest, rich cove forest, and chestnut oak
forest) before reaching the base of Hickory Nut Falls. Park amenities
include restrooms, picnic tables, a restaurant, a gift shop, and the
Great Woodland Adventure, a trail especially for kids. An admission
fee is charged and visitors are provided with a park brochure with
detailed maps.

The Hike

From the paved road, the Four Seasons Trail enters an oak hickory forest and soon
crosses a small wooden bridge, climbs a series of timbered stairs with mountain
laurel and gorge rhododendron, and skirts a small service building at 0.2 mile where
sweet Betsy, giant chickweed, and bloodroot bloom in spring. Soon you'll cross a
second small footbridge with a large patch of orange jewelweed growing along the
margin of a small stream. The trail ascends more steeply up a series of timbered
steps before leveling off along a long wooden footbridge at 0.4 mile.

The oak hickory forest you're hiking through is a good example of a multi-layered
forest with a tall canopy, a subcanopy of smaller trees, a shrub layer, and a ground

layer of mostly herbaceous plants. Some of the more common trees are oaks (chestnut, northern red, and white), mockernut hickory, tulip tree, Carolina silverbell, and magnolias (Fraser and cucumber). Birders may see mixed flocks of tanagers, warblers, and vireos during spring migration. Look (and listen) for pileated woodpeckers tapping on dead trees and fallen logs year round.

You'll quickly cross another wooden footbridge before skirting three huge boulders and a couple more footbridges. On this sheltered slope with deep, nutrient-rich, relatively high-pH soil, the vegetation changes to a rich cove forest. It's here that the wildflowers really take off. Peak flowering is early spring when plants such as sweet Betsy, bloodroot, purple phacelia, blue cohosh, mayapple, Jack-in-the-pulpit, Solomon's seal, plumed Solomon's seal, dwarf crested iris, yellow mandarin, and sweet shrub bloom. If you're hiking in early summer, the upright narrow flowering spikes of black cohosh are striking. Look for pink turtlehead, Canada horsebalm, white snakeroot, and white wood aster in summer or early fall.

At 0.6 mile, you'll climb a steep stairwell to reach the Hickory Nut Falls Trail. At the top of the stairs, turn right and follow the wide gravel trail as it skirts the base of the cliff on the way to the falls. The vegetation alternates between moist cove forest and drier chestnut oak forest with dense thickets of gorge rhododendron and mountain laurel. Hikers in late summer to early fall may see pink turtlehead, white snakeroot, white wood aster, and heartleaf aster. Watch out for poison ivy along the margin of the trail.

Arriving at the lower viewing platform, you'll see a tall, narrow, mostly sliding waterfall flowing over a nearly vertical cliff composed of gneiss (pronounced *nice*), a granite-like rock formed more than 500 million years ago. Notice how large chunks of rock have broken off the mountain, some of which are piled up at the base of the falls.

Hickory Nut Falls is part of Fall Creek, which begins in a natural spring at the top of Chimney Rock Mountain. The actual height of the falls (404 feet as listed by the park) has been a subject of some debate. Regardless of actual height, there's no doubt that it's one of the tallest waterfalls in the region. From the base of the falls, Fall Creek continues eastward down a rocky ravine, eventually emptying into the French Broad River.

As you continue on the short trail to the upper viewing platform at 1.2 miles, look for ninebark, a loosely branched shrub with shedding bark and dense clusters of white flowers; the tiny blue bell-shaped flowers of southern harebell; and the yellow flower heads of whorled coreopsis, all of which bloom in summer or fall. Other plants growing in cracks, crevices, and small ledges on the nearly vertical cliff are rock alumroot, dwarf crested iris, galax, whorled coreopsis, violets, and goldenrod, along with stunted gorge rhododendron.

Plants in the spray cliff zone are generally sparse. Those that do occur mainly grow on narrow ledges and crevices where soil collects and roots can grow, thereby anchoring the plant to the substrate. Perhaps the most conspicuous plant in the spray cliff zone is sundrops—look for its large yellow flowers from spring through summer. Other plants in the spray cliff zone include tassel rue, mountain dwarf dandelion, rock alumroot, mountain meadowrue, and various ferns.

The north-facing cliff of Hickory Nut Falls has an unusually cool moist microclimate that harbors species normally found at much higher elevations, including deerhair bulrush, a rare grass-like plant with wiry leaves that normally occurs at elevations above 5,000 feet in North Carolina, but is growing here at just 2,400 feet.

Birds that normally occur at much higher elevations can also be seen, including common raven and peregrine falcon.

Take time to enjoy the waterfall, the wildflowers, and the cool air draft at the upper falls platform before turning around and retracing your steps to the parking area.

Options. You may want to take the elevator to Chimney Rock and climb the nearly 50 stairs to the top of Chimney Rock before taking the Skyline Trail to Exclamation Point. From late September through October, this area provides an outstanding viewing platform to enjoy the fall colors and to watch broad-winged hawks along with sharp-shinned, Cooper's, and red-shouldered hawks during fall migration. See the park brochure (and accompanying maps) for additional details.

12 / HICKORY NUT FALLS: WHAT TO LOOK FOR

Spring

Jack-in-the-pulpit	*Arisaema triphyllum*	p. 241
Sweet shrub	*Calycanthus floridus*	p. 241
Cutleaf toothwort	*Cardamine concatenata*	p. 210
Blue cohosh	*Caulophyllum thalictroides*	p. 242
Dwarf crested iris	*Iris cristata*	p. 247
Mountain laurel	*Kalmia latifolia*	p. 236
Plumed Solomon's seal	*Maianthemum racemosum*	p. 216
Purple phacelia	*Phacelia bipinnatifida*	p. 243
Mayapple	*Podophyllum peltatum*	p. 208
Yellow mandarin	*Prosartes lanuginosa*	p. 263
Gorge rhododendron, Punctatum	*Rhododendron minus*	p. 237
Bloodroot	*Sanguinaria canadensis*	p. 209
Giant chickweed	*Stellaria pubera*	p. 214
Poison ivy	*Toxicodendron radicans*	p. 223
Sweet Betsy	*Trillium cuneatum*	p. 240
Perfoliate bellwort	*Uvularia perfoliata*	p. 256
Mapleleaf viburnum	*Viburnum acerifolium*	NI
Sweet white violet	*Viola blanda*	p. 219
Halberdleaf yellow violet	*Viola hastata*	p. 254
Roundleaf yellow violet	*Viola rotundifolia*	NI
Common blue violet	*Viola sororia*	p. 247
Yellowroot	*Xanthorhiza simplicissima*	p. 240

Spring–Summer

Leather flower	*Clematis viorna*	NI
Strawberry bush, Hearts-a-bustin'	*Euonymus americanus*	p. 264
Galax, Skunkweed	*Galax urceolata*	p. 224
Rattlesnake hawkweed	*Hieracium venosum*	p. 256
Cliff saxifrage	*Hydatica petiolaris*	p. 220
Sundrops	*Oenothera fruticosa*	p. 257
Hairy beardtongue	*Penstemon canescens*	p. 245
Solomon's seal	*Polygonatum biflorum*	p. 217
Mountain meadowrue	*Thalictrum clavatum*	p. 226
Poison ivy	*Toxicodendron radicans*	p. 223
Deerhair bulrush	*Trichophorum cespitosum*	NI
Canada violet	*Viola canadensis*	p. 220

Summer

Black cohosh	*Actaea racemosa*	p. 226
False goatsbeard	*Astilbe biternata*	p. 224
Whorled coreopsis	*Coreopsis major*	p. 259
Beggar's ticks	*Desmodium nudiflorum*	p. 238
Ashy hydrangea	*Hydrangea cinerea*	NI
Orange jewelweed	*Impatiens capensis*	p. 268
Mountain laurel	*Kalmia latifolia*	p. 236
Wood nettle	*Laportea canadensis*	p. 265
Yellow passion flower	*Passiflora lutea*	NI
Ninebark	*Physocarpus opulifolius*	NI
Kudzu	*Pueraria montana*	NI
Rosebay rhododendron	*Rhododendron maximum*	p. 230
Cranefly orchid	*Tipularia discolor*	p. 246
Tassel rue	*Trautvetteria caroliniensis*	p. 228

Summer–Fall

Hog peanut	*Amphicarpaea bracteata*	p. 238
Southern harebell	*Campanula divaricata*	p. 250
Pink turtlehead	*Chelone lyonii*	p. 239
Canada horsebalm	*Collinsonia canadensis*	p. 261
White wood aster	*Eurybia divaricata*	p. 231
Rock alumroot	*Heuchera villosa*	p. 230
Mountain dwarf dandelion	*Krigia montana*	p. 258
Pokeweed	*Phytolacca americana*	p. 227
Jumpseed	*Polygonum virginianum*	NI
Wideleaf spiderwort	*Tradescantia subaspera*	p. 250

Fall

White snakeroot	*Ageratina altissima*	p. 232
Witch hazel	*Hamamelis virginiana*	p. 262
Curtis's goldenrod	*Solidago curtisii*	p. 261
Heartleaf aster	*Symphyotrichum cordifolium*	p. 251
Canada violet	*Viola canadensis*	p. 220

NI = species not included in the wildflower profiles (Part IV)

13 / Pearson's Falls

TRYON GARDEN CLUB

Highlights	Abundant wildflowers and a scenic 90-foot waterfall
Flowering season	March through mid-October
Peak flowering	Late March through April
Trail length	0.6 mile out and back
Trail rating	Easy
Elevation	1,620–1,800 feet
Nearest town	Saluda, Polk County, N.C.
Contact	828-749-3031; www.pearsonsfalls.org
Directions	From I-26, take exit 59 (Saluda) and head west on Ozone Drive 1.1 miles to where it ends at U.S. 176. Turn left onto U.S. 176 and travel 2.5 miles, then turn right onto Pearson Falls Road. Continue for 0.9 mile and turn left into the driveway at the sign for Pearson's Falls. After paying a small fee, continue a short distance to the parking area. GPS: N35 13.051 W82 19.958
Overview	If you like short hikes with abundant spring wildflowers and a majestic waterfall, you'll want to visit Pearson's Falls. This site has attracted nature lovers, wildflower enthusiasts, birders, gardeners, and picnickers for generations. To prevent the area from being logged, the Tryon Garden Club purchased the waterfall and surrounding glen in 1931, and continues to do an outstanding job maintaining the site as a nature preserve. A short easy trail along a scenic creek takes you through a rich cove forest packed with wildflowers. Amenities include restrooms, picnic tables, and a trailhead kiosk illustrating plants currently in bloom.

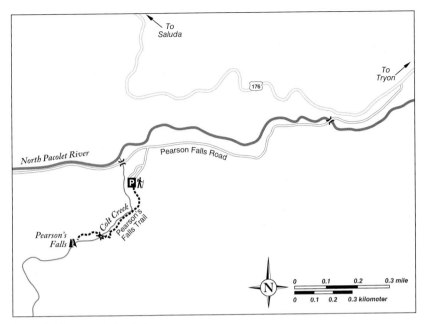

Pearson's Falls, Tryon Garden Club

The Hike

The hike begins at the kiosk at the far (upper) end of the parking area and follows the creek upstream to the base of the waterfall. Before starting out, admire the grove of eastern hemlocks in the parking area. These robust trees are currently being treated to ward off the hemlock woolly adelgids that have decimated hemlocks throughout much of its range.

The first part of the hike goes from the trailhead to a series of stone steps, a distance of about 100 yards. Plants vary dramatically in the length of their growing season, as illustrated by the wildflowers growing along this section of the trail. Species such as yellow trout lily, Virginia spring beauty, and cutleaf toothwort are known as spring ephemerals because their growing season lasts only about four weeks (they emerge in early spring but go dormant once the canopy trees leaf out). In contrast, bloodroot, Jack-in-the-pulpit, and giant chickweed persist as leafy plants under a shaded canopy before going dormant in late summer or fall. A third group of spring wildflowers, including acute-lobed hepatica, foamflower, and Oconee bells have leaves that persist year round.

Other spring flowering plants along the first part of the trail include three trilliums—the purple flowers of sweet Betsy, the white (fading to pink) flowers of large-flowered trillium, and sweet white trillium. Look for these four violets along the trail—halberdleaf yellow violet, roundleaf yellow violet, common blue violet, and Canada violet. You may also hear the clear flute-like songs of male wood thrushes at dawn and from late afternoon until dusk.

Larger, more robust wildflowers include Solomon's seal and plumed Solomon's seal. These two species are similar vegetatively, but differ in that the flowers and fruits of Solomon's seal hang beneath the leafy stem; while those of plumed Solomon's seal are clustered at the stem tip. Blue cohosh and black cohosh also look similar vegetatively, but differ in their flowers. Blue cohosh has yellowish green to purple-green flowers, while black cohosh has tassel-like white flowers in long narrow upright racemes. False goatsbeard, like blue and black cohosh, has large pinnately compound leaves, but produces tiny whitish flowers in densely branched inflorescences.

The second part of the trail begins at the series of stone steps and ends at the stone bridge. Canopy trees in this rich cove forest include white basswood, sugar maple, yellow buckeye, sweet birch, eastern hemlock, and white ash (some with name tags). An exotic wood boring beetle known as the emerald ash borer is currently threatening both white and green ash in the southeastern United States.

Look and listen for red-bellied woodpeckers. In addition to foraging on insects by hammering at wood, they catch insects in flight, and consume fruits, nuts, and seeds (including acorns), some of which they store in tree crevices for later use.

The small shrub with peeling bark and silver-backed leaves is silverleaf hydrangea. See if you can spot wild ginger. It's a low-growing plant with urn-shaped maroon flowers hidden beneath the heart-shaped leaves. The upside-down white flowers of Dutchman's britches resemble a pair of knickers hanging out to dry, hence the common name. Another interesting plant is yellow mandarin—it produces nodding yellowish-green, bell-shaped flowers in spring that develop into striking orange-red fruits by late summer.

As you continue up the trail, you'll see a large moss-covered rock outcrop with a bronze plaque on the left side of the trail at 0.2 mile. The continuously moist substrate (due to seepage flow) harbors moisture-loving plants such as brook lettuce, early saxifrage, and mountain meadowrue, along with orange jewelweed, wood nettle, Jack-in-the-pulpit, and sweet trillium. You might also notice liverworts growing in a narrow ledge near the base of the rock—they form a dense prostrate mat of leaf-like structures with a forked branching pattern.

Just past the seepage rock, veer right and admire the elegant stone bridge that crosses the creek. Small cascades can be seen along the creek just above and below the bridge. A dense patch of rosebay rhododendron dominates the rocky streamside community. Birders may notice Louisiana waterthrush along the stream or hear the loud call of a Carolina wren. Upstream, the steep slopes on either side of the creek form a cove that shelters the site from intense sunlight and drying winds, resulting in a persistently moist soil. If the leaves aren't too dense, you'll have a nice view of Pearson's Falls at the head of the cove.

From the stone bridge to the base of the waterfall, you'll see many of the same wildflowers observed earlier, including fall-flowering species such as white wood aster, Curtis's goldenrod, and white snakeroot. Notice the difference in vegetation on the slope adjacent to the trail versus the slope on the far side of the creek. The far slope is a typical acidic cove forest with a dense understory of rhododendrons (and relatively few wildflowers); in contrast, the trail takes you through a rich cove forest with a less acidic, more nutrient-rich soil that is covered with wildflowers.

As you continue up the trail, you'll see a small area on the left with a couple of picnic tables. Here, flowering dogwood, Carolina silverbell, and spicebush bloom in early spring, as do mayapple, blue cohosh, Canada mayflower, and large-flowered trillium. Keen observers may notice walking fern, a rare plant that forms small prostrate clumps on a large boulder or two in this area.

On your right, about 25 yards up the trail is a rocky seepage slope with a variety of spring wildflowers, including sweet Betsy, large-flowered trillium, Canada violet, and a dense patch of early saxifrage.

The trail ends at 0.3 mile with a fabulous view of a 90-foot waterfall cascading and free falling over multiple steps and ledges. Plants in the spray cliff zone are clustered mainly on the edge of the falls and beneath ledges, including rosebay rhododendron, silverleaf hydrangea, rock alumroot, umbrella leaf, orange jewelweed, and white wood aster. Various insects, snails, and salamanders also live in the spray cliff zone. One morning a dead beaver was found at the base of the falls, apparently having succumbed to a trip over the falls.

Look for cardinal flower near the water's edge, just up from where the trail ends—its intensely red-to-scarlet flowers attract ruby-throated hummingbirds from midsummer through fall. Hummingbirds obtain carbohydrates from the nectar in flowers and meet their protein needs by foraging on insects gleaned from spider webs, captured in the air, or removed from flowers. The ruby-throated hummingbird is the only hummingbird to breed in eastern North America.

After enjoying the waterfall, retrace your steps to enjoy this wildflower-rich trail again.

13 / PEARSON'S FALLS: WHAT TO LOOK FOR

Spring

Acute-lobed hepatica	*Anemone acutiloba*	p. 207
Wood anemone	*Anemone quinquefolia*	p. 209
Puttyroot, Adam and Eve	*Aplectrum hyemale*	NI
Jack-in-the-pulpit	*Arisaema triphyllum*	p. 241
Wild ginger	*Asarum canadense*	p. 242
Sweet shrub	*Calycanthus floridus*	p. 241
Cutleaf toothwort	*Cardamine concatenata*	p. 210
Blue cohosh	*Caulophyllum thalictroides*	p. 242
Fairywand, Devil's bit	*Chamaelirium luteum*	p. 210
Virginia spring beauty	*Claytonia virginica*	NI
Dutchman's britches	*Dicentra cucullaria*	p. 208
Umbrella leaf	*Diphylleia cymosa*	p. 215
Yellow trout lily	*Erythronium americanum*	NI
Spicebush	*Lindera benzoin*	p. 263
Plumed Solomon's seal	*Maianthemum racemosum*	p. 216
Brook lettuce	*Micranthes micranthidifolia*	p. 217
Early saxifrage	*Micranthes virginiensis*	NI
Mayapple	*Podophyllum peltatum*	p. 208
Solomon's seal	*Polygonatum biflorum*	p. 217
Yellow mandarin	*Prosartes lanuginosa*	p. 263
Bloodroot	*Sanguinaria canadensis*	p. 209
Oconee bells	*Shortia galacifolia*	NI
Giant chickweed	*Stellaria pubera*	p. 214
Foamflower	*Tiarella cordifolia*	p. 218
Sweet Betsy	*Trillium cuneatum*	p. 240
Large-flowered trillium	*Trillium grandiflorum*	p. 214
Sweet white trillium	*Trillium simile*	NI
Halberdleaf yellow violet	*Viola hastata*	p. 254
Roundleaf yellow violet	*Viola rotundifolia*	NI
Common blue violet	*Viola sororia*	p. 247

Spring–Summer

False goatsbeard	*Astilbe biternata*	p. 224
Pipsissewa, Striped wintergreen	*Chimaphila maculata*	p. 222
Speckled wood lily	*Clintonia umbellulata*	p. 222
Silverleaf hydrangea	*Hydrangea radiata*	NI
Broadleaf waterleaf	*Hydrophyllum canadense*	NI
Canada mayflower	*Maianthemum canadense*	p. 225
Mountain meadowrue	*Thalictrum clavatum*	p. 226
Canada violet	*Viola canadensis*	p. 220

Summer

Black cohosh	*Actaea racemosa*	p. 226
Rattlesnake orchid	*Goodyera pubescens*	p. 229
Wood nettle	*Laportea canadensis*	p. 265
Rosebay rhododendron	*Rhododendron maximum*	p. 230
Cranefly orchid	*Tipularia discolor*	p. 246

Summer–Fall

Hog peanut	*Amphicarpaea bracteata*	p. 238
Pink turtlehead	*Chelone lyonii*	p. 239
Rock alumroot	*Heuchera villosa*	p. 230
Orange jewelweed	*Impatiens capensis*	p. 268
Cardinal flower	*Lobelia cardinalis*	p. 269
Indian pipe, Ghost flower	*Monotropa uniflora*	p. 231

Fall

White snakeroot	*Ageratina altissima*	p. 232
Beechdrops	*Epifagus virginiana*	p. 233
White wood aster	*Eurybia divaricata*	p. 231
Witch hazel	*Hamamelis virginiana*	p. 262
Curtis's goldenrod	*Solidago curtisii*	p. 261
Heartleaf aster	*Symphyotrichum cordifolium*	p. 251
Canada violet	*Viola canadensis*	p. 220

NI = species not included in the wildflower profiles (Part IV)

14 / Moore Cove Falls

PISGAH NATIONAL FOREST

Highlights	A short hike to a picturesque waterfall with good spring wildflowers
Flowering season	Mid-March through mid-October
Peak flowering	April
Trail length	1.4 miles out and back
Trail rating	Easy
Elevation	2,600–2,900 feet
Nearest town	Brevard, Transylvania County, N.C.
Contact	Pisgah Ranger District; 828-877-3265; www.fs.usda.gov/nfsnc
Directions	From the junction of U.S. 64 and U.S. 276 in Brevard, drive 6.6 miles north on U.S. 276 and park on the pull-off to the right by the kiosk (just before crossing the bridge). GPS: N35 18.294 W82 46.466
Overview	This pleasant hike parallels a small creek that runs through an acidic cove forest with numerous spring wildflowers, including three species of trillium. The short trail ends at a scenic waterfall that free falls 50 feet over an overhanging bluff. The waterfall is most impressive after a good rain as dry periods reduce the creek

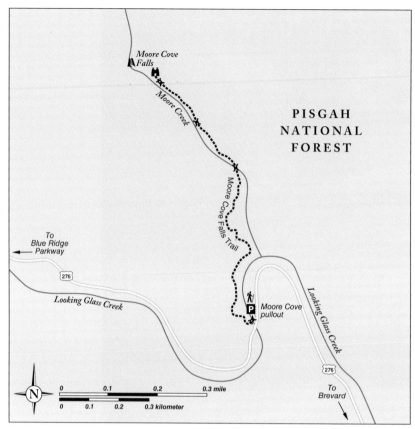

Moore Cove Falls, Pisgah National Forest

to a trickle. In winter, long periods of cold may be followed by icicles hanging from the top of the falls, with the splash zone freezing into a hollow cone.

The Hike

The trail begins at the kiosk and immediately crosses a footbridge over Looking Glass Creek where you get a bird's eye view of red maple, river birch, and witch hazel. After crossing the footbridge, the easy-to-follow trail climbs steeply for a short distance. Along the upper bank, look for galax, sweet white violet, and Indian cucumber root. As the trail levels off, notice the paucity of wildflowers under the rosebay rhododendron near the creek; in contrast, the slope to your left has good spring wildflower displays, including foamflower, giant chickweed, sweet white violet, wood anemone, and Solomon's seal. If you're hiking in late summer or fall, look for white wood aster, Curtis's goldenrod, and beechdrops, a root parasite on American beech. In summer, you may hear the tea-kettle, tea-kettle sound of a male Carolina wren, a small bird with one of the loudest songs in the forest.

Cross a small tributary via a footbridge at 0.1 mile and look for dimpled trout lily, wood anemone, dwarf crested iris, and Jack-in-the-pulpit in spring. Keen observers may also notice the inconspicuous inflorescences of cranefly orchid in summer (in fall through early spring, you'll see its distinctive leaves but not its flowers).

As you walk through this acidic cove forest, notice the tall trees including American beech, Fraser magnolia, white basswood, tulip tree, red maple, and sweet birch. Rows of small shallow holes on the trunks of trees are sapwells made by yellow-bellied sapsuckers. A winter resident in the Southeast, they feed on sap and on insects attracted to the sap. The sapwells also attract hummingbirds. Once common, eastern hemlock has mostly died off due to an infestation of hemlock woolly adelgids, a sap-sucking insect inadvertently introduced from Asia.

Look for Robin's plantain, dwarf cinquefoil, and plumed Solomon's seal before skirting a huge boulder on the left side of the trail. A fully extended five foot long black rat snake was warming itself in the sunlight on a narrow ledge on the boulder one cool spring morning as I walked by. On another occasion, I saw a black rat snake drop nearly 5 feet from a rosebay rhododendron to the ground, before slithering away.

As the trail gradually climbs and winds to the left, look for spring wildflowers such as Solomon's seal, foamflower, and dimpled trout lily, along with sweet white violet, common blue violet, blue cohosh, and giant chickweed. Hikers in fall may see white snakeroot, white wood aster, and heartleaf aster. From here to the falls are good spring wildflower displays, except where shrub thickets or New York fern blanket the slopes.

You'll soon come to the first of three footbridges crossing Moore Creek at 0.4 mile. Just before the first crossing, look for scattered clumps of wake robin (most plants have purple flowers but white-flowered individuals also occur).

Shortly after crossing the creek, you may notice mayapple, foamflower, Robin's plantain, and dwarf crested iris growing near the first of two long footbridges. Wild hydrangea, mountain doghobble, and wood nettle grow along the second long footbridge. Unfortunately, a few clumps of multiflora rose, an exotic invasive shrub, occur in the moist soil along the two footbridges (perhaps the Forest Service will remove them; if not, it's likely to spread since birds consume its fleshy red fruits and disperse the seeds in their droppings).

As the trail gently rises and falls, look for more clumps of wake robin, along with southern nodding trillium, a relatively rare species with white nodding flowers and purple anthers. In summer, rattlesnake orchid blooms, while fall hikers can enjoy white wood aster, white snakeroot, and heartleaf aster.

Cross Moore Creek a second time at 0.5 mile and look for the arching stems of mountain doghobble along the stream. It produces dense clusters of small urn-shaped white flowers in spring with a fragrance that varies from cloyingly sweet to musky.

The spring wildflower show continues as you head up the trail, including more wake robin along with dense mats of dwarf crested iris and plantainleaf sedge (notice the unusually wide leaves for a sedge). Jack-in-the-pulpit is also here.

As you approach the third footbridge over Moore Creek at 0.6 mile, you can see the falls at the head of the cove. Notice the numerous tulip trees with narrow trunks reaching high into the canopy. This dense stand likely colonized the cove in the early 1900s, after much of the Pisgah National Forest was logged. The highway (U.S. 276) that brought you to the trailhead was originally a railroad route that hauled out the cut timber.

The last 100 yards before reaching the falls is a gradual climb with good spring wildflowers, including foamflower, wake robin (with both purple and white flower color forms), and Vasey's trillium. The flowers of wake robin have a fetid odor, which attracts flies and beetles that function as pollinators. Vasey's trillium has larger flowers with a pleasantly sweet fragrance. Showy orchis also grows here and flowers in spring.

The trail ends at a large viewing platform at 0.7 mile where Moore Cove Falls cascades over a small series of steps before free falling 50 feet to the rocks below. Plants in the spray cliff zone include mountain meadowrue, wood nettle, and various ferns. Rosebay rhododendron and mountain laurel grow on the margin of the spray cliff, and a leafy stem or two of Virginia creeper sometimes dangles over the multi-colored bluff.

An overhang, as seen here at Moore Cove Falls, occurs when the rock on top is more resistant to erosion than the rock beneath it. To get a close-up view, take the spur trail on the far side of the platform to the cave-like area beneath the overhang where you can view the falls (and surrounding landscape) from an unusual perspective. Be careful—the wet rocks are slippery!

Enjoy the scenery before retracing your steps back to the trailhead.

Options. You may want to stop and view Looking Glass Falls. It's located one mile south of the Moore Cove trailhead on the left side of U.S. 276. You can see this stunning 60-foot waterfall from the roadside or get a closer look by taking the stone steps down to the base. If you'd like to cool off on a hot summer day, consider going to Sliding Rock, a 60-foot natural rockslide with a 6-foot deep pool at the base. It's located one mile north of the Moore Cove trailhead along U.S. 276. Managed by the U.S. Forest Service, a small admission fee is charged during the summer season.

14 / MOORE COVE FALLS: WHAT TO LOOK FOR

Spring

Wood anemone	*Anemone quinquefolia*	p. 209
Jack-in-the-pulpit	*Arisaema triphyllum*	p. 241
Plantainleaf sedge	*Carex plantaginea*	NI
Blue cohosh	*Caulophyllum thalictroides*	p. 242
Robin's plantain	*Erigeron pulchellus*	p. 216
Dimpled trout lily	*Erythronium umbilicatum*	p. 253
Showy orchis	*Galearis spectabilis*	p. 234
Dwarf crested iris	*Iris cristata*	p. 247
Mountain laurel	*Kalmia latifolia*	p. 236
Mountain doghobble	*Leucothoe fontanesiana*	p. 213
Plumed Solomon's seal	*Maianthemum racemosum*	p. 216
Indian cucumber root	*Medeola virginiana*	p. 264
Partridge berry	*Mitchella repens*	p. 223
Mayapple	*Podophyllum peltatum*	p. 208
Solomon's seal	*Polygonatum biflorum*	p. 217
Dwarf cinquefoil	*Potentilla canadensis*	p. 253
Yellow mandarin	*Prosartes lanuginosa*	p. 263
Bloodroot	*Sanguinaria canadensis*	p. 209
Giant chickweed	*Stellaria pubera*	p. 214
Foamflower	*Tiarella cordifolia*	p. 218
Wake robin, Stinking Willie	*Trillium erectum*	p. 243

Southern nodding trillium	*Trillium rugelii*	NI
Vasey's trillium	*Trillium vaseyi*	p. 244
Sweet white violet	*Viola blanda*	p. 219
Halberdleaf yellow violet	*Viola hastata*	p. 254
Common blue violet	*Viola sororia*	p. 247

Spring–Summer

Strawberry bush, Hearts-a-bustin'	*Euonymus americanus*	p. 264
Galax, Skunkweed	*Galax urceolata*	p. 224
Canada violet	*Viola canadensis*	p. 220

Summer

Rattlesnake orchid	*Goodyera pubescens*	p. 229
Wild hydrangea	*Hydrangea arborescens*	p. 225
Wood nettle	*Laportea canadensis*	p. 265
Rosebay rhododendron	*Rhododendron maximum*	p. 230
Cranefly orchid	*Tipularia discolor*	p. 246

Summer–Fall

Joe Pye weed	*Eutrochium fistulosum*	p. 239
Cave alumroot	*Heuchera parviflora*	NI

Fall

White snakeroot	*Ageratina altissima*	p. 232
Beechdrops	*Epifagus virginiana*	p. 233
White wood aster	*Eurybia divaricata*	p. 231
Witch hazel	*Hamamelis virginiana*	p. 262
Curtis's goldenrod	*Solidago curtisii*	p. 261
Heartleaf aster	*Symphyotrichum cordifolium*	p. 251
Canada violet	*Viola canadensis*	p. 220

NI = species not included in the wildflower profiles (Part IV)

15 / Twin Falls

PISGAH NATIONAL FOREST

Highlights	Scenic cove forests with numerous wildflowers and several waterfalls
Flowering season	Late March through mid-October
Peak flowering	Mid-April to mid-May
Trail length	4.0 mile partial loop
Trail rating	Easy to moderate
Elevation	2,600–3,070 feet
Nearest town	Brevard, Transylvania County, N.C.
Contact	Pisgah Ranger District; 828-877-3265; www.fs.usda.gov/nfsnc
Directions	From the junction of U.S. 64 and U.S. 276 in Brevard, drive 2.1 miles north on U.S. 276 and turn right on F.R. 477. Take the gravel road for 2.7 miles to a small pullout on the right, beneath a power line crossing. GPS: N35 18.891 W82 44.955

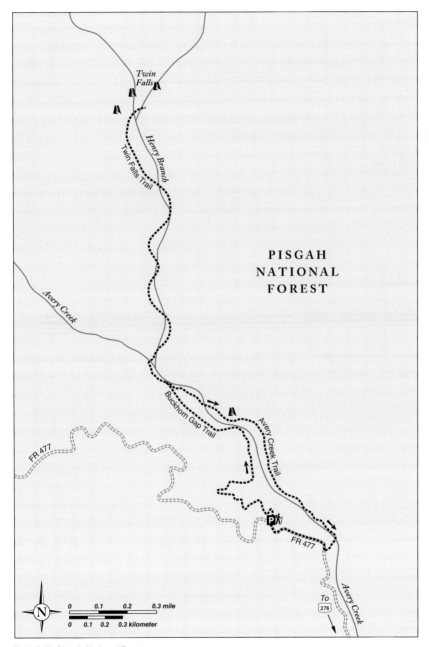

Twin Falls, Pisgah National Forest

Overview This pleasant hike through rich and acidic cove forests follows a small creek upstream with numerous crossings on narrow log footbridges before reaching Twin Falls at 2.0 miles. Twin Falls is a set of two waterfalls, separated by a ridge, each consisting of sheer drops and cascades. The surrounding slopes are rich in spring wildflowers, including dimpled trout lily, showy orchis, bloodroot, and Vasey's trillium. On the return leg, you're rewarded with good views of Avery Falls, several nice cascades, an old beaver pond, and more wildflowers.

The Hike

The Buckhorn Gap Trail (orange blazes) begins at the pullout and quickly descends into an acidic cove forest with canopy trees such as sweet birch, tulip tree, Fraser magnolia, and red maple. Mountain laurel and rosebay rhododendron are common shrubs. Spring wildflowers along the old logging road include dimpled trout lily, foamflower, wood anemone, dwarf crested iris, partridge berry, and four violets (sweet white, common blue, roundleaf yellow, and halberdleaf yellow). If you're hiking in summer or fall, look for rattlesnake orchid, false nettle, cranefly orchid, Indian pipe, and white wood aster.

As you hike down the trail, look and listen for birds. Cove forests have an abundance of nesting songbirds, including colorful birds such as rose-breasted grosbeak, blue-headed vireo, and scarlet tanager.

At 0.9 mile, the Avery Creek Trail comes in on the right (note this junction as you'll want to follow this trail on the return loop). Both trails turn left and soon cross a tributary via a log footbridge. Continue on the Buckhorn Gap Trail by turning right and crossing Avery Creek on the second of many crossings via a log footbridge. At this and other crossings, bypass the horse ford and follow the trail a short distance upstream to a footlog to make a dry crossing. Yellowroot and mountain doghobble grow along the creek as do trout lily, wood anemone, and Quaker ladies, all of which flower in spring.

At the T-junction (1.0 mile), go left and continue to follow the orange-blazed trail as it takes you upstream. Common shrubs along the rocky streamside include rosebay rhododendron, yellowroot, wild hydrangea, and mountain doghobble. You'll occasionally see a dense carpet of ferns (especially New York fern) blanketing slopes and streamside flats. Spring wildflowers include mayapple, dwarf cinquefoil, foamflower, and Robin's plantain, along with wild geranium, Vasey's trillium, and trout lily. In summer or fall, look for wood nettle, wild hydrangea, long-bristled smartweed, black-eyed Susan, and heal all.

Continue to follow the trail upstream through an acidic cove forest until you come to the junction with the Twin Falls Trail at 1.7 miles. Go left on the Twin Falls Trail (blue blazes) and cross the creek three more times via footlogs. After the third crossing, look to your left for a small unnamed waterfall. Wildflowers include fairywand, Indian cucumber root, and wideleaf spiderwort. Painted trillium is also here.

As the trail ascends toward the main falls, the vegetation changes from an acidic cove forest to a rich cove forest and the diversity and abundance of wildflowers increases. Tulip tree is the dominant canopy tree. Common shrubs include spicebush, witch hazel, and wild hydrangea. Look for spring wildflowers, including mayapple, giant chickweed, showy orchis, Robin's plantain, and Jack-in-the-pulpit.

Take the trail to the left of the primitive campsite to view the falls and to explore additional wildflowers along the slopes including bloodroot, giant chickweed, wood anemone, dimpled trout lily, Solomon's seal, Vasey's trillium, black cohosh, and puttyroot.

At 2.0 miles, the trail crosses the creek at the base of the left half of Twin Falls and continues a short distance to the tributary at the base of the right half of Twin Falls. The slopes above this part of the trail are rich in wildflowers, including large clumps of Vasey's trillium and scattered Jack-in-the-pulpit.

Each waterfall is a series of cascades and free falls, the left one nearly 80 feet high, the right falls about 60 feet. Plants in the spray cliff community include rosebay rhododendron, mountain doghobble, rock alumroot, mountain meadowrue, and early saxifrage. These same species also occur in the rocky streamside community, as does wild hydrangea, yellowroot, woodnettle, white wood aster, and white snakeroot. Dense shrubs on the margins of streams provide habitat for the Acadian flycatcher, an acrobatic bird that can fly forward or backward as it forages for insects.

After enjoying the scenery, retrace your steps by following the orange blazed trail to the junction with the Avery Creek Trail at 3.0 miles (passed earlier on the hike) and go left. Follow the Avery Creek Trail (blue blazes), crossing the creek via two footlogs, skirting a primitive campsite, and then crossing the creek via two more footlogs before reaching Avery Falls, a 20-foot free fall with a small plunge pool at the base at 3.3 miles.

Continuing down the trail, you'll pass several cascades. Spring wildflowers include wake robin, mayapple, and foamflower, along with summer- or fall-flowering species such as wild hydrangea, heal all, and pale spiked lobelia.

At the junction with the Clawhammer Cove Trail (3.6 miles), continue on the Avery Creek Trail by going right. Cross Avery Creek via a long footlog and look for Jack-in-the-pulpit, Solomon's seal, wake robin, and yellowroot. Several small boardwalks take you over boggy areas with orange jewelweed, goldenrod, and white wood aster. Narrowleaf red turtlehead, a rare species that flowers in fall, also grows here.

Just before the trail heads up the ridge, look to your left to see an old beaver pond (now a meadow with scattered young trees). The large standing dead trees (snags) were killed when the pond formed. The snags currently provide food for decomposers (including fungi and invertebrates) and nesting sites for birds (notice the cavities high up the trunks).

As you follow the trail up the ridge through a rosebay rhododendron thicket, look for pipevine, a twining vine with large heart-shaped leaves. It's the larval (caterpillar) host plant of pipevine swallowtail butterflies. At the junction with the main road, turn right and walk about 0.25 mile to the pullout where the trailhead is located.

15 / TWIN FALLS: WHAT TO LOOK FOR

Spring

Wood anemone	*Anemone quinquefolia*	p. 209
Jack-in-the-pulpit	*Arisaema triphyllum*	p. 241
Fairywand, Devil's bit	*Chamaelirium luteum*	p. 210
Robin's plantain	*Erigeron pulchellus*	p. 216
Dimpled trout lily	*Erythronium umbilicatum*	p. 253
Showy orchis	*Galearis spectabilis*	p. 234
Wild geranium	*Geranium maculatum*	p. 235
Quaker ladies	*Houstonia caerulea*	NI

Dwarf crested iris	*Iris cristata*	p. 247
Mountain laurel	*Kalmia latifolia*	p. 236
Mountain doghobble	*Leucothoe fontanesiana*	p. 213
Spicebush	*Lindera benzoin*	p. 263
Indian cucumber root	*Medeola virginiana*	p. 264
Early saxifrage	*Micranthes virginiensis*	NI
Partridge berry	*Mitchella repens*	p. 223
Mayapple	*Podophyllum peltatum*	p. 208
Solomon's seal	*Polygonatum biflorum*	p. 217
Dwarf cinquefoil	*Potentilla canadensis*	p. 253
Bloodroot	*Sanguinaria canadensis*	p. 209
Giant chickweed	*Stellaria pubera*	p. 214
Foamflower	*Tiarella cordifolia*	p. 218
Wake robin, Stinking Willie	*Trillium erectum*	p. 243
Painted trillium	*Trillium undulatum*	p. 219
Vasey's trillium	*Trillium vaseyi*	p. 244
Sweet white violet	*Viola blanda*	p. 219
Halberdleaf yellow violet	*Viola hastata*	p. 254
Roundleaf yellow violet	*Viola rotundifolia*	NI
Common blue violet	*Viola sororia*	p. 247
Yellowroot	*Xanthorhiza simplicissima*	p. 240

Spring–Summer

Black cohosh	*Actaea racemosa*	p. 226
Puttyroot, Adam and Eve	*Aplectrum hyemale*	NI
Pipevine, Dutchman's pipe	*Aristolochia macrophylla*	p. 244
Pipsissewa, Striped wintergreen	*Chimaphila maculata*	p. 222
Strawberry bush, Hearts-a-bustin'	*Euonymus americanus*	p. 264
Galax, Skunkweed	*Galax urceolata*	p. 224
Japanese honeysuckle	*Lonicera japonica*	NI
Mountain meadowrue	*Thalictrum clavatum*	p. 226

Summer

False nettle	*Boehmeria cylindrica*	NI
Beggar's ticks	*Desmodium nudiflorum*	p. 238
Rattlesnake orchid	*Goodyera pubescens*	p. 229
Wild hydrangea	*Hydrangea arborescens*	p. 225
Wood nettle	*Laportea canadensis*	p. 265
Rosebay rhododendron	*Rhododendron maximum*	p. 230
Cranefly orchid	*Tipularia discolor*	p. 246
Wideleaf spiderwort	*Tradescantia subaspera*	p. 250

Summer–Fall

Hog peanut	*Amphicarpaea bracteata*	p. 238
Joe Pye weed	*Eutrochium fistulosum*	p. 239
Rock alumroot	*Heuchera villosa*	p. 230
Orange jewelweed	*Impatiens capensis*	p. 268
Pale spiked lobelia	*Lobelia spicata*	NI
Indian pipe, Ghost flower	*Monotropa uniflora*	p. 231
Long-bristled smartweed	*Polygonum caespitosum*	NI
Jumpseed	*Polygonum virginianum*	NI
Heal all	*Prunella vulgaris*	p. 249
Black-eyed Susan	*Rudbeckia hirta*	NI

Fall

White snakeroot	*Ageratina altissima*	p. 232
Narrowleaf red turtlehead	*Chelone obliqua*	NI
White wood aster	*Eurybia divaricata*	p. 231
Witch hazel	*Hamamelis virginiana*	p. 262
Goldenrod	*Solidago* species	NI

NI = species not included in the wildflower profiles (Part IV)

16 / Rainbow Falls

GORGES STATE PARK AND PISGAH NATIONAL FOREST

Highlights	Four waterfalls along a scenic river with good wildflower displays
Flowering season	Late-March through mid-October
Peak flowering	Mid-April through May
Trail length	4.0 miles out and back
Trail rating	Moderate
Elevation	2,925–2,470 feet
Nearest town	Sapphire, Transylvania County, N.C.
Contact	828-966-9099; www.ncparks.gov
Directions	From the junction of N.C. 281 south and U.S. 64 in Lake Toxaway, drive south on N.C. 281 for 0.9 mile and turn left into Gorges State Park. Follow the park road for 1.6 miles to the Grassy Ridge parking area on the right. The trailhead is located at the lower end of the parking area, near the kiosk. GPS: N35 05.329 W82 57.113
Overview	It's hard to find a better waterfall hike than the Rainbow Falls Trail. Beginning in Gorges State Park, the trail soon enters Pisgah National Forest where it follows the Horsepasture River (a designated Wild and Scenic River) as it plummets over four waterfalls, including Rainbow Falls, one of the most spectacular waterfalls in the southern Appalachians. An added bonus is the diversity of wildflowers and plant communities along the trail. You may want to stop at the visitor center (on your right, 1.0 mile after entering Gorges State Park) for maps, information, interesting exhibits, and restrooms. The park is located along the Blue Ridge Escarpment, where the mountains drop down to the piedmont. In the upper escarpment, rivers descend

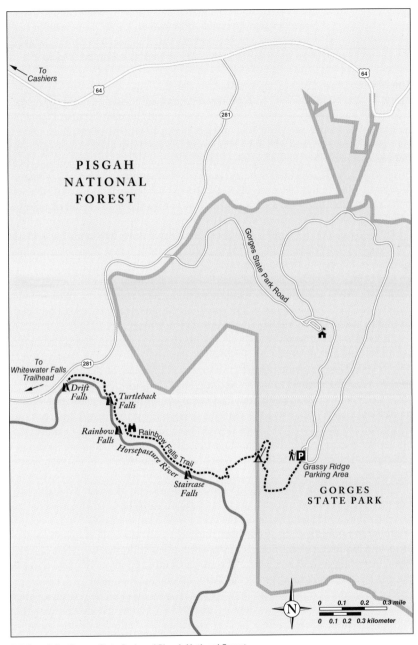

To Cashiers

64

64

281

PISGAH
NATIONAL
FOREST

Gorges State Park Road

To
Whitewater Falls
Trailhead

281

Drift
Falls

Turtleback
Falls

Rainbow
Falls

Rainbow Falls Trail

Horsepasture River

Staircase
Falls

Grassy Ridge
Parking Area

GORGES
STATE PARK

N

0   0.1   0.2   0.3 mile

0   0.1 0.2 0.3 kilometer

Rainbow Falls, Gorges State Park and Pisgah National Forest

gradually, but as the escarpment steepens, rivers run through steep-walled gorges with numerous waterfalls. A small picnic area, an information kiosk, and portable toilets are located near the trailhead. A 0.5-mile hike from the trailhead leads to a walk-in campground.

The Hike

The wide gravel trail marked with orange tags gradually descends through a pine-oak-heath community with dry, shallow, acidic soil. Canopy dominants include chestnut oak, scarlet oak, white oak, and red maple, along with pitch pine and eastern white pine. The twisted trunks of mountain laurel form a nearly impenetrable thicket. Other shrubs include rosebay rhododendron, gorge rhododendron, bear huckleberry, and lowbush blueberry. Look for root sprouts of American chestnut along with chinquapin, a closely related shrub whose lower leaf surface is densely hairy rather than smooth. A dense shrub layer limits the density and diversity of wildflowers along this portion of the trail.

At the T-junction (0.3 mile), go right and continue downhill. In spring, look for the flowers of fairywand, trailing arbutus, and partridge berry, while hikers in late summer to fall may notice southern harebell and striped gentian.

Just before crossing a wet weather tributary at 0.7 mile, you may notice spring wildflowers such as foamflower, Catesby's trillium, Solomon's seal, plumed Solomon's seal, speckled wood lily, yellow star grass, Robin's plantain, and three violets (roundleaf yellow, halberdleaf yellow, and common blue).

The vegetation changes from pine-oak-heath to oak hickory forest just before signposts indicate you're leaving Gorges State Park and entering the national forest. Mature oak forests provide habitat for a variety of breeding birds, including wood thrush, ovenbird, eastern wood-pewee, and black-and-white warbler.

At 1.0 mile, bypass the side trail that veers left for Stairway Falls (but make a mental note, as you may want to visit this falls on the return loop) and continue hiking toward Rainbow Falls. Rock hop across a larger tributary at 1.1 miles, and immediately skirt a primitive campsite with Catesby's trillium, plumed Solomon's seal, sessileleaf bellwort, solitary pussytoes, and sweet shrub, all of which bloom in spring.

After gently rising and falling, the trail climbs steeply through an acidic cove forest as it follows the Horsepasture River upstream. Look for galax, partridge berry, and poke milkweed along the trail. Milkweeds are the larval (caterpillar) host plants of monarch butterflies. Shrubs include rosebay rhododendron, gorge rhododendron, and mountain laurel. Short spur trails allow you to explore the Horsepasture River, including several nice pools. The river is loud with plenty of white water as the fast-flowing water tumbles over and around endless boulders.

The trail climbs more steeply as it approaches an overlook at 1.5 miles, where you're rewarded with a fantastic view of Rainbow Falls, a near vertical cascade about 125 feet high with a large plunge pool at the base. Few waterfalls in the southern Appalachians are as powerful as this one, especially after a good rain. When the water levels are up, the falls hitting the pool create a thunderous roar along with a mist that is sometimes blown up the hillside, soaking hikers in the viewing area. If the light is right, you may see a long arching rainbow in the mist. The large boulders at the base of the falls were once part of the rock face.

The viewing area is rich in spring wildflowers, including Catesby's trillium, Solomon's seal, and Robin's plantain, along with dwarf iris, yellow star grass, wood anemone, and sweet white violet. In summer or fall, look for wild sweet William, cowbane, and flowering spurge, along with whorled coreopsis, cutleaf coneflower, and other members of the sunflower family. Follow the path to the lower observation deck to get a closer look of the falls, but stay on the trail, as the hillside is susceptible to erosion.

On the far side of the gorge, on a cliff above the falls, is a dense stand of heath shrubs, including rosebay rhododendron, gorge rhododendron, and mountain laurel. Eastern white pine grows on the ridgeline. Look for the large white flowers of Fraser magnolia in spring.

After enjoying the view, continue on the main trail 0.2 mile to Turtleback Falls, a short but wide waterfall that drops off a ledge that resembles a turtle's back. In summer, you'll likely see people sliding (or jumping) off the rock into the pool below. Doing so is risky, as there may be rocks and other debris close to the surface, and the strong currents have overpowered swimmers, resulting in several drownings.

To reach Drift Falls, follow the trail upstream for an additional 0.2 mile. The main trail ends at a fence with a no trespassing sign; from here, take the narrow trail to the left to get a view of the falls without crossing onto private property. The waterfall slides rather than falls 40 feet down smooth bedrock. Tag alder, common elderberry, yellowroot, Joe Pye weed, and Appalachian bluet grow along the rocky streambed.

After enjoying the falls, retrace your steps back to the parking area.

Options. If you'd like to see a fourth waterfall (and are willing to follow a short but steep side trail to get there), backtrack on the main trail 0.9 mile to the large tributary (with the primitive campsite) and continue up the hill for another 0.1 mile. The spur trail is on your right, marked by a carsonite post. At the base of a steep slope, the narrow trail continues downstream through an acidic cove forest to a pool at the base of Staircase Falls. The scenic waterfall cascades over a long series of stairs and ledges where the Horsepasture River has cut into the rock of the gorge.

16 / RAINBOW FALLS: WHAT TO LOOK FOR

Spring

Wood anemone	*Anemone quinquefolia*	p. 209
Solitary pussytoes	*Antennaria solitaria*	NI
Jack-in-the-pulpit	*Arisaema triphyllum*	p. 241
Sweet shrub	*Calycanthus floridus*	p. 241
Fairywand, Devil's bit	*Chamaelirium luteum*	p. 210
Trailing arbutus	*Epigaea repens*	p. 207
Robin's plantain	*Erigeron pulchellus*	p. 216
Strawberry bush, Hearts-a-bustin'	*Euonymus americanus*	p. 264
Yellow star grass	*Hypoxis hirsuta*	NI
Dwarf iris	*Iris verna*	NI
Mountain doghobble	*Leucothoe fontanesiana*	p. 213
Plumed Solomon's seal	*Maianthemum racemosum*	p. 216
Solomon's seal	*Polygonatum biflorum*	p. 217
Dwarf cinquefoil	*Potentilla canadensis*	p. 253
Heal all	*Prunella vulgaris*	p. 249
Gorge rhododendron, Punctatum	*Rhododendron minus*	p. 237
Foamflower	*Tiarella cordifolia*	p. 218
Catesby's trillium	*Trillium catesbaei*	p. 212

Sessileleaf bellwort	*Uvularia sessilifolia*	NI
Lowbush blueberry	*Vaccinium pallidum*	NI
Sweet white violet	*Viola blanda*	p. 219
Halberdleaf yellow violet	*Viola hastata*	p. 254
Roundleaf yellow violet	*Viola rotundifolia*	NI
Common blue violet	*Viola sororia*	p. 247
Yellowroot	*Xanthorhiza simplicissima*	p. 240

Spring–Summer

Pipsissewa, Striped wintergreen	*Chimaphila maculata*	p. 222
Speckled wood lily	*Clintonia umbellulata*	p. 222
Galax, Skunkweed	*Galax urceolata*	p. 224
Bear huckleberry	*Gaylussacia ursina*	NI
Bowman's root	*Gillenia trifoliata*	NI
Virginia heartleaf	*Hexastylis virginica*	NI
Appalachian bluet	*Houstonia serpyllifolia*	p. 248
Mountain laurel	*Kalmia latifolia*	p. 236
Indian cucumber root	*Medeola virginiana*	p. 264
Partridge berry	*Mitchella repens*	p. 223

Summer

Poke milkweed	*Asclepias exaltata*	p. 228
Chinquapin	*Castanea pumila*	NI
Whorled coreopsis	*Coreopsis major*	p. 259
Beggar's ticks	*Desmodium nudiflorum*	p. 238
Common fleabane	*Erigeron philadelphicus*	NI
Rattlesnake orchid	*Goodyera pubescens*	p. 229
Silverleaf hydrangea	*Hydrangea radiata*	NI
Wild sweet William	*Phlox maculata*	NI
Sweet azalea	*Rhododendron arborescens*	NI
Rosebay rhododendron	*Rhododendron maximum*	p. 230
Common elderberry	*Sambucus canadensis*	p. 221

Summer–Fall

Yarrow	*Achillea millefolium*	p. 221
False nettle	*Boehmeria cylindrica*	NI
Southern harebell	*Campanula divaricata*	p. 250
Flowering spurge	*Euphorbia corollata*	NI
Joe Pye weed	*Eutrochium fistulosum*	p. 239
Orange jewelweed	*Impatiens capensis*	p. 268
Mountain dwarf dandelion	*Krigia montana*	p. 258
Cowbane	*Oxypolis rigidior*	NI
Heal all	*Prunella vulgaris*	p. 249
Cutleaf coneflower	*Rudbeckia laciniata*	p. 260

Fall

White wood aster	*Eurybia divaricata*	p. 231
Striped gentian	*Gentiana decora*	NI
Witch hazel	*Hamamelis virginiana*	p. 262
Curtis's goldenrod	*Solidago curtisii*	p. 261

NI = species not included in the wildflower profiles (Part IV)

17 / Whitewater Falls

NANTAHALA NATIONAL FOREST

Highlights	A spectacular waterfall with abundant spring wildflowers
Flowering season	April through September
Peak flowering	Mid-April through early May
Trail length	2.0 miles out and back
Trail rating	Moderate
Elevation	2,600–2,200 feet
Nearest town	Sapphire, Transylvania County, N.C.
Contact	Nantahala Ranger District; 828-524-6441; www.fs.usda.gov/nfsnc
Directions	At the intersection of U.S. 64 and N.C. 281, between Cashiers and Lake Toxaway, drive south on N.C. 281 for 8.4 miles and turn left at the sign for Whitewater Falls. GPS: N35 01.818 W83 00.972

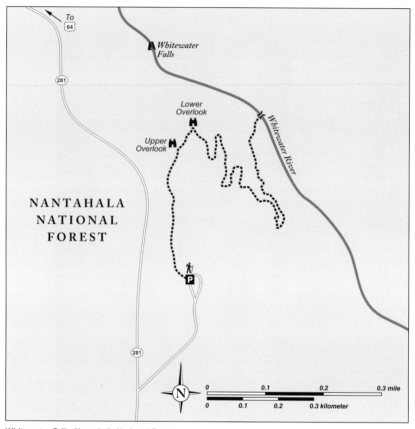

Whitewater Falls, Nantahala National Forest

Overview Whitewater Falls is one of the most spectacular waterfalls in the eastern United States. It's also one of the highest, with two sheer drops and cascades totaling 411 feet. It's especially beautiful in autumn when the leaves of the adjoining deciduous forest are brightly colored. A 0.25-mile paved wheelchair accessible walkway with good wildflower displays ascends 200 feet to the upper viewing area of Whitewater Falls. The trail goes down 150 wooden steps to a lower viewing area (with even better views of the falls). Energetic hikers can continue on the trail as it descends 500 feet to the Whitewater River, passing through a rich cove forest with abundant spring wildflowers. Botanically, the Whitewater River Gorge is best known for its incredible diversity of mosses—its 268 species of mosses represent about one-quarter of the total known species of moss in eastern North America. Facilities include restrooms, picnic tables, and a shelter. A small day-use fee is payable at a drop box in the parking area.

The Hike

From the kiosk at the upper end of the parking area begin two paved paths. Follow the narrower path on the left for about 25 yards and cross a short footbridge to a wooded area with several picnic tables. A variety of spring wildflowers grow here, including pale yellow trillium, halberdleaf yellow violet, Vasey's trillium, plumed Solomon's seal, Solomon's seal, and doll's eyes. Woody plants include silverleaf hydrangea, sweet shrub, and Carolina silverbell.

Continue on the paved path as it ascends to the upper overlook. In spring through early summer look for the greenish yellow flowers of tulip tree, the pinkish flowers of gorge rhododendron and mountain laurel, and the white bowl-shaped flowers of multiflora rose (an exotic invasive species that the Forest Service is trying to eradicate from this area). Spring herbaceous wildflowers include Robin's plantain, common blue violet, and cinquefoil. Hikers in midsummer to fall are likely to see bearsfoot, cutleaf coneflower, wideleaf spiderwort, white snakeroot, and orange jewelweed.

The upper viewing area at 0.25 mile provides good views of Whitewater Falls, a spectacular waterfall that alternates free falls and cascades over a span of 411 feet. The vegetation in the river gorge is mostly acidic cove forest with trees such as eastern white pine, red maple, Carolina silverbell, Fraser magnolia, and scattered hemlocks.

For even better views of the falls, walk down the long series of wooden stairs to the lower viewing platform. Be careful, as leaves on the steps, here and elsewhere along the trail, can be slippery.

Framing the view of the falls from the observation platform are two hemlocks—the tree on the left is an eastern hemlock, the one on the right is a Carolina hemlock (each has been chemically treated for adelgids). The best way to tell them apart is to look at their needle-like leaves—the leaves of Carolina hemlock are arranged all around the twigs (like a bottlebrush) whereas the needles of eastern hemlock are more or less in a single plane (like a feather). Other trees growing on the edge of the platform are black gum, witch hazel, and eastern white pine.

From the lower viewing platform, the trail descends steeply via another long series of wooden steps through an acidic cove forest with gorge rhododendron and rosebay rhododendron. Past the stairs, look for roundleaf yellow violet and the daisy-like flowers of Robin's plantain in spring. Notice the bright leaf undersides that give silverleaf hydrangea its name.

At the T-junction, go left (toward Laurel Valley). As the trail descends via several switchbacks, you'll pass through an acidic cove forest with rosebay rhododendron and gorge rhododendron. Wildflowers are sparse under the dense shrubs.

Listen for the fee-bee-fee-bay song of Carolina chickadees along the trail. Year round residents, Carolina chickadees forage in flocks with migrating warblers and other songbirds in fall and spring, gleaning insects from foliage and tree bark. So, listening for chickadees will help you spot the migrants!

As you continue down the trail, you'll come to a relatively open slope at 0.8 mile where the dense shrub layer is replaced by a dense carpet of wildflowers. Among the showiest plants in this rich cove forest are three trilliums—pale yellow trillium has upright yellow flowers, Catesby's trillium has white nodding flowers that turn pink with age, and Vasey's trillium (the last to bloom) has large nodding maroon flowers that are partially hidden under its three leaves.

Other spring wildflowers on the slopes above and below the trail are foamflower, mayapple, halberdleaf yellow violet, blue cohosh, Jack-in-the-pulpit, yellow mandarin, doll's eyes, Solomon's seal, and plumed Solomon's seal. If you're hiking in late summer or early fall, look for the flowers of Canada horsebalm, mountain bunch-flower, white wood aster, and white snakeroot, along with the striking reddish-orange fruits and seeds of strawberry bush. Considered toxic to humans, various songbirds, wild turkeys, and white-tailed deer eat the fruits of strawberry bush. So, just because you see a bird or mammal eating a fruit (or other part of the plant), does not mean it's edible for you!

Overhead, look for Carolina silverbell, white basswood, and yellow buckeye, all of which have bee-pollinated flowers. In contrast, beetles pollinate the large, fragrant, creamy-white flowers of Fraser magnolia as well as the maroon-to-brown spicy scented flowers of sweet shrub.

At 1.0 mile, the trail reaches the river. Follow the large boulders downstream a few yards to the wide footbridge over the Whitewater River. Even though you cannot see the falls from the river corridor, the roar of the rushing water weaving its way through giant boulders is exhilarating. Notice the nice pools below the bridge.

Plants growing in the rocky streamside habitat include rosebay rhododendron and gorge rhododendron along with yellowroot, sweet white violet, and Appalachian bluet. It's interesting to see flowering dogwood growing among the boulders along the river since you typically associate this species with the forest understory (and home landscapes!). The showy blooms of flowering dogwood consist of four large, petal-like white bracts surrounding a cluster of small flowers, each of which may develop into a bright red berry-like fruit.

On the far side of the bridge, look for devil's walkingstick, a fitting name given the sharp-pointed prickles on its narrow trunk. It produces dense clusters of small greenish-yellow flowers in summer that mature into purplish-black fruits in fall. The flowers are actively visited by bees, wasps, and tiger swallowtail butterflies, and the fruits are eaten and the seeds dispersed by various songbirds, including wood thrush, northern cardinal, and brown thrashers.

The river's edge is a great place to relax on a boulder, have a picnic lunch, and enjoy the sights and sounds of the river before retracing your steps to the parking area.

17 / WHITEWATER FALLS: WHAT TO LOOK FOR

Spring

Doll's eyes, White baneberry	*Actaea pachypoda*	p. 213
Wood anemone	*Anemone quinquefolia*	p. 209
Sweet shrub	*Calycanthus floridus*	p. 241
Blue cohosh	*Caulophyllum thalictroides*	p. 242
Robin's plantain	*Erigeron pulchellus*	NI
Strawberry bush, Hearts-a-bustin'	*Euonymus americanus*	p. 264
Appalachian bluet	*Houstonia serpyllifolia*	p. 248
Plumed Solomon's seal	*Maianthemum racemosum*	p. 216
Indian cucumber root	*Medeola virginiana*	p. 264
Mayapple	*Podophyllum peltatum*	p. 208
Solomon's seal	*Polygonatum biflorum*	p. 217
Yellow mandarin	*Prosartes lanuginosa*	p. 263
Giant chickweed	*Stellaria pubera*	p. 214
Foamflower	*Tiarella cordifolia*	p. 218

Catesby's trillium	*Trillium catesbaei*	p. 212
Pale yellow trillium	*Trillium discolor*	NI
Vasey's trillium	*Trillium vaseyi*	p. 244
Sweet white violet	*Viola blanda*	p. 219
Halberdleaf yellow violet	*Viola hastata*	p. 254
Roundleaf yellow violet	*Viola rotundifolia*	NI
Common blue violet	*Viola sororia*	p. 247
Yellowroot	*Xanthorhiza simplicissima*	p. 240

Spring–Summer

Jack-in-the-pulpit	*Arisaema triphyllum*	p. 241
Galax, Skunkweed	*Galax urceolata*	p. 224
Mountain laurel	*Kalmia latifolia*	p. 236
Partridge berry	*Mitchella repens*	p. 223
Gorge rhododendron, Punctatum	*Rhododendron minus*	p. 237
Multiflora rose	*Rosa multiflora*	NI

Summer

Devil's walkingstick	*Aralia spinosa*	NI
Beggar's ticks	*Desmodium nudiflorum*	p. 238
Southern bush honeysuckle	*Diervilla sessilifolia*	NI
Common fleabane	*Erigeron philadelphicus*	NI
Silverleaf hydrangea	*Hydrangea radiata*	NI
Wood nettle	*Laportea canadensis*	p. 265
Rosebay rhododendron	*Rhododendron maximum*	p. 230
Cranefly orchid	*Tipularia discolor*	p. 246
Wideleaf spiderwort	*Tradescantia subaspera*	p. 250
Mountain bunchflower	*Veratrum parviflorum*	NI

Summer–Fall

Canada horsebalm	*Collinsonia canadensis*	p. 261
Asiatic dayflower	*Commelina communis*	p. 249
Rock alumroot	*Heuchera villosa*	p. 230
Orange jewelweed	*Impatiens capensis*	p. 268
Yellow jewelweed	*Impatiens pallida*	NI
Pokeweed	*Phytolacca americana*	p. 227
Cutleaf coneflower	*Rudbeckia laciniata*	p. 260
Bearsfoot, Yellow leafcup	*Smallanthus uvedalius*	p. 260

Fall

White snakeroot	*Ageratina altissima*	p. 232
Common ragweed	*Ambrosia artemisiifolia*	p. 266
White wood aster	*Eurybia divaricata*	p. 231
Pale spiked lobelia	*Lobelia spicata*	NI
Curtis's goldenrod	*Solidago curtisii*	p. 261

NI = species not included in the wildflower profiles (Part IV)

18 / Panthertown Valley

NANTAHALA NATIONAL FOREST

Highlights	Three waterfalls, scenic views, and a diverse flora
Flowering season	April through late September
Peak flowering	May through June
Trail length	3.4 mile loop trail
Trail rating	Moderate
Elevation	4,095–3,630 feet
Nearest town	Cashiers, Jackson County, N.C.
Contact	Nantahala Ranger District; 828-524-6441; www.fs.usda.gov/nfsnc
Directions	From the junction of U.S. 64 and N.C. 107 in Cashiers, travel east on U.S. 64 for 2.0 miles and turn left onto Cedar Creek Road. Drive 2.3 miles before turning right onto Breedlove Road. Follow Breedlove Road for 3.5 miles to a parking area that ends at a gate (the last 0.2 mile is on a gravel road). GPS: N35 10.068 W83 02.391
Overview	If you haven't been to Panthertown Valley, you'll want to add it to your list of places to visit. Because of its massive granite domes, valley floors, and scenic waterfalls, it's sometimes referred to as the Yosemite of the East. The 6,700-acre tract in the Nantahala National Forest contains a large network of hiking trails. Thanks to the Friends of Panthertown, some of the trails are now marked (including the ones included in this hike description) with the standard brown carsonite trail signs used by the Forest Service. The loop trail described here descends to the valley, where you'll see three waterfalls and numerous wildflowers. By October, the wildflowers are few, but the fall colors really kick in.

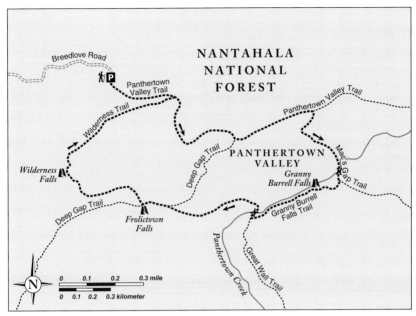

Panthertown Valley, Nantahala National Forest

The Hike

From the gate at the end of the parking area, follow the Panthertown Valley Trail (#474) downhill through a deciduous forest with red oak, white oak, chestnut oak, hickory, red maple, and tulip tree. Good wildflower displays line the gravel roadbed, including spring flowering Robin's plantain, common blue violet, dwarf cinquefoil, wild strawberry, Catesby's trillium, and pink lady's slipper. In summer, look for the nodding white flowers of poke milkweed, the bright pink flowers of Carolina phlox, the yellow flower heads of black-eyed Susan, the orange-to-red flowers of flame azalea, and the white flower heads of basil bee balm, oxeye daisy, and white wood aster.

There are timber rattlesnakes in Panthertown. Watch for them basking in warm spots along the trail. Black bears are also here—look for their scat, tracks, and markings (on tree trunks) along the trail. If you camp in the area, you'll likely hear coyotes howling in the night. Be wary of yellow jackets—not just at Panthertown, but on any hike in summer or fall. Stepping on or near an underground nest can cause them to come swarming out, inflicting multiple painful stings. If you disturb a yellow jacket colony, walk slowly away and don't wave your arms since swift movements will only attract more yellow jackets.

At 0.4 mile, bypass the side trail to Wilderness Falls on the right (on the return loop, you'll come back to this junction). Just around the bend, the trail levels off on a rocky flat with stunning views of Panthertown Valley, including granite domes rising high above the valley floor. The stunted pines growing on the rocky flat are pitch pines, a fire adapted species that, unlike most pines, can regenerate from stump sprouts following topkill by fire.

The showy white flowers of smooth serviceberry put on quite a show in early spring. Even more spectacular are the pink-to-purple flower clusters of Catawba rhododendron in late spring. At ground level, look for the flowers of mountain dwarf dandelion, wintergreen, and Curtiss' milkwort in summer.

As the trail descends, the vegetation transitions to an acidic cove forest with a variety of shrubs, including sweet azalea, mountain laurel, gorge rhododendron, sweet shrub, witch hazel, and mountain sweet pepperbush. Scattered root sprouts of American chestnut can also be seen. The introduced fungus that caused the chestnut blight in the 1930s killed the above-ground part of the trees but not their roots. As a result, some of the large chestnut trees of the past persist today as root sprouts in the forest understory.

Bypass the Deep Gap Trail (#449) at 0.7 mile and stay on the main trail as it narrows, passing through a dense thicket of rosebay rhododendron and mountain laurel. If you're wondering about all the sand along the trail, it's derived from quartz in the granite rock.

Continue down the trail for another 0.2 mile to a four-way junction and turn right onto Mac's Gap Trail. Just as the trail reaches the valley floor (1.0 mile), you'll pass a primitive campsite and the remains of an old homestead on your left, with lots of fly poison and scattered Catesby's trillium. Toxic alkaloids deter most animals from feeding on the foliage of fly poison but theridiid spiders often perch in the flowers, where they ambush potential pollinators.

Shortly after the campsite, take the right fork through a clearing marked by dense patches of galax, running cedar, and partridge berry. As the trail passes through a small open field you may notice various members of the sunflower family, including yarrow, oxeye daisy, common fleabane, and goldenrod.

Walk through a grove of eastern white pine (planted for Christmas trees, but never harvested). Pine plantations lack the diversity of birds, plants, and other organisms that occur in a more natural forest.

Cross Panthertown Creek via a footbridge at 1.2 miles. The tea-colored water comes from tannins in decaying vegetation leaching into the slow-moving water. Look for rosebay rhododendron, southern bush honeysuckle, and Joe Pye weed along the creek. The pinkish flower heads of Joe Pye weed are a magnet for butterflies, including tiger swallowtails, great spangled fritillary, red admiral, painted lady, viceroy, and monarchs. Goldfinches glean seeds from the fruiting heads of Joe Pye in autumn.

On the far side of Panthertown creek, you'll soon come to a fork in the trail. Take the Granny Burrell Falls Trail (#486) to the right and immediately enter a rosebay rhododendron tunnel.

As you follow the trail upstream, listen for the sound of the falls, and take one of the short spur trails to the right to get a close-up view of Granny Burrell Falls (1.4 miles). The falls is a classic example of a sliding waterfall, with water sliding (rather than falling) down a smooth sloping rock face about 15 feet. Rosebay rhododendron and mountain laurel grow on the margin of the falls. Below the falls, the river flows over multi-colored bedrock for about 100 feet before emptying into a large shallow pool with a dense thicket of rosebay rhododendron on the rim.

The trail continues upstream through a rosebay rhododendron tunnel. Looking at the twisted mass of stems which forms a nearly impenetrable wall makes you appreciate the individuals who create and maintain trails like this.

At the T-junction (1.6 miles), turn right onto the Great Wall Trail (#489) and immediately rock hop or wade across Panthertown Creek. On the far side of the creek, the trail continues through an acidic cove forest with New York fern, fly poison, Catesby's trillium, and poke milkweed. Look for the conspicuously yellow-, black-, and white-striped caterpillars of monarch butterflies on the leaves of poke milkweed.

The gently undulating trail ascends more steeply as it approaches a ridge with a T-junction at 2.0 miles. Turn left at the junction and follow the Deep Gap Trail (#449) downhill. Just before reaching the creek, you'll come to a junction with side trails going left and right. The trail to the left is a short steep scramble to the base of Frolictown Falls, a small waterfall with a near vertical 15-foot drop with rosebay rhododendron and mountain doghobble on the margin.

After enjoying the falls, return to the main trail and follow the side trail to the right (the Wilderness Trail). The trail winds its way through an acidic cove forest with eastern white pine, red maple, and dying eastern hemlocks in the overstory, with dense thickets of mountain doghobble and rosebay rhododendron in the understory. Yellow birch is also here, easily recognized by its peeling silvery bark. You'll pass through several boggy areas, where Catesby's trillium, painted trillium, and pink lady's slipper add a splash of color in spring.

Lady slipper orchids use a form of deception to attract pollinators (bumblebees) as the large colorful flowers, nectar guides, and sweet fragrance falsely advertise a food reward. Most lady slipper flowers fail to mature a fruit because of lack of pollination, but when a fruit does mature, it produces thousands of tiny seeds that are dispersed in the wind.

The trail ascends more steeply as it approaches Wilderness Falls at 2.5 miles, an impressive sliding waterfall that drops 65 feet over smooth rock. Of the three waterfalls on the loop, it's by far the tallest and most impressive.

From the falls, the trail weaves its way upslope under a dense rosebay rhododendron tunnel before veering to the right and leveling off as it passes through a slightly more open tunnel of mountain laurel and rosebay rhododendron. As the trail continues, look for spring to early summer wildflowers, including bearcorn, galax, common blue violet, halberdleaf yellow violet, wood anemone, bowman's root, and Catesby's trillium. At the T-junction, turn left and follow the Panthertown Valley Trail 0.4 mile back to the trailhead.

Options. There are numerous trails in Panthertown Valley, some marked, others not. Before exploring the area further, I'd recommend purchasing a copy of Burt Kornegay's *A Guide's Guide to Panthertown.* It's available at many local outfitters as well as from Slickrock Expeditions' website.

18 / PANTHERTOWN VALLEY: WHAT TO LOOK FOR

Spring

Wood anemone	*Anemone quinquefolia*	p. 209
Bearcorn, Squawroot	*Conopholis americana*	p. 255
Pink lady's slipper	*Cypripedium acaule*	p. 235
Robin's plantain	*Erigeron pulchellus*	p. 216
Wild strawberry	*Fragaria virginiana*	p. 212
Dwarf iris	*Iris verna*	NI
Mountain doghobble	*Leucothoe fontanesiana*	p. 213
Canada mayflower	*Maianthemum canadense*	p. 225
Plumed Solomon's seal	*Maianthemum racemosum*	p. 216
Solomon's seal	*Polygonatum biflorum*	p. 217
Dwarf cinquefoil	*Potentilla canadensis*	p. 253

Catesby's trillium	*Trillium catesbaei*	p. 212
Painted trillium	*Trillium undulatum*	p. 219
Sessileleaf bellwort	*Uvularia sessilifolia*	NI
Sweet white violet	*Viola blanda*	p. 219
Halberdleaf yellow violet	*Viola hastata*	p. 254
Common blue violet	*Viola sororia*	p. 247

Spring–Summer

Sweet shrub	*Calycanthus floridus*	p. 241
Pipsissewa, Striped wintergreen	*Chimaphila maculata*	p. 222
Galax, Skunkweed	*Galax urceolata*	p. 224
Bowman's root	*Gillenia trifoliata*	NI
Mountain laurel	*Kalmia latifolia*	p. 236
Indian cucumber root	*Medeola virginiana*	p. 264
Heal all	*Prunella vulgaris*	p. 249
Flame azalea	*Rhododendron calendulaceum*	p. 267
Catawba rhododendron	*Rhododendron catawbiense*	p. 236
Gorge rhododendron, Punctatum	*Rhododendron minus*	p. 237

Summer

Colicroot	*Aletris farinosa*	NI
Fly poison	*Amianthium muscitoxicum*	NI
Poke milkweed	*Asclepias exaltata*	p. 228
Mountain sweet pepperbush	*Clethra acuminata*	NI
Whorled coreopsis	*Coreopsis major*	p. 259
Southern bush honeysuckle	*Diervilla sessilifolia*	NI
Common fleabane	*Erigeron philadelphicus*	NI
Wintergreen	*Gaultheria procumbens*	p. 229
Rattlesnake orchid	*Goodyera pubescens*	p. 229
Decumbent St. Andrew's cross	*Hypericum stragalum*	NI
Whorled loosestrife	*Lysimachia quadrifolia*	p. 258
Partridge berry	*Mitchella repens*	p. 223
Basil bee balm	*Monarda clinopodia*	p. 227
Small's ragwort	*Packera anonyma*	NI
Carolina phlox	*Phlox carolina*	NI
Sweet azalea	*Rhododendron arborescens*	NI
Rosebay rhododendron	*Rhododendron maximum*	p. 230
Fire pink	*Silene virginica*	p. 267
Wild raisin	*Viburnum cassinoides*	NI

Summer–Fall

Yarrow	*Achillea millefolium*	p. 221
Southern harebell	*Campanula divaricata*	p. 250
Oxeye daisy	*Chrysanthemum leucanthemum*	NI
Flowering spurge	*Euphorbia corollata*	NI
White wood aster	*Eurybia divaricata*	p. 231
Joe Pye weed	*Eutrochium fistulosum*	p. 239
Pineweed	*Hypericum gentianoides*	NI
Mountain dwarf dandelion	*Krigia montana*	p. 258
Indian pipe	*Monotropa uniflora*	p. 231
Common evening primrose	*Oenothera biennis*	NI
Cowbane	*Oxypolis rigidior*	NI
Curtiss' milkwort	*Polygala curtissii*	NI
Black-eyed Susan	*Rudbeckia hirta*	NI

Fall

White snakeroot	*Ageratina altissima*	p. 232
Common ragweed	*Ambrosia artemisiifolia*	p. 266
Witch hazel	*Hamamelis virginiana*	p. 262
Heal all	*Prunella vulgaris*	p. 249
Goldenrod	*Solidago* species	NI
New York ironweed	*Vernonia noveboracensis*	p. 246

NI = species not included in the wildflower profiles (Part IV)

19 / Rufus Morgan Falls

NANTAHALA NATIONAL FOREST

Highlights	Rich cove forest with abundant wildflowers and a long cascading waterfall
Flowering season	Mid-March through mid-October
Peak flowering	April through early May
Trail length	1 mile out and back
Trail rating	Easy to moderate
Elevation	3,225–3,475 feet
Nearest town	Franklin, Macon County, N.C.
Contact	Nantahala Ranger District; 828-524-6441; www.fs.usda.gov/nfsnc/
Directions	From the intersection of U.S. 64 and Business 441 in Franklin, travel west on U.S. 64 for 3.7 miles. Turn right onto Old Murphy Road (at the Wayah Bald sign) and drive 0.2 mile, before turning left onto Wayah Road. Travel 6.5 miles on Wayah Road, then turn left on F.R. 388. Follow the gravel road for 2 miles to a small parking area on the right. GPS: N35 08.804 W83 32.862

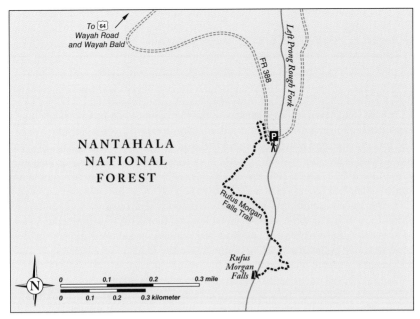

To [64]
Wayah Road
and Wayah Bald

Left Prong Rough Fork

FR 388

NANTAHALA
NATIONAL
FOREST

Rufus Morgan Falls Trail

Rufus Morgan Falls

N

| 0 | 0.1 | 0.2 | 0.3 mile |
| 0 | 0.1 | 0.2 | 0.3 kilometer |

Rufus Morgan Falls, Nantahala National Forest

Overview This short hike to a scenic waterfall takes you through a rich cove forest with abundant spring wildflowers, including two bellworts, three trilliums, and five violets. The falls' name honors Reverend Albert Rufus Morgan, a poet, minister, hiker, and conservationist. At one time, he personally maintained 50 miles of the Appalachian trail. A hike to Rufus Morgan Falls coupled with an outing to nearby Wayah Bald makes a memorable day trip.

The Hike

As the easily followed trail ascends from the parking area, you'll pass spring wildflowers such as foamflower, common blue violet, and halberdleaf yellow violet. You may also see a few scattered showy orchis. The rich cove forest you're hiking through includes trees such as yellow buckeye, white basswood, Carolina silverbell, tulip tree, and both striped and red maple.

In the forest understory, look for witch hazel, buffalo nut, wild hydrangea, and the root sprouts of American chestnut. You may also notice pipevine, a twining vine with large heart-shaped leaves and small flowers with a sharply bent flower tube. Look closely for pipevine swallowtail caterpillars (black, with orange spots) feeding on the leaves of pipevine. In most forests, the caterpillars of butterflies and moths consume more leaves than all other plant-feeding organisms combined.

As you continue upslope, the spring wildflowers are plentiful, including bloodroot, acute-lobed hepatica, speckled wood lily, Solomon's seal, plumed Solomon's seal, blue cohosh, cucumber root, yellow mandarin, early meadowrue, and three species of trillium—wake robin, large-flowered trillium, and Vasey's trillium. In summer, look for the blue-to-purplish 3-petaled flowers of wideleaf spiderwort and the drooping white umbels of poke milkweed. Fall flowering species include white snakeroot, heartleaf aster, Curtis's goldenrod, and witch hazel.

In mature cove forests where large snags (dead standing trees) are present, various woodpeckers may be seen (or heard), including downy, hairy, and red-headed woodpeckers, all of which drill the bark of trees for insects. Woodpeckers also eat fleshy fruits such as sumac and mistletoe, as well as seeds and nuts.

At 0.25 mile, the trail veers sharply to the right and crosses a footbridge over a creek (the Left Prong of Rough Fork) where foamflower, sweet white violet, mountain meadowrue, and wood nettle grow in the moist soil. The stinging hairs of wood nettle deter many, but not all, animals from feeding on the foliage. For example, white-tailed deer, snails, and the caterpillars of some butterflies and moths are known to feed on the leaves of wood nettle.

As the trail continues upslope, you'll see many of the species previously encountered along with mayapple, Canada violet (which blooms from spring through early fall), whorled loosestrife, and large-flowered bellwort. Bumblebee queens crawl up large-flowered bellwort's nodding yellow flowers to suck up sugar-rich nectar as an energy source and to obtain pollen for raising their broods.

Follow the trail upstream to a small sliding waterfall with the much larger Rufus Morgan Falls visible up the slope. Look for spring-flowering broadleaf toothwort, wake robin, and Jack-in-the-pulpit near the stream. If you're hiking in summer to early fall, you may notice pink turtlehead and white wood aster as well as the large brown seeds and leathery pods of yellow buckeye along the trail. Seeds of yellow buckeye exposed to direct sunlight or dry conditions quickly lose viability, which may partially explain why yellow buckeye is restricted to moist sheltered forests.

At 0.5 mile, turn right at the junction and follow the spur trail 75 yards through a rich cove forest to the falls. Along the way, you may see wake robin, large-flowered trillium, Vasey's trillium, and large-flowered bellwort in spring, and Canada horsebalm, white snakeroot, and Curtis's goldenrod in summer to early fall.

Rufus Morgan Falls is a long narrow waterfall that cascades and slides about 65 feet down a mostly bare rock face. The spray cliff includes mountain meadowrue, rosebay rhododendron, and various mosses. Because mosses obtain water and nutrients directly from the air, they can grow on bare rock. In contrast, flowering plants are restricted to areas where their roots can harvest water and nutrients from soil that has accumulated in cracks and ledges on the rock substrate.

Near the base of the falls and along the rocky streamside, look for spring wildflowers, including dimpled trout lily, early meadowrue, Canada violet, blue cohosh, broadleaf toothwort, Jack-in-the-pulpit, wake robin, and doll's eyes. You may notice doll's eyes' round white fruits (with a prominent black spot at the tips of bright red stalks) in late summer through fall.

The slope to the right of the falls is an acidic cove forest with a dense understory of rosebay rhododendron. The left side of the falls is a rich cove forest with few shrubs and good wildflower displays.

Stand near the base of the falls to experience the cool air flowing off the falls and listen to the sound of the falls as it mingles with the sounds of the creek below. It's the combination of sight and sound that makes a waterfall. After enjoying the falls, follow the spur trial back to the main trail and turn left to return to the trailhead.

Options. If you have time, visit the nearby Wayah Bald, the area's highest point, at 5,342 feet. On a clear day, the stone observation tower at the summit provides panoramic views of the southern Appalachians in Georgia, Tennessee, and the Carolinas. The best time to visit is late spring to early summer when the rhododendrons, azaleas, and other wildflowers are most likely to bloom. To get to Wayah Bald from the Rufus Morgan Falls parking area, follow the gravel road back to the junction with Wayah Road and turn left. Continue on Wayah Road for 2.7 miles and turn right onto Forest Service Road 69. Follow the gravel road for 4.5 miles to the Wayah Bald parking area. A 0.3-mile trail leads to the observation tower. Both the Appalachian Trail and the Bartram Trail cross Wayah Bald at the observation tower so there is ample opportunity to add additional miles to your hike.

19 / RUFUS MORGAN FALLS: WHAT TO LOOK FOR

Spring

Doll's eyes, White baneberry	*Actaea pachypoda*	p. 213
Acute-lobed hepatica	*Anemone acutiloba*	p. 207
Wood anemone	*Anemone quinquefolia*	p. 209
Jack-in-the-pulpit	*Arisaema triphyllum*	p. 241
Broadleaf toothwort	*Cardamine diphylla*	NI
Blue cohosh	*Caulophyllum thalictroides*	p. 242
Bearcorn, Squawroot	*Conopholis americana*	p. 255
Umbrella leaf	*Diphylleia cymosa*	p. 215
Dimpled trout lily	*Erythronium umbilicatum*	p. 253
Showy orchis	*Galearis spectabilis*	p. 234
Dwarf crested iris	*Iris cristata*	p. 247
Plumed Solomon's seal	*Maianthemum racemosum*	p. 216
Mayapple	*Podophyllum peltatum*	p. 208
Solomon's seal	*Polygonatum biflorum*	p. 217
Yellow mandarin	*Prosartes lanuginosa*	p. 263
Heal all	*Prunella vulgaris*	p. 249
Bloodroot	*Sanguinaria canadensis*	p. 209
Early meadowrue	*Thalictrum dioicum*	NI
Foamflower	*Tiarella cordifolia*	p. 218
Wake robin, Stinking Willie	*Trillium erectum*	p. 243
Large-flowered trillium	*Trillium grandiflorum*	p. 214
Vasey's trillium	*Trillium vaseyi*	p. 244
Large-flowered bellwort	*Uvularia grandiflora*	NI
Sessileleaf bellwort	*Uvularia sessilifolia*	NI
Sweet white violet	*Viola blanda*	p. 219
Halberdleaf yellow violet	*Viola hastata*	p. 254
Roundleaf yellow violet	*Viola rotundifolia*	NI
Common blue violet	*Viola sororia*	p. 247

Spring–Summer

Black cohosh	*Actaea racemosa*	p. 226
Pipevine, Dutchman's pipe	*Aristolochia macrophylla*	p. 244
False goatsbeard	*Astilbe biternata*	p. 224
Speckled wood lily	*Clintonia umbellulata*	p. 222
Indian cucumber root	*Medeola virginiana*	p. 264
Mountain meadowrue	*Thalictrum clavatum*	p. 226
Canada violet	*Viola canadensis*	p. 220

Summer

Poke milkweed	*Asclepias exaltata*	p. 228
Beggar's ticks	*Desmodium nudiflorum*	p. 238
Wild hydrangea	*Hydrangea arborescens*	p. 225
Wood nettle	*Laportea canadensis*	p. 265
Whorled loosestrife	*Lysimachia quadrifolia*	p. 258
Rosebay rhododendron	*Rhododendron maximum*	p. 230
Flowering raspberry	*Rubus odoratus*	NI
Wideleaf spiderwort	*Tradescantia subaspera*	p. 250

Summer–Fall

Hog peanut	*Amphicarpaea bracteata*	p. 238
Pink turtlehead	*Chelone lyonii*	p. 239
Canada horsebalm	*Collinsonia canadensis*	p. 261
White wood aster	*Eurybia divaricata*	p. 231
Basal bee balm	*Monarda clinopodia*	p. 227
Indian pipe, Ghost flower	*Monotropa uniflora*	p. 231
Heal all	*Prunella vulgaris*	p. 249

Fall

White snakeroot	*Ageratina altissima*	p. 232
Witch hazel	*Hamamelis virginiana*	p. 262
Curtis's goldenrod	*Solidago curtisii*	p. 261
Heartleaf aster	*Symphyotrichum cordifolium*	p. 251
Canada violet	*Viola canadensis*	p. 220

NI = species not included in the wildflower profiles (Part IV)

20 / Deep Creek

GREAT SMOKY MOUNTAINS NATIONAL PARK

Highlights	Scenic hike with three waterfalls and numerous wildflowers
Flowering season	March through mid-October
Peak flowering	Mid-April through early May
Trail length	2.4-mile loop trail
Trail rating	Easy to moderate
Elevation	1,850–2,260 feet
Nearest town:	Bryson City, Swain County, N.C.
Contact	865-436-1200; www.nps.gov/grsm/planyourvisit/waterfalls.htm
Directions	From downtown Bryson City, follow the signs leading to National Park/Deep Creek and then Deep Creek Campground. As you enter the National Park, continue past the campground entrance and picnic area to a large parking lot on the left. GPS: N35 27.871 W83 26.049

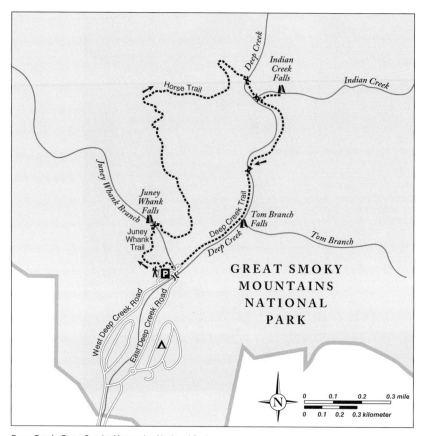

Deep Creek, Great Smoky Mountains National Park

Overview   This delightful loop trail has it all—three waterfalls, a beautiful creek, and abundant wildflowers. Just before entering the National Park, roadside entrepreneurs wave enthusiastically trying to get you to pull over and rent inner tubes. Many families acquiesce and have fun tubing down Deep Creek. The soft light, low humidity, cool air, and vibrant colors (spring wildflowers and autumn leaves) make spring and fall a great time to be out on the trail. Nearby facilities include a campground, picnic area, and restrooms. On the sign adjacent to the trailhead, the trail described here is labeled the three waterfalls loop trail.

The Hike

From the north side of the parking area, take the signed trail to Juney Whank Falls. Wildflowers appear right from the start—common blue violet, buttercup, common fleabane, orange daylily (an escaped cultivar), a pink-flowered phlox, thimbleweed, great blue lobelia, leafy elephant's foot, and flowering dogwood.

The trail immediately ascends a small hill and then winds to the left through a cove forest. At the T-junction, veer to the right and follow the Juney Whank Trail upslope to a stairway that descends to a footbridge with spring wildflowers such as rue anemone, bloodroot, Solomon's seal, and plumed Solomon's seal. The daisy-like flowers of Robin's plantain, the pink-to-lavender flowers of showy orchis, and the relatively rare southern nodding trillium also flower in spring.

Directly across from the footbridge at 0.25 mile is Juney Whank Falls. The viewing area is about as close as you're ever going to get to a waterfall. The upper portion of the falls consists of slides and cascades about 40 feet high that are lined with rosebay rhododendron and mountain laurel. In the spray cliff, look for yellow jewel-weed, wideleaf spiderwort, and rock alumroot. Below the footbridge, the cascades continue another 50 feet before disappearing into the forest.

Continue across the footbridge and up the slope. In quick succession, take the right fork at the first junction and the left fork at the second junction and follow the signed Deep Creek Horse Trail. Initially flat, the trail climbs steadily for about 0.5 mile through an acidic cove forest with spring wildflowers such as sweet white violet, speckled wood lily, and giant chickweed. Loosely scattered along the trail are cardinal flower and striped gentian, but they don't bloom until midsummer or fall. Mountain laurel and rosebay rhododendron form dense thickets along the small tributary that parallels the trail.

The trail tops off on a relatively dry ridge at 0.8 mile, then descends into an acidic cove forest with mountain laurel, rosebay rhododendron, flame azalea, and striped maple. In spring, look for pink lady's slipper, southern nodding trillium, and fairywand, along with abundant Robin's plantain and partridge berry along the trail. Fairywand gets its name from the dense elongated cluster of small white flowers on a wand-like stalk.

At the junction (1.3 miles), turn right and cross the footbridge where the bright-pink-to-rose-purple flowers of wild geranium stand out in spring. Rosebay rhodo-dendron, wild hydrangea, and wood nettle bloom in summer. On the far side of the footbridge is a dense patch of forsythia, a remnant planting from an old homestead.

Go right at the T-junction (1.4 miles) and follow the Deep Creek Trail through an acidic cove forest. As you cross the wide bridge, pause to enjoy the sights and sounds of Deep Creek. You may see a belted kingfisher perched on a bare branch above the stream, or diving to catch a fish with its straight, pointed bill. It's one of our few bird species in which the female is more brightly colored than the male.

Within a hundred yards, you'll come to a second wide bridge over Deep Creek. Just before crossing it, take the short spur trail to the right to explore the river flat (an alluvial forest) with good spring wildflower displays, including wake robin, southern nodding trillium, Solomon's seal, and spicebush. Yellow jewelweed and common wingstem flower in summer and fall.

Cross the bridge and immediately turn left, following the Indian Creek Trail upslope through an acidic cove forest. After about 100 yards, veer left and follow the short spur trail as it descends to a viewing area of Indian Creek Falls at 1.6 miles. The sliding cascade drops into a nice pool with rosebay rhododendron and mountain doghobble along the water's edge. Mountain doghobble forms dense thickets that are difficult to walk through, hence the common name. Birders may spot Acadian flycatchers and various warblers in this area.

After enjoying the falls, backtrack to the Deep Creek Trail and turn left, following the old roadbed and gentle slope as it runs alongside the scenic creek. From late spring through summer, you'll see lots of kids (adults too) hauling colorful tubes up this part of the trail, then floating downstream. The trail provides excellent wildflower displays, including spring-flowering species such as dwarf crested iris, foamflower, fire pink, Carolina vetch, and common alumroot. Heal all, which can also be seen here, is unusual in that you can find it in flower from spring through fall.

Cross another wide bridge over Deep Creek at 2.0 miles. As you continue down the trail, you may notice spring wildflowers such as bloodroot, showy orchis, bishop's cap, and dwarf crested iris. Shrubs with showy flowers in summer include rosebay rhododendron, wild hydrangea, and flowering raspberry. In moist flats along the creek, look for cardinal flower, orange jewelweed, great blue lobelia, and Joe Pye weed in summer to fall. Those that linger may notice ruby-throated hummingbirds visiting the flowers of cardinal flower and orange jewelweed, bumblebees working the flowers of great blue lobelia, and butterflies sipping nectar on the flower heads of Joe Pye weed.

At 2.2 miles, a row of benches facing the creek is a good landmark for Tom Branch Falls, a narrow multi-level cascade that drops 75 feet into the far side of Deep Creek. The crescendo of sounds made by the rushing water reflects the waterfall as well as the riffles along Deep Creek. In winter to early spring (or after a good rain), it's one of the more scenic waterfalls in the park.

In summer, Tom Branch Falls is partially obscured by rosebay rhododendron, mountain laurel, and mountain doghobble, and the water level may be so low that you barely notice the falls. The large tree on the near side of the creek directly opposite the falls is a white oak. Look for yellowroot at its base and poison ivy climbing the trunk. Yellowroot is rarely washed away during floods because its underground stems (rhizomes) anchor the plant to the substrate and its short stature and flexible stems reduce resistance to the force of flowing water.

From Tom Branch Falls, continue on the Deep Creek Trail another 0.2 mile to the parking area and trailhead. Along the way, look for the flowers of fire pink in spring, rosebay rhododendron in early summer, and white wood aster in autumn.

Options. Consider taking a ride on the Great Smoky Mountains Railroad from nearby Bryson City to the Nantahala River Gorge. Current schedules on this half-day excursion can be obtained at www.gsmr.com or by calling 800-872-4681.

20 / DEEP CREEK: WHAT TO LOOK FOR

Spring

Doll's eyes, White baneberry	*Actaea pachypoda*	p. 213
Fairywand, Devil's bit	*Chamaelirium luteum*	p. 210
Pink lady's slipper	*Cypripedium acaule*	p. 235
Trailing arbutus	*Epigaea repens*	p. 207
Robin's plantain	*Erigeron pulchellus*	p. 216
Showy orchis	*Galearis spectabilis*	p. 234
Wild geranium	*Geranium maculatum*	p. 235
Common alumroot	*Heuchera americana*	NI
Dwarf crested iris	*Iris cristata*	p. 247
Mountain doghobble	*Leucothoe fontanesiana*	p. 213

Plumed Solomon's seal	*Maianthemum racemosum*	p. 216
Bishop's cap	*Mitella diphylla*	NI
Mayapple	*Podophyllum peltatum*	p. 208
Solomon's seal	*Polygonatum biflorum*	p. 217
Buttercup	*Ranunculus* species	NI
Bloodroot	*Sanguinaria canadensis*	p. 209
Giant chickweed	*Stellaria pubera*	p. 214
Rue anemone	*Thalictrum thalictroides*	p. 211
Foamflower	*Tiarella cordifolia*	p. 218
Wake robin, Stinking Willie	*Trillium erectum*	p. 243
Southern nodding trillium	*Trillium rugelli*	NI
Carolina vetch	*Vicia caroliniana*	NI
Sweet white violet	*Viola blanda*	p. 219
Halberdleaf yellow violet	*Viola hastata*	p. 254
Common blue violet	*Viola sororia*	p. 247
Yellowroot	*Xanthorhiza simplicissima*	p. 240

Spring–Summer

Thimbleweed	*Anemone virginiana*	NI
Sweet shrub	*Calycanthus floridus*	p. 241
New Jersey tea	*Ceanothus americanus*	NI
Speckled wood lily	*Clintonia umbellulata*	p. 222
Common fleabane	*Erigeron philadelphicus*	NI
Forsythia	*Forsythia x intermedia*	NI
Orange daylily	*Hemerocallis fulva*	NI
Mountain laurel	*Kalmia latifolia*	p. 236
Indian cucumber root	*Medeola virginiana*	p. 264
Partridge berry	*Mitchella repens*	p. 223
Heal all	*Prunella vulgaris*	p. 249
Flame azalea	*Rhododendron calendulaceum*	p. 267
Lyreleaf sage	*Salvia lyrata*	NI
Fire pink	*Silene virginica*	p. 267
Poison ivy	*Toxicodendron radicans*	p. 223

Summer

Black cohosh	*Actaea racemosa*	p. 226
Appalachian oak leach	*Aureolaria laevigata*	NI
Pipsissewa, Striped wintergreen	*Chimaphila maculata*	p. 222
Asiatic dayflower	*Commelina communis*	p. 249
Beggar's ticks	*Desmodium nudiflorum*	p. 238
Rattlesnake orchid	*Goodyera pubescens*	p. 229
Wild hydrangea	*Hydrangea arborescens*	p. 225
Wood nettle	*Laportea canadensis*	p. 265
Whorled loosestrife	*Lysimachia quadrifolia*	p. 258
Rosebay rhododendron	*Rhododendron maximum*	p. 230
Flowering raspberry	*Rubus odoratus*	NI
Rose pink	*Sabatia angularis*	NI
Cranefly orchid	*Tipularia discolor*	p. 246
Wideleaf spiderwort	*Tradescantia subaspera*	p. 250

Southern harebell	*Campanula divaricata*	p. 250
Canada horsebalm	*Collinsonia canadensis*	p. 261
Leafy elephant's foot	*Elephantopus carolinianus*	NI
Joe Pye weed	*Eutrochium fistulosum*	p. 239
Rock alumroot	*Heuchera villosa*	p. 230
Orange jewelweed	*Impatiens capensis*	p. 268
Yellow jewelweed	*Impatiens pallida*	NI
Cardinal flower	*Lobelia cardinalis*	p. 269
Great blue lobelia	*Lobelia siphilitica*	p. 251
Goldenrod	*Solidago* species	NI
Common wingstem	*Verbesina alternifolia*	p. 262

Fall

White wood aster	*Eurybia divaricata*	p. 231
Striped gentian	*Gentiana decora*	NI
Witch hazel	*Hamamelis virginiana*	p. 262
Heal all	*Prunella vulgaris*	p. 249
Heartleaf aster	*Symphyotrichum cordifolium*	p. 251

NI = species not included in the wildflower profiles (Part IV)

21 / Chasteen Creek Cascade

GREAT SMOKY MOUNTAINS NATIONAL PARK

Highlights	Streamside hike with a rich diversity of spring wildflowers
Flowering season	Mid-March through late October
Peak flowering	Mid-April through mid-May
Trail length	4 miles out and back
Trail rating	Easy to moderate
Elevation	2,270–2,675 feet
Nearest town	Cherokee, Swain County, N.C.
Contact	865-436-1200; www.nps.gov/grsm
Directions	From Cherokee, drive north on U.S. 441 (Newfound Gap Road) into Great Smoky Mountains National Park. Continue past the Oconaluftee Visitor Center for 3.1 miles then turn right at the sign for the Smokemont Campground. Cross the Oconaluftee River and turn left into the campground. Follow the road all the way back to the end of the D section and park on the right near the signed trailhead for the Bradley Fork Trail. In early spring, sections C and D of the campground may be closed, so you'll need to park in the B section parking area and walk an additional 0.4 mile to the trailhead. GPS: N35 33.785 W83 18.646

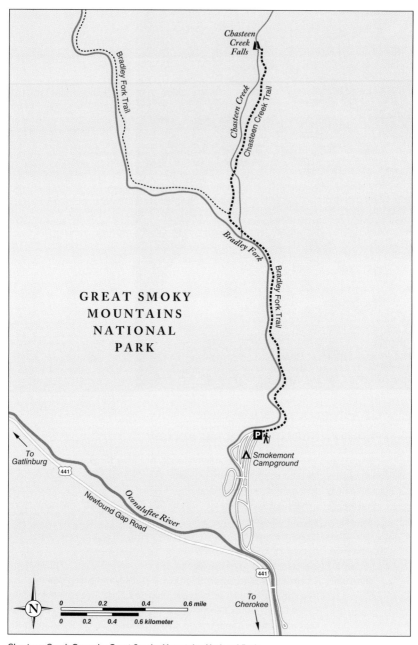

Chasteen Creek Cascade, Great Smoky Mountains National Park

Overview   Much of the hike is a gentle ascent on the Bradley Fork Trail, a former gravel roadbed that parallels Bradley Fork, a scenic stream. The trail winds its way through acidic cove forest, with scattered patches of rich cove forest, and a narrow band of alluvial forest along the stream. The waterfall (a 20-foot cascade) is small, but the setting is lovely and numerous wildflowers line the trail. Restroom facilities are available seasonally at the campground.

The Hike

The Bradley Fork Trail begins in an acidic cove forest at the end of section D of the Smokemont Campground. Right from the start, look for spring wildflowers such as common blue violet, sweet white violet, buttercup, Robin's plantain, and wild geranium. If you're hiking in late summer or fall, you may notice great blue lobelia, heal all, and heartleaf aster. From the trailhead, climb a short hill with good spring wildflower displays, including rue anemone, foamflower, the white and maroon flowers of wake robin, Solomon's seal, plumed Solomon's seal, and yellow mandarin. If you're hiking in summer, keep an eye out for wild hydrangea, false goatsbeard, spikenard, and wood nettle.

At 0.1 mile, a horse trail comes in from the right. Look for spring wildflowers such as wild ginger, longspur violet, creeping phlox, and Robin's plantain on the bank above the trail. You may want to take a few minutes to explore the horse trail since it runs through a rich cove forest with numerous wildflowers.

As the Bradley Fork Trail gently meanders up and down look for spicebush, a common shrub that produces dense clusters of tiny yellow flowers in early spring and showy red fruits in late summer. Spicebush is an important larval host plant of the spicebush swallowtail butterfly and its high-fat fruits are an important food source for fall migrants, including gray catbird, eastern kingbird, and great crested flycatcher.

The trail skirts a small field with summer-to-fall-flowering species such as black-eyed Susan, Asiatic dayflower, heal all, common evening primrose, beggar's ticks, and both common ragweed and giant ragweed (if your nose begins to run or you start sneezing in late summer or early fall, ragweed pollen is likely the cause). The fall-ripening nuts produced by a large black walnut tree on the left side of the trail across from the small field are consumed by black bears, white tailed deer, and eastern grey squirrels. The leaves, roots, and fruit husks of black walnut release a chemical known as juglone into the soil that inhibits the growth of many plants.

Bypass a second horse trail on the right at 0.25 mile and continue on the Bradley Fork Trail through an acidic cove forest. If you come upon a group of horseback riders on the trail, it's best to step aside and let them pass. You may see butterflies (especially pipevine swallowtails) aggregating on horse droppings, from which they obtain moisture and salts.

After passing a small tributary at 0.3 mile, look for foamflower, large-flowered trillium, creeping phlox, dwarf crested iris, plumed Solomon's seal, mountain dog-hobble, and flowering dogwood, all of which flower in spring.

As the trail continues, you may notice additional spring wildflowers, including lousewort, showy orchis, wild geranium, wild stonecrop, and fringed phacelia, which forms dense white patches that resemble snow. In moist flats along the stream, crimson bee balm, orange jewelweed, yellow jewelweed, great blue lobelia, common wingstem, and cutleaf coneflower create a vivid palette of colors from summer to fall.

I'm always amazed to see orange and yellow jewelweed plants 3–6 feet tall and nearly as wide, since they are annual plants that begin each spring as tiny seedlings. Fringed phacelia is another annual, but individuals are tiny by comparison. In contrast, nearly all other forest plants in undisturbed habitats are perennials.

At 1.2 miles, cross a footbridge over Chasteen Creek, and turn right onto the Chasteen Creek Trail. As the trail narrows and gradually ascends, you'll pass a boggy area on the right with cinnamon fern, rosebay rhododendron, orange jewelweed, long-bristled smartweed, and great blue lobelia. A few yards up the trail, there's an old homestead on the right with remnant garden plants including periwinkle (blue flowers), forsythia (yellow flowers), and Japanese quince (pink flowers).

As you cross a second footbridge over Chasteen Creek at 1.4 miles, look for the flowers of brook lettuce and broadleaf toothwort in spring, wild hydrangea in early summer, and pink turtlehead in summer to fall. Dense thickets of rosebay rhododendron grow along the creek and up the slope under a canopy of sweet birch in this acidic cove forest. Once common, eastern hemlock is becoming increasingly rare due to hemlock woolly adelgids, an exotic insect inadvertently introduced from Asia.

Continuing up the trail, look for scattered clumps of pink lady's slipper and prostrate mats of partridge berry. On a steep bank on the right side of the trail at 1.6 miles is a dense patch of Fraser's sedge, a rare species with long strap-shaped leaves and terminal clusters of tiny white flowers. You may also notice foamflower, Indian cucumber root, Vasey's trillium, and the white-to-blue flowers of acute-lobed hepatica on this slope.

A bit further up the trail, look for wake robin, wild geranium, Robin's plantain, Jack-in-the-pulpit, and creeping phlox. In summer, keen observers may spot the inconspicuous greenish-purple-to-brown flowers of cranefly orchid. Night-flying moths pollinate its flowers.

At just under 2.0 miles, take the left fork at the Y-junction. Go past the hitching post (for horses) and follow the narrow spur trail along the creek about 100 yards to the falls. Keep an eye out for three orchids—showy orchis and yellow lady's slipper bloom in spring and rattlesnake orchid flowers in summer.

As you approach the falls, look for Fraser's sedge, Jack-in-the-pulpit, sweet white violet, and roundleaf yellow violet. At the end of the trail, you may notice a prostrate mat of mountain wood sorrel—it has clover-like leaves and pink-striped flowers in summer. The pink stripes help guide insect pollinators to the center of the flower where the nectar is located.

The 20-foot cascade over smoothly worn sandstone is nearly as wide as it is tall. Rosebay rhododendron, mountain laurel, and moss-covered rocks frame the cascade. Adjoining the falls is an acidic cove forest dominated by sweet birch. The leaves and twigs of sweet birch have a pleasant wintergreen fragrance.

Enjoy this peaceful setting before retracing your steps to the trailhead.

Spring

Doll's eyes, White baneberry	*Actaea pachypoda*	p. 213
Acute-lobed hepatica	*Anemone acutiloba*	p. 207
Jack-in-the-pulpit	*Arisaema triphyllum*	p. 241
Wild ginger	*Asarum canadense*	p. 242
Broadleaf toothwort	*Cardamine diphylla*	NI
Japanese quince	*Chaenomeles japonica*	NI
Fraser's sedge	*Cymophyllus fraseriana*	p. 215
Pink lady's slipper	*Cypripedium acaule*	p. 235
Yellow lady's slipper	*Cypripedium parviflorum*	NI
Robin's plantain	*Erigeron pulchellus*	p. 216
Forsythia	*Forsythia x intermedia*	NI
Showy orchis	*Galearis spectabilis*	p. 234
Wild geranium	*Geranium maculatum*	p. 235
Dwarf crested iris	*Iris cristata*	p. 247
Mountain doghobble	*Leucothoe fontanesiana*	p. 213
Spicebush	*Lindera benzoin*	p. 263
Plumed Solomon's seal	*Maianthemum racemosum*	p. 216
Lousewort, Wood betony	*Pedicularis canadensis*	p. 255
Fringed phacelia	*Phacelia fimbriata*	p. 211
Mayapple	*Podophyllum peltatum*	p. 208
Solomon's seal	*Polygonatum biflorum*	p. 217
Yellow mandarin	*Prosartes lanuginosa*	p. 263
Buttercup	*Ranunculus* species	NI
Mountain stonecrop	*Sedum ternatum*	p. 218
Rue anemone	*Thalictrum thalictroides*	p. 211
Foamflower	*Tiarella cordifolia*	p. 218
Wake robin, Stinking Willie	*Trillium erectum*	p. 243
Large-flowered trillium	*Trillium grandiflorum*	p. 214
Vasey's trillium	*Trillium vaseyi*	p. 244
Periwinkle	*Vinca* species	NI
Sweet white violet	*Viola blanda*	p. 219
Halberdleaf yellow violet	*Viola hastata*	p. 254
Longspur violet	*Viola rostrata*	NI
Roundleaf yellow violet	*Viola rotundifolia*	NI
Common blue violet	*Viola sororia*	p. 247

Spring–Summer

False goatsbeard	*Astilbe biternata*	p. 224
Strawberry bush, Hearts-a-bustin'	*Euonymus americanus*	p. 264
Mountain laurel	*Kalmia latifolia*	p. 236
Indian cucumber root	*Medeola virginiana*	p. 264
Brook lettuce	*Micranthes micranthidifolia*	p. 217
Partridge berry	*Mitchella repens*	p. 223
Creeping phlox	*Phlox stolonifera*	NI
Mountain meadowrue	*Thalictrum clavatum*	p. 226

Summer

Black cohosh	*Actaea racemosa*	p. 226
Thimbleweed	*Anemone virginiana*	NI
Spikenard	*Aralia racemosa*	p. 265
Oxeye daisy	*Chrysanthemum leucanthemum*	NI
Beggar's ticks	*Desmodium nudiflorum*	p. 238
Leafy elephant's foot	*Elephantopus carolinianus*	NI
Common fleabane	*Erigeron philadelphicus*	NI
Rattlesnake orchid	*Goodyera pubescens*	p. 229
Wild hydrangea	*Hydrangea arborescens*	p. 225
Wood nettle	*Laportea canadensis*	p. 265
Mountain wood sorrel	*Oxalis montana*	p. 237
Rosebay rhododendron	*Rhododendron maximum*	p. 230
Black-eyed Susan	*Rudbeckia hirta*	NI
Cranefly orchid	*Tipularia discolor*	p. 246
Poison ivy	*Toxicodendron radicans*	p. 223
Wideleaf spiderwort	*Tradescantia subaspera*	p. 250

Summer–Fall

Common ragweed	*Ambrosia artemisiifolia*	p. 266
Giant ragweed	*Ambrosia trifida*	NI
Hog peanut	*Amphicarpaea bracteata*	p. 238
Pink turtlehead	*Chelone lyonii*	p. 239
Canada horsebalm	*Collinsonia canadensis*	p. 261
Asiatic dayflower	*Commelina communis*	p. 249
Flowering spurge	*Euphorbia corollata*	NI
Orange jewelweed	*Impatiens capensis*	p. 268
Yellow jewelweed	*Impatiens pallida*	NI
Great blue lobelia	*Lobelia siphilitica*	p. 251
Crimson bee balm	*Monarda didyma*	p. 269
Common evening primrose	*Oenothera biennis*	NI
Long-bristled smartweed	*Polygonum caespitosum*	NI
Heal all	*Prunella vulgaris*	p. 249
Cutleaf coneflower	*Rudbeckia laciniata*	p. 260
Common wingstem	*Verbesina alternifolia*	p. 262

Fall

White wood aster	*Eurybia divaricata*	p. 231
Witch hazel	*Hamamelis virginiana*	p. 262
Curtis's goldenrod	*Solidago curtisii*	p. 261
Heartleaf aster	*Symphyotrichum cordifolium*	p. 251

NI = species not included in the wildflower profiles (Part IV)

22 / Big Creek

GREAT SMOKY MOUNTAINS NATIONAL PARK

Highlights	Two waterfalls, a gorgeous pool, numerous wildflowers
Flowering season	Early March through October
Peak flowering	April through mid-May
Trail length	4 miles out and back
Trail rating	Easy to moderate
Elevation	1,800–2,420 feet
Nearest town	Waterville, Haywood County, N.C.
Contact	865-436-1200; www.nps.gov/grsm/planyourvisit/waterfalls.htm
Directions	The trail is located along Big Creek on the northwestern side of Great Smoky Mountains National Park just off I-40 at the North Carolina-Tennessee border. From I-40 take the Waterville Road exit (exit 451, just inside Tennessee). Turn left after crossing the Pigeon River and proceed 2.3 miles to an intersection. Continue straight past the ranger station to a large parking area at the end of the road. GPS: N35 45.113 W83 06.615

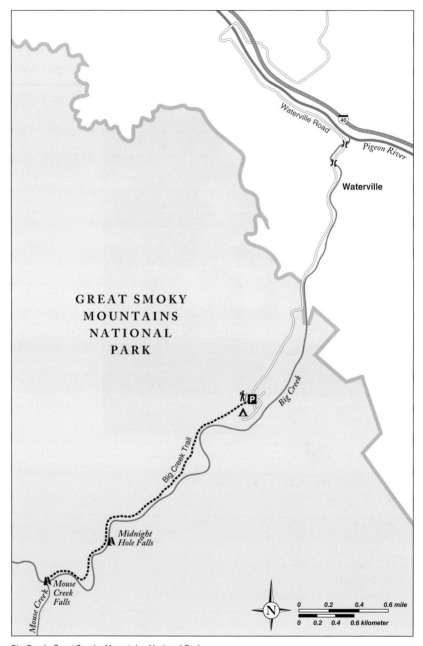

Big Creek, Great Smoky Mountains National Park

Overview   The Big Creek Trail in the northwestern section of Great Smoky
          Mountains National Park is a popular destination for hikers, folks
          who fish, and, to a lesser degree, horseback riders. The trail is wide,
          relatively smooth, and never steep, as it gains just 500 feet over the
          2.0-mile hike to Mouse Creek Falls. A cascading stream, enchanting
          pools, two scenic waterfalls, wildflowers, and both rich and acidic
          cove forests make this a wonderful hike. Restrooms, a picnic area,
          and a campground are located close to the parking area.

The Hike

From the parking area, hike back on the main road for about 50 yards and turn left
onto the signed Big Creek Trail. Right from the start, look for spring wildflowers such
as yellow trillium, common blue violet, bloodroot, golden ragwort, buttercup, and
lyreleaf sage. Poison ivy also grows along the trail. As the trail ascends slightly, you
may notice the blue flowers of dwarf crested iris, the daisy-like flowers of Robin's
plantain, and the white star-shaped flowers of giant chickweed in spring.

Even though the first part of the trail is high above Big Creek, you'll probably hear
the sound of the river rushing past huge boulders. As you look toward the creek,
notice the tall trees rising above the floodplain, including tulip tree, sycamore, sweet
gum, and red maple. Bats, including big brown, hoary, and little brown bats roost
under the loose bark of sycamores and other trees in alluvial forests. River otters are
sometimes seen along the lower sections of Big Creek.

The trees along the floodplain and adjoining slopes became established after the
area was heavily logged in the early 1900s. The current trail follows the old narrow
gauge railroad bed that was used to haul out the cut timber.

Good wildflower displays can be seen along a series of rock outcrops on the steep
banks above the trail at 0.3 mile. In spring, look for the scarlet red tubular flowers of fire pink along with the showy bowl-shaped flowers of purple phacelia. Less
conspicuous are the small white flowers of wild stonecrop and common alumroot.
In early to mid-summer, look for the tubular pinkish-purple flowers of hairy beardtongue. Hikers in summer to fall may see erect dayflower, tall bellflower, southern
harebell, Curtis's goldenrod, heartleaf aster, white snakeroot, flowering raspberry,
wild hydrangea, and both yellow and orange jewelweed.

Where the trail veers away from Big Creek at 0.6 mile, you may notice spring
wildflowers such as yellow trillium, purple phacelia, fringed phacelia, and wild geranium, along with squirrel corn, sweet white violet, Canada violet, and doll's eyes.
In some years, yellow jewelweed blankets large areas of this rich cove forest from
summer through early fall.

As the trail swings back to the river at 0.9 mile, look for old tree trunks lying like
beached whales along the rocky stream bank; the surge in the creek following heavy
rainstorms moves fallen trees downstream as if they were matchsticks.

As you continue up the trail, notice the large boulder field on the slope above the
trail. Erosion caused by stripping the mountainside of trees in the early 1900s likely
exposed these underlying boulders.

Today, the forested slopes along the trail consist of a patchwork of rich and
acidic cove forests with deciduous trees such as white basswood, yellow buckeye,
red maple, striped maple, sweet birch, Carolina silverbell, and Fraser magnolia.

As the trail continues its gradual ascent, you'll pass through an acidic cove forest
with dense thickets of rosebay rhododendron. Rosebay thickets became more wide-

spread in the southern Appalachians after large-scale logging in the 1900s and again after the chestnut blight opened up the forest in the 1930s. Along the margin of the trail, look for sweet white violet and dwarf crested iris in spring and wild hydrangea and cranefly orchid in summer. Heal all is common from spring through fall.

At 1.5 miles, look for a small unmarked side trail to the left that descends to Midnight Hole Falls, a scenic cascade between two huge boulders dropping 6 feet into a lovely large pool. The beauty of this site more than makes up for the size of the falls. Large sycamores flank the pool as do small mats of Appalachian bluet. Depending on the light, the color of the pool fluctuates from dark green to near black (which may explain the name). It's easily one of the best swimming holes in the southern Appalachians.

From Midnight Hole, the trail continues through an acidic cove forest with the rushing water of Big Creek immediately to your left. The clear cold water provides good habitat for rainbow trout. At 2.0 miles, you'll come to an easily missed unmarked side trail to the left (look for a horse hitching rail followed by a narrow spur trail leading to the creek). As you veer left on the spur trail, keep an eye out for wake robin and plumed Solomon's seal in spring and rattlesnake orchid and cranefly orchid in summer.

The short side trail ends at a viewing area with Mouse Creek Falls on the far side of Big Creek. This small but beautiful waterfall drops about 15–20 feet into a small pool before cascading another 10–15 feet into Big Creek. Rosebay rhododendron and moss-covered rocks frame the falls. The adjoining acidic cove forest is dominated by red maple and yellow birch, with dense thickets of rosebay rhododendron and mountain doghobble in the understory.

Red maple is one of the most abundant and widely distributed trees in eastern North America. It's also one of the first native trees to bloom each year, with flowers opening as early as January.

After enjoying the scenery, retrace your steps back to the trailhead.

Options. You may want to continue past the falls to explore more of the Big Creek Trail. The trail crosses Big Creek on a sturdy carriage bridge and ends at Walnut Bottoms, 3.3 miles beyond Mouse Creek Falls.

22 / BIG CREEK: WHAT TO LOOK FOR

Spring

Doll's eyes, White baneberry	*Actaea pachypoda*	p. 213
Wood anemone	*Anemone quinquefolia*	p. 209
Speckled wood lily	*Clintonia umbellulata*	p. 222
Bearcorn, Squawroot	*Conopholis americana*	p. 255
Squirrel corn	*Dicentra canadensis*	NI
Robin's plantain	*Erigeron pulchellus*	p. 216
Wild geranium	*Geranium maculatum*	p. 235
Common alumroot	*Heuchera americana*	NI
Appalachian bluet	*Houstonia serpyllifolia*	p. 248
Dwarf crested iris	*Iris cristata*	p. 247
Mountain doghobble	*Leucothoe fontanesiana*	p. 213

Plumed Solomon's seal	*Maianthemum racemosum*	p. 216
Indian cucumber root	*Medeola virginiana*	p. 264
Purple phacelia	*Phacelia bipinnatifida*	p. 243
Fringed phacelia	*Phacelia fimbriata*	p. 211
Solomon's seal	*Polygonatum biflorum*	p. 217
Buttercup	*Ranunculus* species	NI
Lyreleaf sage	*Salvia lyrata*	NI
Bloodroot	*Sanguinaria canadensis*	p. 209
Mountain stonecrop	*Sedum ternatum*	p. 218
Fire pink	*Silene virginica*	p. 267
Giant chickweed	*Stellaria pubera*	p. 214
Early meadowrue	*Thalictrum dioicum*	NI
Rue anemone	*Thalictrum thalictroides*	p. 211
Foamflower	*Tiarella cordifolia*	p. 218
Wake robin, Stinking Willie	*Trillium erectum*	p. 243
Yellow trillium	*Trillium luteum*	p. 254
Sweet white violet	*Viola blanda*	p. 219
Halberdleaf yellow violet	*Viola hastata*	p. 254
Common blue violet	*Viola sororia*	p. 247

Spring–Summer

False goatsbeard	*Astilbe biternata*	p. 224
Sweet shrub	*Calycanthus floridus*	p. 241
Strawberry bush, Hearts-a-bustin'	*Euonymus americanus*	p. 264
Rattlesnake hawkweed	*Hieracium venosum*	p. 256
Partridge berry	*Mitchella repens*	p. 223
Golden ragwort	*Packera aurea*	p. 257
Heal all	*Prunella vulgaris*	p. 249
Poison ivy	*Toxicodendron radicans*	p. 223
Canada violet	*Viola canadensis*	p. 220

Summer

Spikenard	*Aralia racemosa*	p. 265
Beggar's ticks	*Desmodium nudiflorum*	p. 238
Common fleabane	*Erigeron philadelphicus*	NI
Rattlesnake orchid	*Goodyera pubescens*	p. 229
Wild hydrangea	*Hydrangea arborescens*	p. 225
Wood nettle	*Laportea canadensis*	p. 265
Indian pipe, Ghost flower	*Monotropa uniflora*	p. 231
Hairy beardtongue	*Penstemon canescens*	p. 245
Rosebay rhododendron	*Rhododendron maximum*	p. 230
Flowering raspberry	*Rubus odoratus*	NI
Cranefly orchid	*Tipularia discolor*	p. 246

Summer–Fall

Hog peanut	*Amphicarpaea bracteata*	p. 238
Southern harebell	*Campanula divaricata*	p. 250
Tall bellflower	*Campanulastrum americanum*	NI
Canada horsebalm	*Collinsonia canadensis*	p. 261
Erect dayflower	*Commelina erecta*	NI
Orange jewelweed	*Impatiens capensis*	p. 268
Yellow jewelweed	*Impatiens pallida*	NI

Fall

White snakeroot	*Ageratina altissima*	p. 232
Witch hazel	*Hamamelis virginiana*	p. 262
Heal all	*Prunella vulgaris*	p. 249
Curtis's goldenrod	*Solidago curtisii*	p. 261
Heartleaf aster	*Symphyotrichum cordifolium*	p. 251
Canada violet	*Viola canadensis*	p. 220

NI = species not included in the wildflower profiles (Part IV)

Tennessee

23 / Abrams Falls

GREAT SMOKY MOUNTAINS NATIONAL PARK

Highlights	Impressive waterfall, scenic river, numerous wildflowers
Flowering season	Mid-March through late October
Peak flowering	Early April through mid-May
Trail length	5 miles out and back
Trail rating	Moderate
Elevation	1,770–1,460 feet
Nearest town	Townsend, Blount County, Tenn.
Contact	865-436-1200; www.nps.gov/grsm/planyourvisit/waterfalls.htm
Directions	Drive the one-way Cades Cove Loop Road in Great Smoky Mountains National Park for 4.9 miles and turn right onto a signed gravel road that ends at a parking area. GPS: N35 35.480 W83 51.180
Overview	The Abrams Falls Trail, off the Cades Cove Loop Road, is one of the most popular waterfall destinations in Great Smoky Mountains National Park. The easy to follow trail follows Abrams Creek much of the way. The mostly calm creek is diverted into a narrow chute at Abrams Falls, transforming it into a powerful waterfall. The falls drop 20 feet over a sandstone ledge into one of the largest plunge pools in the region. The force of the falls throws spray over 50 feet, forming ice on the vegetated banks in winter and creating natural air conditioning in summer. Arrive early to avoid the crowds; basic restrooms are available in the parking area.

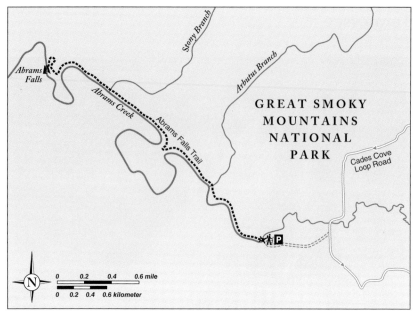

Abrams Falls, Great Smoky Mountains National Park

The Hike

From the parking area, enter the forest and immediately cross the footbridge over Abrams Creek. Go left at the T-junction and follow the Abrams Creek Trail upstream through an acidic cove forest. Rosebay rhododendron is abundant along the creek—its showy pinkish-white flowers bloom in early summer. Soon, the trail begins winding its way up the first of three ridges. Here and elsewhere along the trail, you'll see galax, trailing arbutus, partridge berry, and little brown jugs, each of which has thick evergreen leaves. Look for the unusual flowers of little brown jugs partially hidden under the leaf litter at the base of the plant.

At the top of the ridge (0.5 mile), the trail curves right and begins to descend. Notice the dense stand of eastern white pine and scattered eastern hemlock on the slope with rosebay rhododendron in the understory. At the base of the slope, you'll cross a footlog over a small creek.

The relatively flat trail follows Abrams Creek through an acidic cove forest with mountain laurel, mountain doghobble, and yellowroot, all of which flower in spring. Along the creek, look for the red tubular flowers of cardinal flower and the showy pink flower heads and tall leafy shoots of Joe Pye weed in summer through early fall. You may see ruby-throated hummingbirds visiting the flowers of cardinal flower and various butterflies on the flower heads of Joe Pye weed.

At 1.0 mile, the trail begins a gradual ascent of Arbutus Ridge. Mountain laurel is common as are ground-hugging plants such as partridge berry, solitary pussytoes, rattlesnake hawkweed, and grassleaf golden aster. Long dense hairs give grassleaf golden aster a silvery sheen that reflects light and moderates the surface temperature of the plant, thereby reducing evaporative water loss, an important feature given the dry habitats it occupies.

The trail tops out on Arbutus Ridge, under an open canopy of eastern white pine, Virginia pine, and eastern hemlock. Birders may spot brown-headed nuthatch, Carolina chickadee, and tufted titmouse excavating insects from the bark of pines.

On the far side of the ridgetop, a rocky bank immediately above the trail has good wildflower displays including spring-flowering bleeding hearts, giant chickweed, Solomon's seal, plumed Solomon's seal, and common alumroot. If you're hiking in summer through early fall, look for the small, bell-shaped, pale blue flowers of southern harebell, the yellow flower heads of goldenrod, and both white and blue-flowered asters.

The trail descends through a forest that is recovering from a tornado that swept through the area in 2011, snapping the trunks of tall trees and blowing others over. As you follow the trail down, look for spring wildflowers such as Catesby's trillium, common blue violet, white milkweed, dwarf cinquefoil, and Robin's plantain, along with the maroon to brown spicy-scented flowers of sweet shrub. Robust perennials that benefit from the increased light associated with the relatively open canopy include pokeweed, fireweed, Joe Pye weed, and goldenrod, which bloom in summer through early fall.

As the trail approaches the creek at the base of the slope, moisture levels increase and the vegetation reverts to an acidic cove forest with rosebay rhododendron, mountain laurel, mountain doghobble, and devil's walkingstick in the understory. In spring, look for Catesby's trillium, fairywand, halberdleaf yellow violet, and sweet white violet, along with dense patches of galax and scattered clumps of gaywings, a low-growing plant with showy pink-to-purple flowers in small clusters.

The nearly level trail parallels Abrams Creek for nearly 0.5 mile, crossing Stony Branch via a footlog along the way. As you hike through this acidic cove forest, look for the blue flowers of dwarf crested iris and the white pea-shaped flowers of Carolina vetch in spring. From late spring into summer, the narrow white flowering stalks of galax stand out like beacons of light. Along this section of trail, I saw an adult black bear with her two cubs feeding on plants on the far side of the creek. On a subsequent visit, a cub was feeding on leaves high up in a tree. It's not unusual to find bear scat along the trail.

As you ascend one last ridge, look for gaywings, partridge berry, wood anemone, dwarf cinquefoil, and yellow star grass in spring, along with wild hydrangea, whorled coreopsis, and grassleaf golden aster in summer. Near the ridgetop (2.2 miles), the trail passes through a pine-oak-heath community with eastern white pine, Virginia pine, and pitch pine in the canopy and mountain laurel and bear huckleberry in the understory. The charred bark on trees is a sign of past fire.

On the far side of the ridge, the trail descends through a pine forest with more dense mats of trailing arbutus, partridge berry, and galax. In a moist sheltered area near the base of the slope, look for Catesby's trillium, sweet white violet, and gaywings in spring. There's also a nice patch of Indian cucumber root. As its fruits ripen in fall, the basal portion of the whorled leaves turn scarlet. The contrasting colors of the fruits and leaves attract birds that consume the fruits and disperse the seeds.

Near the footbridge over Wilson Creek, look for orange jewelweed, cardinal flower, and white wood aster in summer through early fall.

As the trail descends, take the side trail to the left and immediately cross the footlog to reach Abrams Falls at 2.5 miles. The short but powerful waterfall drops 20 feet, creating a tremendous splash in a plunge pool that is about 100 feet long and nearly as wide. Swimmers beware! Strong currents and an undertow have resulted in several drownings. Spray cliff plants include rosebay rhododendron, yellowroot, rock alumroot, mountain meadowrue, and white wood aster. You might see a river otter frolicking in the pool or a northern water snake (which resembles a copperhead but is nonvenomous) basking in the sun along the shore. Early morning sunlight hitting the mist from the falls makes a beautiful rainbow.

Find yourself a nice boulder and take in the sights at this turnaround point.

Options. For an enjoyable day trip, combine a hike to Abrams Falls with exploring the Cades Cove Loop Road (you can pick up an auto tour map at the information area at the beginning of the loop). Expect vehicles to travel very slowly on the 11-mile loop as drivers creep along looking for wildlife such as white-tailed deer, grazing horses, wild turkey (showing off their plumage), and black bear. You can also stop to view old cabins, churches, and farms in the picturesque valley.

23 / ABRAMS FALLS: WHAT TO LOOK FOR

Spring

Wood anemone	*Anemone quinquefolia*	p. 209
Solitary pussytoes	*Antennaria solitaria*	NI
Fairywand, Devil's bit	*Chamaelirium luteum*	p. 210
Bleeding heart	*Dicentra eximia*	NI
Trailing arbutus	*Epigaea repens*	p. 207
Robin's plantain	*Erigeron pulchellus*	p. 216
Common alumroot	*Heuchera americana*	NI
Little brown jugs	*Hexastylis arifolia*	NI
Yellow star grass	*Hypoxis hirsuta*	NI
Dwarf crested iris	*Iris cristata*	p. 247
Mountain doghobble	*Leucothoe fontanesiana*	p. 213
Plumed Solomon's seal	*Maianthemum racemosum*	p. 216
Gaywings	*Polygala paucifolia*	NI
Solomon's seal	*Polygonatum biflorum*	p. 217
Dwarf cinquefoil	*Potentilla canadensis*	p. 253
Giant chickweed	*Stellaria pubera*	p. 214
Catesby's trillium	*Trillium catesbaei*	p. 212
Wake robin, Stinking Willie	*Trillium erectum*	p. 243
Carolina vetch	*Vicia caroliniana*	NI
Sweet white violet	*Viola blanda*	p. 219
Halberdleaf yellow violet	*Viola hastata*	p. 254
Common blue violet	*Viola sororia*	p. 247
Yellowroot	*Xanthorhiza simplicissima*	p. 240

Spring–Summer

White milkweed	*Asclepias variegata*	NI
False goatsbeard	*Astilbe biternata*	p. 224
Sweet shrub	*Calycanthus floridus*	p. 241
Pipsissewa, Striped wintergreen	*Chimaphila maculata*	p. 222
Strawberry bush, Hearts-a-bustin'	*Euonymus americanus*	p. 264
Galax, Skunkweed	*Galax urceolata*	p. 224
Bear huckleberry	*Gaylussacia ursina*	NI
Rattlesnake hawkweed	*Hieracium venosum*	p. 256
Mountain laurel	*Kalmia latifolia*	p. 236
Indian cucumber root	*Medeola virginiana*	p. 264
Partridge berry	*Mitchella repens*	p. 223
Mountain meadowrue	*Thalictrum clavatum*	p. 226

Summer

Devil's walkingstick	*Aralia spinosa*	NI
False nettle	*Boehmeria cylindrica*	NI
New Jersey tea	*Ceanothus americanus*	NI
Butterfly pea	*Clitoria mariana*	NI
Whorled coreopsis	*Coreopsis major*	p. 259
Beggar's ticks	*Desmodium nudiflorum*	p. 238
Wintergreen	*Gaultheria procumbens*	p. 229
Wild hydrangea	*Hydrangea arborescens*	p. 225
Whorled loosestrife	*Lysimachia quadrifolia*	p. 258
Rosebay rhododendron	*Rhododendron maximum*	p. 230
Cranefly orchid	*Tipularia discolor*	p. 246

Summer–Fall

Southern harebell	*Campanula divaricata*	p. 250
Fireweed	*Erechtites hieracifolia*	NI
Flowering spurge	*Euphorbia corollata*	NI
Joe Pye weed	*Eutrochium fistulosum*	p. 239
Rattlesnake orchid	*Goodyera pubescens*	p. 229
Rock alumroot	*Heuchera villosa*	p. 230
Orange jewelweed	*Impatiens capensis*	p. 268
Cardinal flower	*Lobelia cardinalis*	p. 269
Pokeweed	*Phytolacca americana*	p. 227
Grassleaf golden aster	*Pityopsis graminifolia*	p. 259

Fall

White wood aster	*Eurybia divaricata*	p. 231
Witch hazel	*Hamamelis virginiana*	p. 262
Goldenrod	*Solidago* species	NI

NI = species not included in the wildflower profiles (Part IV)

24 / Rainbow Falls

GREAT SMOKY MOUNTAINS NATIONAL PARK

Highlights	Old-growth forests, abundant wildflowers, and an 80-foot waterfall
Flowering season	Late March through mid-October
Peak flowering	Mid-April to early May
Trail length	5.4 miles out and back
Trail rating	Moderate to difficult
Elevation	2,690–4,270 feet
Nearest town	Gatlinburg, Sevier County, Tenn.
Contact	865-436-1200; www.nps.gov/grsm/planyourvisit/waterfalls.htm
Directions	Starting from light #8 in downtown Gatlinburg, turn onto Historic Nature Trail/Airport Road. At 0.7 mile, veer right onto Cherokee Orchard Road and enter Great Smoky Mountains National Park. Continue past the Noah "Bud" Ogle home site to the clearly signed parking area for Rainbow Falls. GPS: N35 40.539 W83 29.142

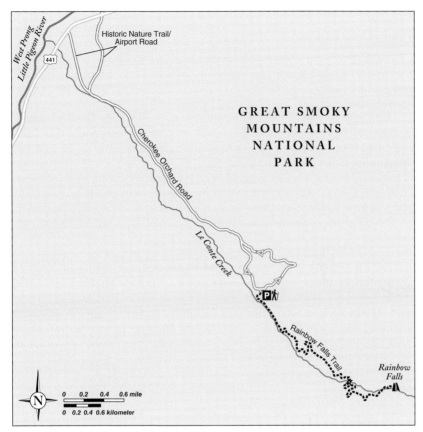

Rainbow Falls, Great Smoky Mountains National Park

Overview As you ascend the slopes of Mount Le Conte on this 5.4-mile round-trip hike, you'll cross scenic Le Conte Creek twice before reaching Rainbow Falls, the highest single-drop waterfall in the Smokies. Along the way you'll pass through several rich and acidic cove forests with huge trees and numerous wildflowers. The moderately strenuous trail is considered to be difficult by some visitors due to the length, elevation gain (1,600 feet), and rocky footing. It's best to get an early start as the trail is often crowded and parking can be a problem. Basic restroom facilities are available near the trailhead.

The Hike

The Rainbow Falls Trail begins at the west end of the parking area across from the restroom. Right from the start, look for yellow trillium, blue cohosh, and halberdleaf yellow violet in spring. If you're hiking in late summer through early fall, you may see yellow jewelweed, white snakeroot, goldenrod, and heartleaf aster here and elsewhere along the trail.

Bypass the fork for the Trillium Gap Trail and continue straight on the Rainbow Falls Trail as it begins a moderate climb. You'll soon be walking through a grove of large old trees (an old-growth forest). Canopy trees in this rich cove forest include yellow buckeye, sugar maple, white ash, tulip tree, white basswood, and Fraser magnolia.

Some huge eastern hemlocks also occur along the trail; unfortunately, many are dead due to an infestation of hemlock woolly adelgids. The eastern hemlocks that are still healthy have been treated with an insecticide to protect them from adelgids, a sap-sucking insect that has devastated eastern hemlocks.

Beneath the tall trees, look for spring wildflowers such as large-flowered trillium, mayapple, Jack-in-the-pulpit, and giant chickweed. You may also notice four violets (roundleaf yellow, longspur, sweet white, and common blue) along the trail. The fern growing on boulders is rock polypody.

In spite of the many hikers using this trail, I've seen black bears on several occasions. In early summer, I watched a young black bear actively feeding on bearcorn (also known as squawroot). The bear went from clump to clump, feeding on both the above and below ground parts. Both the bear and the plant benefit from this interaction—the bear gets food, and the plant's seeds are dispersed in the bear's droppings. On another hike, a black bear dug up a yellow jacket nest adjacent to the trail to feed on the grubs, a good source of protein.

Within 200 hundred yards of the trailhead, you'll see and hear Le Conte Creek as it rushes over a rocky streambed. There are more species of salamanders in the southern Appalachian Mountains than anywhere else in the world, including 30 species in Great Smoky Mountains National Park. Because a salamander's skin must stay moist, adult salamanders generally live in damp habitats such as under leaves, logs, or rocks and along streambeds.

The trail winds away from the creek at 0.8 mile and steepens. You'll soon pass through the first of several rosebay rhododendron thickets with scattered clumps of galax and trailing arbutus.

The vegetation changes from shrub thicket to rich cove forest at 1.4 miles, and the diversity and abundance of wildflowers increase dramatically. Look for spring-flowering dimpled trout lily, Carolina spring beauty, rue anemone, wake robin (the white-color form), foamflower, dwarf crested iris, and Fraser's sedge, a rare species. The bright red flowers of crimson bee balm, the orange flowers of Turk's cap lily, and the white flowers of black cohosh provide a splash of color in summer. The fetid flowers of black cohosh attract carrion flies and beetles that function as pollinators.

At 1.7 miles, the trail crosses Le Conte Creek on a narrow footlog. Like most streams in the park, the water is cold and crystal clear, except after heavy rains when soil particles are carried downstream. Rosebay rhododendron, mountain doghobble, sweet white violet, and mountain wood sorrel grow along the rocky streamside. Few animals feed on mountain wood sorrel as oxalic acid gives its foliage a bitter taste.

The trail ascends via several broad switchbacks through another rich cove forest. Among the spring-to-early-summer-flowering wildflowers are longspur violet, speckled wood lily, Canada mayflower, and wild hydrangea. If you're hiking in late summer to early fall, look for the yellow flowers of cutleaf coneflower, goldenrod, and yellow jewelweed, the white flower heads of white wood aster and white snakeroot, and the blue-to-violet flowers of heartleaf aster.

After passing through another rosebay rhododendron thicket, the trail winds through a more open forest at 2.0 miles with good spring wildflower displays, including dimpled trout lily, yellow mandarin, Solomon's seal, and Canada violet (which continues to bloom through early fall).

As the trail ascends, look and listen for nesting songbirds such as the blue-headed vireo, scarlet tanager, and rose-breasted grosbeak. You may also see or hear chipmunks along the trail. They spend most of the day foraging on the ground for seeds, nuts, berries, roots, mushrooms, insects, and other items, which they store in their cheek pouches. They escape danger by darting into burrows that can be 30 feet long.

At 2.4 miles, you'll come to a scenic 8-foot waterfall (don't worry, this isn't Rainbow Falls). The trail continues through a rich cove forest with numerous spring wildflowers, including Dutchman's britches, Carolina spring beauty, broadleaf toothwort, sweet white violet, Indian cucumber root, and yellow mandarin. After rock hopping across a small tributary at 2.5 miles, look for the pinkish-purple flowers of Catawba rhododendron in late spring and the flowers of pink turtlehead, black cohosh, and mountain wood aster in summer or fall.

After rock-hopping Le Conte Creek, Rainbow Falls is soon before you, plunging some 80 feet over a vertical rock face with streaks of black, green, white, and grey. After a good rain, the swollen creek produces an impressive waterfall that pounds the rocks at the base of the cliff. In dry periods, the falls is only a trickle. Afternoon sunlight hitting the mist from the falls can produce a rainbow, hence the name.

A dense thicket of rosebay rhododendron, with a few Catawba rhododendron, covers the slope to the right of the falls. A variety of wildflowers grow on the boulder-strewn slope between the falls and the narrow footlog over the creek, including crimson bee balm, yellow jewelweed, black cohosh, white wood aster, and wild hydrangea. Notice the large old yellow buckeye trees in the canopy of this rich cove forest.

This is a great place to relax, snap a few photos, and enjoy the wonder of it all before retracing your steps to the parking area.

Options. More adventuresome hikers may want to continue another 4 miles to the summit of Mount Le Conte, the third highest peak in the Great Smoky Mountains.

24 / RAINBOW FALLS: WHAT TO LOOK FOR

Spring

Doll's eyes, White baneberry	*Actaea pachypoda*	p. 213
Acute-lobed hepatica	*Anemone acutiloba*	p. 207
Wood anemone	*Anemone quinquefolia*	p. 209
Jack-in-the-pulpit	*Arisaema triphyllum*	p. 241
Broadleaf toothwort	*Cardamine diphylla*	NI
Blue cohosh	*Caulophyllum thalictroides*	p. 242
Carolina spring beauty	*Claytonia caroliniana*	p. 234
Bearcorn, Squawroot	*Conopholis americana*	p. 255
Fraser's sedge	*Cymophyllus fraseriana*	p. 215
Squirrel corn	*Dicentra canadensis*	NI
Dutchman's britches	*Dicentra cucullaria*	p. 208
Trailing arbutus	*Epigaea repens*	p. 207
Dimpled trout lily	*Erythronium umbilicatum*	p. 253
Showy orchis	*Galearis spectabilis*	p. 234

Dwarf crested iris	*Iris cristata*	p. 247
Mountain doghobble	*Leucothoe fontanesiana*	p. 213
Mayapple	*Podophyllum peltatum*	p. 208
Yellow mandarin	*Prosartes lanuginosa*	p. 263
Giant chickweed	*Stellaria pubera*	p. 214
Rue anemone	*Thalictrum thalictroides*	p. 211
Foamflower	*Tiarella cordifolia*	p. 218
Wake robin, Stinking Willie	*Trillium erectum*	p. 243
Large-flowered trillium	*Trillium grandiflorum*	p. 214
Yellow trillium	*Trillium luteum*	p. 254
Sweet white violet	*Viola blanda*	p. 219
Halberdleaf yellow violet	*Viola hastata*	p. 254
Roundleaf yellow violet	*Viola rotundifolia*	NI
Common blue violet	*Viola sororia*	p. 247

Spring–Summer

Speckled wood lily	*Clintonia umbellulata*	p. 222
Running strawberry bush	*Euonymus obovatus*	NI
Canada mayflower	*Maianthemum canadense*	p. 225
Plumed Solomon's seal	*Maianthemum racemosum*	p. 216
Indian cucumber root	*Medeola virginiana*	p. 264
Bishop's cap	*Mitella diphylla*	NI
Solomon's seal	*Polygonatum biflorum*	p. 217
Catawba rhododendron	*Rhododendron catawbiense*	p. 236
Canada violet	*Viola canadensis*	p. 220
Longspur violet	*Viola rostrata*	NI

Summer

Black cohosh	*Actaea racemosa*	p. 226
Whorled coreopsis	*Coreopsis major*	p. 259
Beggar's ticks	*Desmodium nudiflorum*	p. 238
Galax, Skunkweed	*Galax urceolata*	p. 224
Rattlesnake orchid	*Goodyera pubescens*	p. 229
Wild hydrangea	*Hydrangea arborescens*	p. 225
Mountain laurel	*Kalmia latifolia*	p. 236
Wood nettle	*Laportea canadensis*	p. 265
Turk's cap lily	*Lilium superbum*	p. 268
Whorled loosestrife	*Lysimachia quadrifolia*	p. 258
Partridge berry	*Mitchella repens*	p. 223
Mountain wood sorrel	*Oxalis montana*	p. 237
Rosebay rhododendron	*Rhododendron maximum*	p. 230

Summer–Fall

Pink turtlehead	*Chelone lyonii*	p. 239
Joe Pye weed	*Eutrochium fistulosum*	p. 239
Rock alumroot	*Heuchera villosa*	p. 230
Yellow jewelweed	*Impatiens pallida*	NI
Crimson bee balm	*Monarda didyma*	p. 269
Whorled aster	*Oclemena acuminata*	NI
Cutleaf coneflower	*Rudbeckia laciniata*	p. 260

Fall

White snakeroot	*Ageratina altissima*	p. 232
White wood aster	*Eurybia divaricata*	p. 231
Witch hazel	*Hamamelis virginiana*	p. 262
Goldenrod	*Solidago* species	NI
Heartleaf aster	*Symphyotrichum cordifolium*	p. 251
Canada violet	*Viola canadensis*	p. 220

NI = species not included in the wildflower profiles (Part IV)

25 / Ramsey Cascades

GREAT SMOKY MOUNTAINS NATIONAL PARK

Highlights	Old-growth forests with abundant wildflowers and a 100-foot waterfall
Flowering season	Late March through late October
Peak flowering	Mid-April through mid-May
Trail length	8 miles out and back
Trail rating	Moderately difficult
Elevation	2,090–4,350 feet
Nearest town	Greenbrier, Robertson County, Tenn.
Contact	865-436-1200; www.nps.gov/grsm/planyourvisit/waterfalls.htm
Directions	From the junction of U.S. 441 and U.S. 321 in Gatlinburg (light #3), drive east for 6 miles on U.S. 321 (toward Cosby) and turn right into Greenbrier (look for the Great Smoky Mountains National Park entrance sign on the right). Follow the road along the Middle Prong of the Little Pigeon River for 3.2 miles. At the fork in the road, turn left and cross the wooden bridge. The road ends at the trailhead 1.5 miles from the bridge. GPS: N35 42.159 W83 21.427

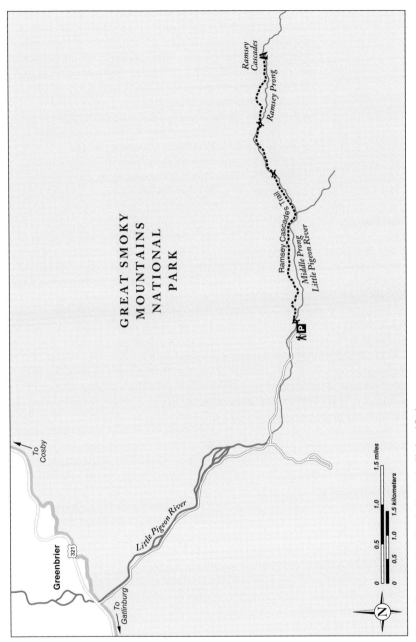

Ramsey Cascades, Great Smoky Mountains National Park

Overview   This moderately strenuous trail is one of the most popular waterfall hikes in the Smokies for good reason. The trail follows a cascading river with crystal-clear water for much of its length. Along the way, you'll hike through some of the best examples of old-growth rich and acidic cove forests in the Smokies. For wildflower enthusiasts, the 2,200-foot gain in elevation along the length of the trail allows you to see a broad spectrum of wildflowers. If you're hiking in mid-May, you'll see the late-spring-flowering species at the lower elevations and the early-spring-flowering species at the higher elevations. The trail ends at Ramsey Cascades, the tallest waterfall in the park and one of the most spectacular. While there are no facilities at the trailhead, you'll pass a small picnic area with toilets 2.8 miles from the junction with U.S. 321.

The Hike

Before you even get to the trailhead, there's a parade of spring wildflowers in the forest immediately above the parking area. Take one of the short spur trails up the slope to see spring wildflowers such as mayapple, bloodroot, yellow trillium, wild geranium, giant chickweed, showy orchis, plumed Solomon's seal, and the white flower form of wake robin. Be mindful of poison ivy as it grows along the ground and up the trunks of trees. Trees in this rich cove forest include yellow buckeye, sugar maple, white basswood, tulip tree, Carolina silverbell, striped maple, and eastern hemlock.

The signed trailhead for Ramsey Cascades is just a few yards from the end of the parking area. From the trailhead, cross the Middle Prong of the Little Pigeon River via a sturdy footbridge, pausing to watch the water tumbling over rocks. Its headwaters are in the distance, high up on the slopes of Mount Guyot, the second highest peak in the Great Smoky Mountains, at 6,621 feet.

The first 1.5 miles of the hike ascend gradually on an old gravel roadbed that parallels the river. The vegetation alternates between acidic cove forest (which includes eastern hemlock in the overstory and dense shrubs in the understory) and rich cove forest (with a greater variety of trees, fewer shrubs, and more wildflowers on the forest floor).

As you cross a small footbridge at 1.3 miles, look for spring wildflowers such as foamflower, rue anemone, longspur violet, yellow trillium, dwarf crested violet, Solomon's seal, plumed Solomon's seal, and bishop's cap. If you're hiking in late summer or fall, you may notice white snakeroot, yellow jewelweed, white wood aster, and heartleaf aster.

At 1.5 miles, the old gravel road flattens out and ends in a short loop (a sign indicates Ramsey Cascades is 2.5 miles). Continue straight on the narrow well-worn trail through a rosebay rhododendron tunnel with painted trillium, speckled wood lily, and Indian cucumber root.

You'll cross a footlog over Ramsey Prong at 2.1 miles. On the far side, look for spring wildflowers such as wake robin, sweet white violet, Jack-in-the-pulpit, and umbrella leaf in this acidic cove forest.

As you continue up the trail, listen for the calls of red squirrels, sometimes called boomers because of their loud calls. Red squirrels chew the bark of sugar maple branches to create wounds that they subsequently visit to lap up the sugary sap.

They also store seeds and fungi at the base of trees and underground. Unrecovered items may help disperse plants and fungi.

The trail ascends more steeply as it enters an old-growth forest. It's hard to miss the two huge tulip trees—one on either side of the trail with a third one off to the left. Other trees in this rich cove forest include white basswood, yellow birch, sugar maple, yellow buckeye, Fraser magnolia, and eastern hemlock.

The large, widely spaced trees in this old-growth forest allow ample light to reach the forest floor. The abundance of wildflowers in this forest reflects adequate light levels coupled with a moist, nutrient-rich soil. Dutchman's britches, squirrel corn, cutleaf toothwort, and dimpled trout lily are among the first wildflowers to emerge at this elevation. Because they emerge early and die back before the canopy trees leaf out, they are known as spring ephemerals. Other spring wildflowers include blue cohosh, yellow mandarin, foamflower, giant chickweed, and various violets. In summer to fall, you may notice Canada horsebalm, New York ironweed, crimson bee balm, cutleaf coneflower, white snakeroot, goldenrod, and white wood aster.

The trail continues upward through an acidic cove forest with a dense understory of rosebay rhododendron before crossing a second footlog over Ramsey Prong. After rock hopping across several tributaries, the trail winds through another old-growth rich cove forest with white basswood, eastern hemlock, sugar maple, and yellow birch. Look and listen for woodpeckers, including pileated woodpeckers, one of the most striking birds in the region. Nearly the size of a crow, pileated woodpeckers are mostly black with bold white stripes down the neck and a flaming red crest. They whack at dead standing trees and fallen logs in search of their favorite prey (carpenter ants), but also feed on fruits, including sassafras, flowering dogwood, hackberry, greenbrier, poison ivy, and elderberry.

The slopes beneath the widely spaced trees are covered with wildflowers, including many species already mentioned, along with brook lettuce, broadleaf toothwort, and witch hobble in spring. Summer- to early-fall-flowering species include black cohosh, cranefly orchid, rattlesnake orchid, yellow jewelweed, and Appalachian dodder.

The steep trail traverses another rosebay rhododendron thicket, follows a series of closely spaced stone steps lined with rosebay rhododendron, Catawba rhododendron, and red spruce, and crosses one last tributary before reaching the base of Ramsey Cascades and the end of the trail.

Considered the tallest waterfall in the park, Ramsey Cascades consists of a series of falls and cascades that drop 100 feet over a jumble of boulders into a small pool. Plants in the spray cliff zone include Catawba rhododendron, Appalachian bluet, sweet white violet, and various ferns.

A couple of large flat boulders at the end of the trail provide a good spot to relax and enjoy a close-up view of the falls, but be careful, as the smooth rocks are slippery, especially when wet from the spray of the falls. A cold air draft coupled with mist from the falls quickly cools warm skin. When you're ready, retrace your steps back to the trailhead.

Spring

Doll's eyes, White baneberry	*Actaea pachypoda*	p. 213
Wood anemone	*Anemone quinquefolia*	p. 209
Jack-in-the-pulpit	*Arisaema triphyllum*	p. 241
Cutleaf toothwort	*Cardamine concatenata*	p. 210
Broadleaf toothwort	*Cardamine diphylla*	NI
Blue cohosh	*Caulophyllum thalictroides*	p. 242
Speckled wood lily	*Clintonia umbellulata*	p. 222
Fraser's sedge	*Cymophyllus fraseriana*	p. 215
Squirrel corn	*Dicentra canadensis*	NI
Dutchman's britches	*Dicentra cucullaria*	p. 208
Umbrella leaf	*Diphylleia cymosa*	p. 215
Dimpled trout lily	*Erythronium umbilicatum*	p. 253
Wild strawberry	*Fragaria virginiana*	p. 212
Showy orchis	*Galearis spectabilis*	p. 234
Wild geranium	*Geranium maculatum*	p. 235
Dwarf crested iris	*Iris cristata*	p. 247
Plumed Solomon's seal	*Maianthemum racemosum*	p. 216
Brook lettuce	*Micranthes micranthidifolia*	p. 217
Bishop's cap	*Mitella diphylla*	NI
Golden ragwort	*Packera aurea*	p. 257
Mayapple	*Podophyllum peltatum*	p. 208
Solomon's seal	*Polygonatum biflorum*	p. 217
Dwarf cinquefoil	*Potentilla canadensis*	p. 253
Yellow mandarin	*Prosartes lanuginosa*	p. 263
Bloodroot	*Sanguinaria canadensis*	p. 209
Mountain stonecrop	*Sedum ternatum*	p. 218
Giant chickweed	*Stellaria pubera*	p. 214
Rue anemone	*Thalictrum thalictroides*	p. 211
Foamflower	*Tiarella cordifolia*	p. 218
Poison ivy	*Toxicodendron radicans*	p. 223
Wake robin, Stinking Willie	*Trillium erectum*	p. 243
Yellow trillium	*Trillium luteum*	p. 254
Painted trillium	*Trillium undulatum*	p. 219
Sweet white violet	*Viola blanda*	p. 219
Halbertleaf yellow violet	*Viola hastata*	p. 254
Roundleaf yellow violet	*Viola rotundifolia*	NI
Common blue violet	*Viola sororia*	p. 247

Spring–Summer

Pipevine, Dutchman's pipe	*Aristolochia macrophylla*	p. 244
Pipsissewa, Striped wintergreen	*Chimaphila maculata*	p. 222
Speckled wood lily	*Clintonia umbellulata*	p. 222
Common fleabane	*Erigeron philadelphicus*	NI
Strawberry bush, Hearts-a-bustin'	*Euonymus americanus*	p. 264
Appalachian bluet	*Houstonia serpyllifolia*	p. 248
Lilyleaf twayblade	*Liparis liliifolia*	NI
Indian cucumber root	*Medeola virginiana*	p. 264
Heal all	*Prunella vulgaris*	p. 249
Lyreleaf sage	*Salvia lyrata*	NI
Mountain meadowrue	*Thalictrum clavatum*	p. 226
Canada violet	*Viola canadensis*	p. 220
Longspur violet	*Viola rostrata*	NI

Summer

Black cohosh	*Actaea racemosa*	p. 226
Beggar's ticks	*Desmodium nudiflorum*	p. 238
Galax, Skunkweed	*Galax urceolata*	p. 224
Rattlesnake orchid	*Goodyera pubescens*	p. 229
Wild hydrangea	*Hydrangea arborescens*	p. 225
Mountain laurel	*Kalmia latifolia*	p. 236
Wood nettle	*Laportea canadensis*	p. 265
Partridge berry	*Mitchella repens*	p. 223
Indian pipe, Ghost flower	*Monotropa uniflora*	p. 231
Mountain wood sorrel	*Oxalis montana*	p. 237
Catawba rhododendron	*Rhododendron catawbiense*	p. 236
Rosebay rhododendron	*Rhododendron maximum*	p. 230
Cranefly orchid	*Tipularia discolor*	p. 246

Summer-Fall

White snakeroot	*Ageratina altissima*	p. 232
Hog peanut	*Amphicarpaea bracteata*	p. 238
Tall bellflower	*Campanulastrum americanum*	NI
Canada horsebalm	*Collinsonia canadensis*	p. 261
Appalachian dodder	*Cuscuta rostrata*	p. 232
White wood aster	*Eurybia divaricata*	p. 231
Yellow jewelweed	*Impatiens pallida*	NI
Crimson bee balm	*Monarda didyma*	p. 269
Pokeweed	*Phytolacca americana*	p. 227
Cutleaf coneflower	*Rudbeckia laciniata*	p. 260
New York ironweed	*Vernonia noveboracensis*	p. 246

Fall

Witch hazel	*Hamamelis virginiana*	p. 262
Heal all	*Prunella vulgaris*	p. 249
Goldenrod	*Solidago* species	NI
Heartleaf aster	*Symphyotrichum cordifolium*	p. 251
Canada violet	*Viola canadensis*	p. 220

NI = species not included in the wildflower profiles (Part IV)

South Carolina

26 / Jones Gap Falls

JONES GAP STATE PARK

Highlights	Scenic river hike with good spring wildflowers and a 50-foot waterfall
Flowering season	Late March to mid-October
Peak flowering	April
Trail length	3.0 miles out and back
Trail rating	Easy to moderate
Elevation	1,415–1,780 feet
Nearest town	Marietta, Greenville County, S.C.
Contact	864-836-3647; www.southcarolinaparks.com
Directions	From the junction of U.S. 276 and S.C. 11 in Cleveland, go west on U.S. 276 and drive 1.4 miles, then turn right (north) on River Falls Road. Continue on River Falls Road (which becomes Jones Gap Road) for 5.4 miles to the main gate for Jones Gap State Park, and turn right into the designated parking area. A small fee is charged per visitor. GPS: N35 07.517 W82 34.237

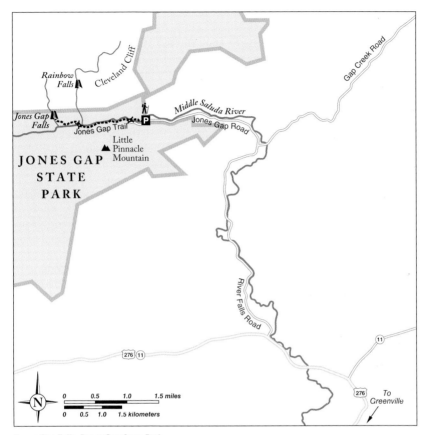

Jones Gap Falls, Jones Gap State Park

Overview Originally an old wagon route, the trail to Jones Gap Falls is within
sight of the Middle Saluda River most of the way. Designated a
scenic river, the Middle Saluda has large boulders, small cascades,
riffles, and pools that harbor three species of trout. Expect to get
your feet wet as you rock hop over several small tributaries. You
may also want to find a nice boulder along the river to relax and dip
your feet into the crystal clear water. Never very wide, the riverbank
plant community (alluvial forest) includes trees such as sweet birch
and thicket-forming shrubs such as rosebay rhododendron and
mountain doghobble. You'll also pass through oak hickory forests
and acidic cove forests with a medley of wildflowers, including
five species of violet, three kinds of trillium, and two species of
bluet. A short spur trail takes you to Jones Gap Falls, where the
river cascades 50 feet down a rock face into a small plunge pool.
Facilities include restrooms, showers, and trailside camping. Parking
is limited, so it's best to arrive early (the park opens at 9 am) if you're
visiting on a weekend from mid-April through late October.

The Hike

The spring wildflowers start off with a bang as the parking area includes foamflower, bloodroot, rue anemone, sweet Betsy, giant chickweed, halberdleaf yellow violet, common blue violet, Jack-in-the-pulpit, Solomon's seal, plumed Solomon's seal, and sweet shrub. Behind the entrance sign at the trailhead is a nice patch of mayapple and Virginia heartleaf.

As you follow the narrow footpath leading into the park, look for bearcorn, longspur violet, and cranefly orchid. In addition to wildflowers, this is a great hike for birders (the park has been designated an Important Bird Area by the National Audubon Society). You may see a variety of birds along the trail, including red-bellied woodpecker, downy woodpecker, red-tailed hawk, raven, white-breasted nuthatch, hermit thrush, and scarlet tanager.

As you cross the arched bridge over the Middle Saluda, pause to enjoy the sights and sounds of the river, surrounded by trees such as sweet birch, yellow buckeye, tulip tree, northern red oak, red maple, sassafras, and flowering dogwood. Many fall and spring migrants use forested stream corridors as avian highways, including Canada warbler and chestnut-sided warbler. The high-fat-content fruits of sassafras and flowering dogwood are an important food source for many fall migrants.

Follow the trail through the picnic area and the old Cleveland fish hatchery, where pink turtlehead, cardinal flower, white wood aster, white snakeroot, tall rattlesnake root, and orange jewelweed bloom in late summer through early fall.

The open forest along this part of the trail is an oak hickory forest with canopy trees such as white oak, chestnut oak, mockernut hickory, eastern white pine, shortleaf pine, and tulip tree. The spiny "balls" on the forest floor indicate sweetgum also grows here.

Restroom facilities are located in the first building to your right. Notice the large healthy eastern hemlock in front of the building; once a dominant canopy species in the region, most have been killed by an infestation of hemlock woolly adelgids.

The second rustic building off to the right is the park headquarters and learning center. Just before crossing the short wooden bridge (0.2 mile), notice the huge boulder on your right as well as the many boulders lining the riverbed. If you're wondering how these boulders got here, there are several possibilities. The boulders lining the riverbed probably became exposed when the Middle Saluda River carved out the gorge. The other boulders may have broken off the ridge and rolled down the slope, or severe erosion following heavy logging in the early 1900s may have brought them to the surface.

To the right, just past the small bridge, is the kiosk that marks the beginning of the Jones Gap Trail (blazed in blue). Take a minute to fill out a hikers' registration card before starting out.

The early part of the trail along the Middle Saluda River showcases a delightful mix of cascades and quiet pools. Spring wildflowers in this narrow alluvial forest include foamflower, dwarf crested iris, roundleaf yellow violet, sweet white violet, longspur violet, and Catesby's trillium. In late summer through early fall, look for beechdrops (a root parasite on American beech). You may also notice the red fruits of strawberry bush, partridge berry, and Jack-in-the-pulpit. Fleshy fruits like these are typically dispersed by birds or small mammals, which consume the pulp and disperse the seeds in their droppings.

At 0.5 mile, the trail narrows and gradually climbs through an acidic cove forest with rosebay rhododendron, gorge rhododendron, and mountain doghobble forming a dense shrub layer. Catesby's trillium, Solomon's seal, and rattlesnake orchid grow in open areas along the trail. The location of the flowers beneath the leafy arching stems of Solomon's seal provides shelter from the potentially damaging effects of wind and rain.

At 0.8 mile, you'll come to another junction (marked by a map of the Mountain Bridge Wilderness Area). Take the trail to the left toward Jones Gap Falls (going straight takes you to Rainbow Falls). As you continue up the trail, look for spring wildflowers, including Catesby's trillium, Vasey's trillium, Indian cucumber root, longspur violet, bearcorn, and partridge berry. The flowers of Catesby's trillium change color from white to pink as they age.

The trail climbs more steeply, veers away from the river, and passes through an acidic cove forest. Among the canopy trees are yellow birch, Fraser magnolia, American beech, red maple, northern red oak, and eastern hemlock. Rosebay rhododendron forms a dense shrub layer. Other understory species include gorge rhododendron, mountain laurel, and striped maple. Along the trail, look for spring wildflowers, including foamflower, Jack-in-the-pulpit, dwarf crested iris, and plumed Solomon's seal.

The trail parallels the river for a short distance, veers away and gently wanders up and down before crossing the Middle Saluda River on a sturdy footbridge at 1.4 miles. Rosebay rhododendron, gorge rhododendron, and mountain doghobble form a dense shrub layer along the river with sweet birch in the canopy.

After crossing the river, the trail bears left, ascends a small hill, and turns left at the T-junction. Rock hop across a tributary and continue up the trail for about 50 yards before turning right on the short spur trail to Jones Gap Falls at 1.5 miles. The falls cascade about 50 feet over a multi-colored staircase of stone with rosebay rhododendron on the margin. The spray cliff is mostly bare rock with scattered clumps of Appalachian bluet and mountain meadowrue. The long leafy branches of an American beech form a dense canopy high above the falls.

On one visit, a young girl coming down the trail called out, "there's air conditioning at the falls." Stand near the plunge pool to experience the cold air drainage before retracing your steps back to the parking area.

Options. From Jones Gap Falls, retrace your steps 0.7 mile to the signed junction of the Jones Gap and Rainbow Falls Trails, turn left, and hike 1.6 miles to Rainbow Falls, a scenic waterfall that free falls nearly 100 feet. The Rainbow Falls Trail (blazed in red) is moderately difficult with an elevation gain of about 1,000 feet.

26 / JONES GAP FALLS: WHAT TO LOOK FOR

Spring

Wood anemone	*Anemone quinquefolia*	p. 209
Jack-in-the-pulpit	*Arisaema triphyllum*	p. 241
Crossvine	*Bignonia capreolata*	NI
Sweet shrub	*Calycanthus floridus*	p. 241
Fairywand, Devil's bit	*Chamaelirium luteum*	p. 210
Bearcorn, Squawroot	*Conopholis americana*	p. 255
Robin's plantain	*Erigeron pulchellus*	p. 216
Dwarf crested iris	*Iris cristata*	p. 247
Mountain laurel	*Kalmia latifolia*	p. 236

Mountain doghobble	*Leucothoe fontanesiana*	p. 213
Plumed Solomon's seal	*Maianthemum racemosum*	p. 216
Indian cucumber root	*Medeola virginiana*	p. 264
Lousewort, Wood betony	*Pedicularis canadensis*	p. 255
Mayapple	*Podophyllum peltatum*	p. 208
Solomon's seal	*Polygonatum biflorum*	p. 217
Dwarf cinquefoil	*Potentilla canadensis*	p. 253
Yellow mandarin	*Prosartes lanuginosa*	p. 263
Bloodroot	*Sanguinaria canadensis*	p. 209
Giant chickweed	*Stellaria pubera*	p. 214
Rue anemone	*Thalictrum thalictroides*	p. 211
Foamflower	*Tiarella cordifolia*	p. 218
Catesby's trillium	*Trillium catesbaei*	p. 212
Sweet Betsy	*Trillium cuneatum*	p. 240
Vasey's trillium	*Trillium vaseyi*	p. 244
Mapleleaf viburnum	*Viburnum acerifolium*	NI
Sweet white violet	*Viola blanda*	p. 219
Halberdleaf yellow violet	*Viola hastata*	p. 254
Longspur violet	*Viola rostrata*	NI
Roundleaf yellow violet	*Viola rotundifolia*	NI
Common blue violet	*Viola sororia*	p. 247
Yellowroot	*Xanthorhiza simplicissima*	p. 240

Spring–Summer

Pipsissewa, Striped wintergreen	*Chimaphila maculata*	p. 222
Strawberry bush, Hearts-a-bustin'	*Euonymus americanus*	p. 264
Galax, Skunkweed	*Galax urceolata*	p. 224
Little brown jugs	*Hexastylis arifolia*	NI
Virginia heartleaf	*Hexastylis virginica*	NI
Woodland bluet	*Houstonia purpurea*	NI
Appalachian bluet	*Houstonia serpyllifolia*	p. 248
Silverleaf hydrangea	*Hydrangea radiata*	NI
Partridge berry	*Mitchella repens*	p. 223
Gorge rhododendron, Punctatum	*Rhododendron minus*	p. 237
Mountain meadowrue	*Thalictrum clavatum*	p. 226
Poison ivy	*Toxicodendron radicans*	p. 223

Summer

Spikenard	*Aralia racemosa*	p. 265
Rattlesnake orchid	*Goodyera pubescens*	p. 229
Wood nettle	*Laportea canadensis*	p. 265
Rosebay rhododendron	*Rhododendron maximum*	p. 230
Cranefly orchid	*Tipularia discolor*	p. 246

Summer–Fall

White snakeroot	*Ageratina altissima*	p. 232
Pink turtlehead	*Chelone lyonii*	p. 239
Asiatic dayflower	*Commelina communis*	p. 249
White wood aster	*Eurybia divaricata*	p. 231
Orange jewelweed	*Impatiens capensis*	p. 268
Cardinal flower	*Lobelia cardinalis*	p. 269
Tall rattlesnake root	*Prenanthes altissima*	NI

Fall

Beechdrops	*Epifagus virginiana*	p. 233
Witch hazel	*Hamamelis virginiana*	p. 262
Pinesap	*Monotropa hypopithys*	NI

NI = species not included in the wildflower profiles (Part IV)

27 / Station Cove Falls

SUMTER NATIONAL FOREST AND OCONEE STATION
STATE HISTORIC SITE

Highlights	Exceptional spring wildflowers in a rich cove forest with a 60-foot waterfall
Flowering season	Mid-February through late October
Peak flowering	Mid-March through April
Trail length	1.8 miles out and back
Trail rating	Easy
Elevation	1,160–1,100 feet
Nearest town	Walhalla, Oconee County, S.C.
Contact	Andrew Pickens Ranger District; 864-638-9568; www.fs.fed.us/wildflowers/regions/southern; Oconee Station State Historic Site; 864-638-0079; www.southcarolinaparks.com
Directions	From Walhalla, drive east on S.C. 183 toward Pickens for 3.5 miles. Turn left (north) onto Christophers Road and go 0.1 mile before

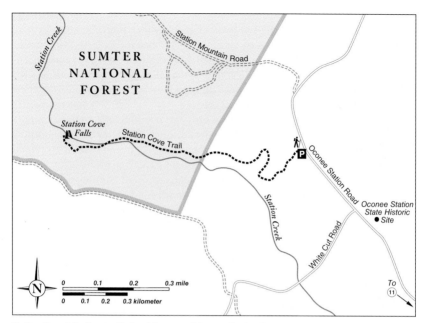

Station Cove Falls, Sumter National Forest and Oconee Station State Historic Site

veering right onto S.C. 11. Follow S.C. 11 for 2.0 miles, turn left (northwest) onto Oconee Station Road (sign indicates Historical Oconee Station), and travel 2.3 miles to a small parking area on the left. The trailhead is located next to the trail information sign. If the small parking lot for Station Cove Falls is full, you can park at the State Historic Site and hike a short, scenic trail to the trailhead for Station Cove Falls. To get there from the parking area for Station Cove Falls, turn around and drive back 0.2 mile on Station Cove Road before turning left at the entrance to the State Historic Site. GPS: N34 50.935 W83 04.470

Overview This short hike in the transition zone between the upper piedmont and Blue Ridge Mountains takes you through a treasure trove of spring wildflowers and ends at a picturesque waterfall. The trail begins in a mixed pine-hardwood forest, winds through a more mature oak hickory forest, goes by an old beaver pond (now a swamp), crosses several small creeks (via wooden footbridges), and enters a broad streamside flat. Wildflowers are most abundant and diverse in the rich cove forest from here to the waterfall, an area influenced by amphibolite, a rock that releases magnesium into the soil, which elevates the soil pH and increases nutrient availability, thereby enabling a large number of species to occupy the site. Station Cove Falls is widely considered to be one of the top early spring wildflower hikes in the region.

The Hike

The trail begins in a mixed pine-hardwood forest in which many of the pines were killed by an infestation of pine bark beetles in 1995 (look for their decaying trunks on the forest floor). Fast-growing trees such as sweetgum, tulip tree, and eastern white pine are rapidly filling in the gap left by the fallen pines. Heath shrubs such as lowbush blueberry, mountain laurel, and sparkleberry are good indicators of the acidic soil that characterizes this part of the trail.

A short loop to the left at 0.2 mile provides an overlook of a wetland created by beavers damming the creek that meanders through the valley. As you continue down the trail, listen for the mating calls of spring peepers and other frogs. Wood ducks nest in larger tree cavities along the stream as well as in the artificial nest boxes in the swamp. Look for sweet Betsy, an early-spring-blooming trillium with maroon (sometimes yellow) flowers atop three whorled leaves. Later in spring, Catesby's trillium, wild geranium, fairywand, and common blue violet dot the trail.

After crossing a small wooden bridge at 0.3 mile, notice the many American beech trees in the forest understory; their persistent bleached leaves stand out in winter and early spring. Wildflowers include the bright yellow flower heads of green and gold, the daisy-like white flower heads of Robin's plantain, and the bright yellow flowers and arrowhead-shaped leaves of halberdleaf yellow violet in spring. Be careful what you touch—poison ivy grows here and elsewhere along the trail!

Near a second footbridge at 0.4 mile, you may notice the yellow-to-reddish-brown two-lipped flowers and ferny leaves of lousewort. Look for bumblebees visiting the flowers for nectar and pollen and pause to take in the oak hickory forest on the slopes to your right. Mature oak forests such as this typically harbor a variety of breeding birds, including wood thrush, black-and-white warbler, scarlet tanager, eastern wood-pewee, and red-eyed vireo.

Below the trail, about 50 feet past the second footbridge, is a dense patch of running cedar, a low-growing evergreen that stands out in winter and early spring. The narrow cones in upright candelabra-like clusters above the foliage release wind-dispersed spores that were used as a flash powder in the early days of photography. As you continue along the trail, look for spring wildflowers such as sweet Betsy, foamflower, and devil's bit.

A third footbridge at 0.5 mile is marked by a dense thicket of mountain dog-hobble—an evergreen shrub with arching stems and white urn-shaped flowers that vary in fragrance from cloyingly sweet to musky. Doghobble spreads vegetatively by rooting at the stem tips, much like blackberries. In summer, look for blue monkshood, a rare species in South Carolina. You may also notice tree stumps chiseled by a beaver's large incisors.

From here to the falls, a cornucopia of spring wildflowers lights up this rich cove forest, including thousands of sweet Betsy plants. Mayapple is also abundant, forming dense patches of large umbrella-like leaves with solitary, nodding white flowers partially hidden under paired leaves. Other spring blooming plants include wild geranium, whorled horsebalm, halberdleaf yellow violet, foamflower, and Solomon's seal.

Immediately after crossing a fourth footbridge at 0.6 mile, take the left fork toward the falls (the right fork goes to Oconee State Park). The trail continues through a streamside flat rich in wildflowers, including bloodroot, foamflower, Jack-in-the-pulpit, and sweet white trillium, along with lots more sweet Betsy and mayapple.

As the trail gently ascends, the adjoining slopes steepen, the creekside flat narrows, and the trail hugs the creek. The trail soon veers left, descends a few steps, and crosses the narrow creek at 0.8 mile via large stones. After crossing the creek, look to your right for a clump of sweet white trillium in early spring, and catch a glimpse of the falls at the head of the cove.

The trail continues through a narrow streamside flat with more spring wildflowers including Canada violet, acute-lobed hepatica, rue anemone, and blue cohosh. By midsummer, a dense patch of wood nettle overtops many of these herbs. Don't worry—the early spring wildflowers will reemerge next year.

Woody plants in the streamside flat include yellow buckeye, spicebush, pawpaw, Carolina silverbell, and white basswood, all of which flower in spring and have insect-pollinated flowers. Trees growing on the steep slopes and shallow soils at the head of the cove are prone to windthrow as indicated by the large number of downed trees.

The trail ends at a picturesque waterfall that drops 60 feet over numerous ledges. The spray cliff community is well developed, including spring-flowering species such as foamflower, and mountain meadowrue, and summer-to-fall-flowering species such as rock alumroot, orange jewelweed, and white turtlehead.

Perhaps the most abundant plant in the spray cliff zone is riverweed—an alga-like flowering plant with deeply dissected narrow leaves that forms dense prostrate mats on bare rock exposed to fast-flowing water, including in rocky streams. Unlike mosses, lichens, and some ferns, few flowering plants are able to grow on bare rock because their roots require soil to absorb water and nutrients.

Look for resurrection fern growing on tree trunks near the falls. In dry conditions, this fern goes dormant—its leaves curl up and turn brown, and it looks dead. After rain, the leaves absorb water, uncurl, and the plant is as alive and green as ever, hence the name. Keen observers may notice the rare walking fern growing on a boulder or two. Be careful—wet rock is more slippery than it looks.

Enjoy the sights at this turnaround point. While peak flowering is early spring, Station Cove Falls makes an interesting hike any time of year.

Options. Visit nearby Oconee Station State Historic Site, which includes two historic structures, a pond, and a short hiking trail that connects to the trailhead for Station Cove Falls. Facilities include restrooms, a picnic area and interpretative signs. It's located 0.2 mile before the parking area for Station Cove Falls on Oconee Station Road.

27 / STATION COVE FALLS: WHAT TO LOOK FOR

Spring

Acute-lobed hepatica	*Anemone acutiloba*	p. 207
Jack-in-the-pulpit	*Arisaema triphyllum*	p. 241
Sweet shrub	*Calycanthus floridus*	p. 241
Blue cohosh	*Caulophyllum thalictroides*	p. 242
Fairywand, Devil's bit	*Chamaelirium luteum*	p. 210
Pink lady's slipper	*Cypripedium acaule*	p. 235
Wild strawberry	*Fragaria virginiana*	p. 212
Showy orchis	*Galearis spectabilis*	p. 234
Wild geranium	*Geranium maculatum*	p. 235

Little brown jugs	*Hexastylis arifolia*	NI
Dwarf crested iris	*Iris cristata*	p. 247
Mountain doghobble	*Leucothoe fontanesiana*	p. 213
Spicebush	*Lindera benzoin*	p. 263
Plumed Solomon's seal	*Maianthemum racemosum*	p. 216
Indian cucumber root	*Medeola virginiana*	p. 264
Pennywort	*Obolaria virginica*	NI
Lousewort, Wood betony	*Pedicularis canadensis*	p. 255
Mayapple	*Podophyllum peltatum*	p. 208
Solomon's seal	*Polygonatum biflorum*	p. 217
Dwarf cinquefoil	*Potentilla canadensis*	p. 253
Bloodroot	*Sanguinaria canadensis*	p. 209
Rue anemone	*Thalictrum thalictroides*	p. 211
Foamflower	*Tiarella cordifolia*	p. 218
Catesby's trillium	*Trillium catesbaei*	p. 212
Sweet Betsy	*Trillium cuneatum*	p. 240
Sweet white trillium	*Trillium simile*	NI
Perfoliate bellwort	*Uvularia perfoliata*	p. 256
Halberdleaf yellow violet	*Viola hastata*	p. 254
Common blue violet	*Viola sororia*	p. 247
Yellowroot	*Xanthorhiza simplicissima*	p. 240

Spring–Summer

Black cohosh	*Actaea racemosa*	p. 226
Pipsissewa, Striped wintergreen	*Chimaphila maculata*	p. 222
Green and gold	*Chrysogonum virginianum*	NI
Whorled horsebalm	*Collinsonia verticillata*	NI
Robin's plantain	*Erigeron pulchellus*	p. 216
Strawberry bush, Hearts-a-bustin'	*Euonymus americanus*	p. 264
Rattlesnake hawkweed	*Hieracium venosum*	p. 256
Appalachian bluet	*Houstonia serpyllifolia*	p. 248
Silverleaf hydrangea	*Hydrangea radiata*	NI
Riverweed	*Podostemum ceratophyllum*	NI
Lyreleaf sage	*Salvia lyrata*	NI
Poison ivy	*Toxicodendron radicans*	p. 223
Canada violet	*Viola canadensis*	p. 220

Summer

Beggar's ticks	*Desmodium nudiflorum*	p. 238
Rattlesnake orchid	*Goodyera pubescens*	p. 229
Wood nettle	*Laportea canadensis*	p. 265
Rosebay rhododendron	*Rhododendron maximum*	p. 230
Cranefly orchid	*Tipularia discolor*	p. 246

Summer–Fall

Blue monkshood	*Aconitum uncinatum*	NI
White snakeroot	*Ageratina altissima*	p. 232
Hog peanut	*Amphicarpaea bracteata*	p. 238
White turtlehead	*Chelone glabra*	NI
Rock alumroot	*Heuchera villosa*	p. 230
Orange jewelweed	*Impatiens capensis*	p. 268
Downy lobelia	*Lobelia puberula*	NI
Indian pipe, Ghost flower	*Monotropa uniflora*	p. 231
Cankerweed	*Prenanthes serpentaria*	NI

Fall

| Beechdrops | *Epifagus virginiana* | p. 233 |
| Canada violet | *Viola canadensis* | p. 220 |

NI = species not included in the wildflower profiles (Part IV)

Georgia

28 / Panther Creek Falls

CHATTAHOOCHEE NATIONAL FOREST

Highlights	Streamside hike with good spring wildflowers and a cascading waterfall
Flowering season	Mid-March through late October
Peak flowering	April–May
Trail length	7.0 miles out and back
Trail rating	Moderate, with a steep descent to the base of the falls
Elevation	1,500–1,100 feet
Nearest town	Tallulah Falls, Habersham County, Ga.
Contact	Chattooga River District; 706-754-6221; www.fs.fed.us
Directions	The turnoff for Panther Creek Recreation Area is about 3 miles south of Tallulah Falls or 3 miles north of Hollywood, Ga., on Historic 441. From the junction of U.S. 441 and Ga. 17 Alternate, travel north on U.S. 441 for 3.0 miles. Turn left onto Glen Hardman Road just south of mile marker 18 and drive 0.1 mile to a stop sign where you'll turn right onto Historic 441 and travel 1.0 mile to the Panther Creek Recreation Area. Park in the pullout on the right side of the road or pay a small fee to park in the lot on the left (includes restroom facilities and a picnic area). The signed trailhead begins on the east side of the road across from the parking lot. GPS: N34 41.931 W83 25.170

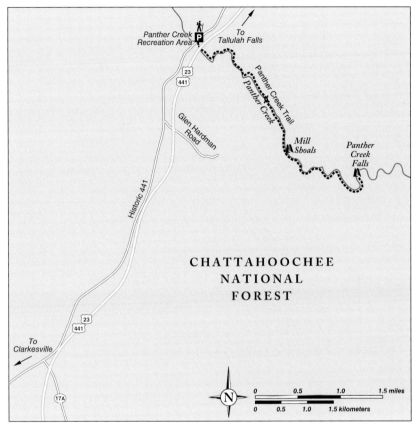

Panther Creek Falls, Chattahoochee National Forest

Overview   This delightful hike follows the banks of Panther Creek for much of the way. The vegetation is mostly acidic cove forest with a mix of piedmont and mountain species. Numerous spring wildflowers bloom along the trail, including colorful displays of mountain laurel and gorge rhododendron in May. The trail descends into a wooded ravine where there is a fine view of Panther Creek Falls, a 60- to 70-foot cascading waterfall that drops into a large pool bordered by a sandy flat. It's a nice spot to wade in the cold water, explore the wildflowers, and have a snack. You may want to get an early start as the trail attracts quite a few hikers, especially on weekends.

The Hike

Near the trailhead, Robin's plantain, lyreleaf sage, common cinquefoil, and whorled loosestrife flower in spring. You may also notice galax, gorge rhododendron, and Solomon's seal in this acidic cove forest. From spring through midsummer, look for barn swallows flying around and under the overpass. Their cup-shaped mud nests are easy to spot under the concrete bridge as are the nests of organ pipe mud daubers.

On the far side of the overpass, the vegetation changes to a mixed pine-hardwood forest, with a dense groundcover of lowbush blueberry. Its sweet edible fruits are consumed by a variety of birds, which disperse the tiny seeds in their droppings. Unlike blueberry, the bland, low-sugar fruits of partridge berry persist on the plant for months. Birding enthusiasts may notice pine warblers, summer tanagers, and yellow-throated vireos gleaning insects from the bark and needles of pines.

Where the trail skirts the creek and moisture levels increase, the vegetation reverts to acidic cove forest with wildflowers such as Indian cucumber root, Catesby's trillium, and halberdleaf yellow violet. As you continue up the trail, notice how Panther Creek has cut into the rock substrate forming a gorge more than 60 feet deep.

At 0.5 mile, the trail crosses an open area below a power line corridor with showy spring wildflowers, including hairy phlox, birdfoot violet, dwarf iris, and green and gold. In summer and fall, look for whorled coreopsis, goldenrod, and compass plant. You might also spot a red-shouldered hawk perched on a tree branch (or utility wire), soaring over the forest, or sitting on a stick nest high up in a tree.

The trail continues through an acidic cove forest with spring-blooming species such as heartleaf, fairywand, trailing arbutus, sweet white violet, and Catesby's trillium.

At 0.8 mile, the trail weaves around a large overhanging boulder then veers to the left away from the creek. Here and elsewhere along the trail, look for clumps of gaywings, a small ground-hugging plant with small airplane-shaped pinkish-purple flowers in spring. I've seen more gaywings along this trail than anywhere else in the region.

The daisy-like flowers of Robin's plantain are commonly seen along trails in spring. Each flower head consists of hundreds of tiny flowers, with showy white-to-lilac-colored ray flowers on the outer rim and yellow disk flowers in the center.

The trail drops down to a creekside flat with a primitive campsite at 1.4 miles. In this acidic cove forest, Catesby's trillium and little brown jugs flower in spring. In summer, look for the flowers of galax, partridge berry, and rosebay rhododendron.

As you cross the wooden footbridge over Panther Creek at 1.9 miles, notice the rocky streamside plants, including mountain doghobble, mountain laurel, rosebay rhododendron, yellowroot, and strawberry bush. As the trail continues, the terrain changes from steep slopes to flat bottomland where dense carpets of dimpled trout lily and Catesby's trillium bloom in early spring. In summer and fall, you may notice fire pink and wideleaf spiderwort along the trail.

Further downstream, the forest opens up with many fallen trunks on the forest floor. The dead trees are mostly eastern white pines, weakened by drought, then killed by pine bark beetles. Appalachian hill cane, a native bamboo, grows well in open bottomland forests such as this. If the timing is right, you may see the showy white blooms of Carolina silverbell, flowering dogwood, and piedmont azalea in spring. On several occasions, I've seen a black rat snake slithering across the trail in this area—they're nonvenomous and unlikely to bother you.

Cross two footbridges over small tributaries, after which the trail passes through an acidic cove forest with spring wildflowers such as mayapple, foamflower, rue anemone, wood anemone, Jack-in-the-pulpit, and mountain doghobble. By early summer, this meadow-like flat is covered in ferns.

At 2.5 miles, the creek bends sharply and the trail ascends to a rock promontory where you get a bird's-eye view of Mill Shoals, a series of cascades where Panther

Creek has cut through solid rock. Some hikers mistake these cascades for the main attraction, but the real waterfall is about a mile up the trail.

Rock hop across a small stream and continue down the trail to a footbridge over another small tributary. Here, the creek bends sharply to the left, and the trail gradually climbs a steep bluff overhanging the creek (cable handrails provide support). Rosebay rhododendron grows along the bluffs as do galax, partridge berry, sweet white violet, and Indian cucumber root.

The trail flattens out a bit and continues following the creek. Rock hop across a larger tributary and follow the trail as it climbs up two more bluffs along the edge of the creek. Cave alumroot, a rare species with round leaf lobes grows in the shaded cliff bases and overhangs. Rock alumroot, a much more common species with sharply lobed leaves is here too, as is poison ivy.

The trail ascends to a rock outcrop just above the brink of the falls, and then drops steeply to the base of the slope, where gaywings, dimpled trout lily, Solomon's seal, plumed Solomon's seal, and wild hydrangea occur. Trees in this acidic cove forest include eastern white pine, eastern hemlock, tulip tree, red maple, sweet birch, and American beech.

Nearly as wide as it is tall, the cascading waterfall slides and free falls over multiple ledges into a large circular pool at the base. Wildflowers in the spray cliff community include orange jewelweed, mountain meadowrue, Joe Pye weed, and rosebay rhododendron.

A sandy beach with scattered boulders at the edge of the large plunge pool provides a nice spot to relax and enjoy the waterfall. You may want to explore the rocky streamside for plants such as foamflower, yellowroot, cinnamon fern, Appalachian bluet, Virginia willow, and silky dogwood. In summer and fall, look for orange jewelweed, cardinal flower, cutleaf coneflower, white wood aster, and Joe Pye weed. You may also notice ruby-throated hummingbirds visiting the flowers of orange jewelweed and cardinal flower for nectar.

When you're ready, return on the same trail to the parking area.

28 / PANTHER CREEK FALLS: WHAT TO LOOK FOR

Spring

Blue star	*Amsonia tabernaemontana*	NI
Wood anemone	*Anemone quinquefolia*	p. 209
Solitary pussytoes	*Antennaria solitaria*	NI
Jack-in-the-pulpit	*Arisaema triphyllum*	p. 241
Crossvine	*Bignonia capreolata*	NI
Fairywand, Devil's bit	*Chamaelirium luteum*	p. 210
Pink lady's slipper	*Cypripedium acaule*	p. 235
Trailing arbutus	*Epigaea repens*	p. 207
Robin's plantain	*Erigeron pulchellus*	p. 216
Dimpled trout lily	*Erythronium umbilicatum*	p. 253
Strawberry bush, Hearts-a-bustin'	*Euonymus americanus*	p. 264
Catchweed bedstraw	*Galium aparine*	NI
Wild geranium	*Geranium maculatum*	p. 235
Yellow star grass	*Hypoxis hirsuta*	NI
Dwarf iris	*Iris verna*	NI
Mountain laurel	*Kalmia latifolia*	p. 236

Mountain doghobble	*Leucothoe fontanesiana*	p. 213
Plumed Solomon's seal	*Maianthemum racemosum*	p. 216
Indian cucumber root	*Medeola virginiana*	p. 264
Hairy phlox	*Phlox amoena*	NI
Woodland phlox	*Phlox divaricata*	p. 248
Mayapple	*Podophyllum peltatum*	p. 208
Gaywings	*Polygala paucifolia*	NI
Solomon's seal	*Polygonatum biflorum*	p. 217
Piedmont azalea	*Rhododendron canescens*	NI
Gorge rhododendron, Punctatum	*Rhododendron minus*	p. 237
Lyreleaf sage	*Salvia lyrata*	NI
Rue anemone	*Thalictrum thalictroides*	p. 211
Foamflower	*Tiarella cordifolia*	p. 218
Catesby's trillium	*Trillium catesbaei*	p. 212
Lowbush blueberry	*Vaccinium pallidum*	NI
Sweet white violet	*Viola blanda*	p. 219
Halberdleaf yellow violet	*Viola hastata*	p. 254
Birdfoot violet	*Viola pedata*	NI
Common blue violet	*Viola sororia*	p. 247
Yellowroot	*Xanthorhiza simplicissima*	p. 240

Spring–Summer

Pipsissewa, Striped wintergreen	*Chimaphila maculata*	p. 222
Green and gold	*Chrysogonum virginianum*	NI
Strawberry bush, Hearts-a-bustin'	*Euonymus americanus*	p. 264
Galax, Skunkweed	*Galax urceolata*	p. 224
Carolina cranesbill	*Geranium carolinianum*	NI
Bowman's root	*Gillenia trifoliata*	NI
Little brown jugs	*Hexastylis arifolia*	NI
Heartleaf	*Hexastylis* species	NI
Rattlesnake hawkweed	*Hieracium venosum*	p. 256
Woodland bluet	*Houstonia purpurea*	NI
Appalachian bluet	*Houstonia serpyllifolia*	p. 248
Virginia willow	*Itea virginica*	NI
Whorled loosestrife	*Lysimachia quadrifolia*	p. 258
Partridge berry	*Mitchella repens*	p. 223
Small's ragwort	*Packera anonyma*	NI
Hairy skullcap	*Scutellaria elliptica*	NI
Fire pink	*Silene virginica*	p. 267
Mountain meadowrue	*Thalictrum clavatum*	p. 226
Poison ivy	*Toxicodendron radicans*	p. 223
Wideleaf spiderwort	*Tradescantia subaspera*	p. 250

Summer

Spikenard	*Aralia racemosa*	p. 265
New Jersey tea	*Ceanothus americanus*	NI
Whorled coreopsis	*Coreopsis major*	p. 259
Beggar's ticks	*Desmodium nudiflorum*	p. 238
Elephant's foot	*Elephantopus tomentosus*	NI
Fleabane	*Erigeron* species	NI
Rattlesnake orchid	*Goodyera pubescens*	p. 229
Wild hydrangea	*Hydrangea arborescens*	p. 225
Rosebay rhododendron	*Rhododendron maximum*	p. 230
Cranefly orchid	*Tipularia discolor*	p. 246

Hog peanut	*Amphicarpaea bracteata*	p. 238
White wood aster	*Eurybia divaricata*	p. 231
Joe Pye weed	*Eutrochium fistulosum*	p. 239
Cave alumroot	*Heuchera parviflora*	NI
Rock alumroot	*Heuchera villosa*	p. 230
Orange jewelweed	*Impatiens capensis*	p. 268
Cardinal flower	*Lobelia cardinalis*	p. 269
Pinesap	*Monotropa hypopithys*	NI
Indian pipe	*Monotropa uniflora*	p. 231
Yellow wood sorrel	*Oxalis stricta*	NI
Grassleaf golden aster	*Pityopsis graminifolia*	p. 259
Heal all	*Prunella vulgaris*	p. 249
Cutleaf coneflower	*Rudbeckia laciniata*	p. 260
Compass plant	*Silphium* species	NI

Fall

Witch hazel	*Hamamelis virginiana*	p. 262

NI = species not included in the wildflower profiles (Part IV)

29 / Anna Ruby Falls

CHATTAHOOCHEE NATIONAL FOREST

Highlights	Streamside hike with abundant spring wildflowers and a double waterfall
Flowering season	Early March to mid-October
Peak flowering	April through early May
Trail length	0.8 mile in and out
Trail rating	Easy but relatively steep
Elevation	1,980–2,450 feet
Nearest town	Helen, White County, Ga.
Contact	Chattooga Ranger District; 706-754-6221; www.fs.usda.gov/nfsga
Directions	From downtown Helen, take Ga. 75 north for about 1.5 miles and turn right onto Ga. 356. Travel on 356 for 1.2 miles, then turn left at the sign for Anna Ruby Falls. Follow the paved road 3.4 miles (mostly through Unicoi State Park) to the large parking lot for the falls. A small per-person fee is charged to enter the parking area for the falls. GPS: N34 42.105 W83 47.361

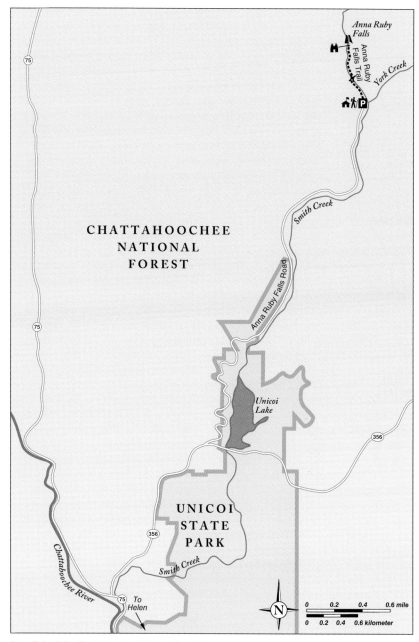

Anna Ruby Falls, Chattahoochee National Forest

Overview   It's hard to find a better short hike than this one. Located near the resort town of Helen, Georgia, the paved wheelchair accessible path follows a cascading creek through a rich cove forest with numerous spring wildflowers. The trail ends at a rare double falls that is one of the most beautiful waterfalls in the region. Two viewing platforms provide an excellent view of the falls. There's often a steady stream of hikers from late spring through the fall leaf-viewing season, so you may want to get an early start to avoid the crowds. Before heading up the trail, take a few minutes to read the interpretive signs and to view the exhibit about moonshine on the far side of the creek directly behind the visitor center. You may even spot a trout in the creek. Facilities include a gift shop, restrooms, picnic tables, and vending machines.

The Hike

The trail begins to the left of the visitor center and is a steady uphill climb to the falls. If you're hiking in spring, you may see a dozen or more spring wildflowers in the first hundred yards, including two species of trillium: sweet Betsy, perhaps the most abundant wildflower along the entire trail, and Vasey's trillium, whose huge maroon flowers dangle beneath the leaves.

Other common spring wildflowers in this rich cove forest include giant chickweed, foamflower, and Jack-in-the-pulpit, along with Robin's plantain, Solomon's seal, and plumed Solomon's seal. You might also spot the scarlet red flowers of fire pink, the dangling pale yellow flowers of yellow mandarin, and the lacy white inflorescences of doll's eyes. Watch out for poison ivy along the trail!

Spring brings not only flowers, but a variety of songbirds to the region. Known as neotropical migrants, many of the birds of eastern forests spend their summer breeding season in North America and their winters in Central or South America. Among the many migrants that add color and song to the spring and summer landscape are wood warblers, indigo buntings, tanagers, and vireos.

If you like violets, enjoy the six species that occur along this trail—sweet white, common blue, roundleaf yellow, yellow woodland, halberdleaf yellow, and Canada violet. Violets are larval (caterpillar) host plants for various fritillary butterflies.

As you cross the sturdy footbridge over Smith Creek at 0.2 mile, take a moment to enjoy the sights and sounds of the cascading stream. Notice the drop in temperature near the creek. Typically, the river is crystal clear, but after a heavy rain, the water turns a dark brown color due to the high sediment load from soil washing into the creek. Just past the bridge is a dense stand of mountain doghobble, easily recognized by its arching stems and alternate evergreen leaves. From spring through early summer, the bright yellow flower heads of golden ragwort add a splash of color along the margin of the stream.

Past the footbridge, the wooded slope on the right side of the trail is an excellent area for wildflowers, including many species already mentioned. Additional spring wildflowers include the nodding pale yellow flowers of perfoliate bellwort, the white flowers of bloodroot and wood anemone, and the brownish-purple to yellow-green flowers of blue cohosh. Look for the drooping white umbels of poke milkweed, the pink-tinged white flowers of whorled horsebalm, and the star-shaped yellow flowers of whorled loosestrife in late spring to early summer. Cutleaf coneflower and roughleaf sunflower bloom in late summer to fall—look for goldfinches gleaning seeds from their fruiting heads in fall.

The rich cove forest in this narrow river gorge includes trees such as yellow buckeye, white basswood, sweet birch, tulip tree, red maple, and Carolina silverbell. The paved path was once a railroad line that hauled out the cut logs when this forest was logged in the late 1800s.

At 0.25 mile, you'll see several huge boulders on the right side of the trail that harbor clumps of rock alumroot and rock polypody. Just past the boulders, on the right side of the trail, you may notice the pink-to-lavender flowers of showy orchis in spring.

As you continue up the trail, you'll see various shrubs in the rocky streamside community, including gorge rhododendron, rosebay rhododendron, mountain doghobble, and yellowroot. In moist cove forests, salamanders are the most abundant vertebrate animal present. They help control insect populations and are eaten by mammals, owls, and snakes.

The lower observation platform at 0.4 mile provides a fabulous view of the falls. On hot summer days, it's also a pleasant spot to bask in the cool air drainage from the falls. Anna Ruby Falls is a rare double waterfall that results from two separate streams flowing down the face of Tray Mountain. Curtiss Creek drops 153 feet and York Creek drops 50 feet over their respective ledges into an area of large boulders (broken off the mountain) and old tree trunks (carried over the falls). At the base of the falls, the two streams fuse to become Smith Creek, which flows into and forms Unicoi Lake, the centerpiece of Unicoi State Park.

Spring wildflowers near the lower observation platform include Vasey's trillium, Jack-in-the-pulpit, blue cohosh, and plumed Solomon's seal. Hikers in late summer through fall may see Canada horsebalm, white wood aster, and Joe Pye weed. You may also notice the bright red fruits of Jack-in-the-pulpit.

Continue up the trail a short distance to the upper observation platform. As you cross Smith Creek on a second footbridge, listen to the roar of the water as it tumbles over the boulder-strewn stream. If you're hiking in autumn, look for the yellow flower clusters of witch hazel. You may also notice galls, shaped like a witch's hat, on the upper surface of the leaves.

As you walk up the wooden steps to the upper viewing platform, you may notice various spring wildflowers, including foamflower, Vasey's trillium, black cohosh, plumed Solomon's seal, and giant chickweed.

A large healthy eastern hemlock grows alongside the upper viewing platform, a welcome sight since most hemlocks in the region have been killed by hemlock woolly adelgids in recent years.

Just to the right of the hemlock are two Carolina silverbell trees—look for the nodding, white, bell-shaped flowers in spring and the pod-like winged fruits in summer to fall. Other conspicuous plants include wild hydrangea, orange jewelweed, and pokeweed.

In the spray cliff community, look for the flowers of golden ragwort, brook lettuce, and rosebay rhododendron in late spring–early summer. White wood aster and Canada horsebalm bloom in summer and early fall.

Relax and enjoy the scenery at this turnaround point.

Options. If you're up for more hiking (or simply want to escape the crowds), the Smith Creek Trail departs from the lower observation deck and continues 4.6 miles over Hickory Nut Ridge on a pleasant forested trail to the Unicoi State Park campground. If you don't want to hike the full distance, consider hiking a portion of it before backtracking to the Anna Ruby FallsTrail.

29 / ANNA RUBY FALLS: WHAT TO LOOK FOR

Spring

Doll's eyes, White baneberry	*Actaea pachypoda*	p. 213
Tag alder	*Alnus serrulata*	NI
Wood anemone	*Anemone quinquefolia*	p. 209
Jack-in-the-pulpit	*Arisaema triphyllum*	p. 241
Sweet shrub	*Calycanthus floridus*	p. 241
Broadleaf toothwort	*Cardamine diphylla*	NI
Blue cohosh	*Caulophyllum thalictroides*	p. 242
Robin's plantain	*Erigeron pulchellus*	p. 216
Showy orchis	*Galearis spectabilis*	p. 234
Mountain doghobble	*Leucothoe fontanesiana*	p. 213
Plumed Solomon's seal	*Maianthemum racemosum*	p. 216
Solomon's seal	*Polygonatum biflorum*	p. 217
Yellow mandarin	*Prosartes lanuginosa*	p. 263
Gorge rhododendron, Punctatum	*Rhododendron minus*	p. 237
Bloodroot	*Sanguinaria canadensis*	p. 209
Giant chickweed	*Stellaria pubera*	p. 214
Foamflower	*Tiarella cordifolia*	p. 218
Sweet Betsy	*Trillium cuneatum*	p. 240
Vasey's trillium	*Trillium vaseyi*	p. 244
Perfoliate bellwort	*Uvularia perfoliata*	p. 256
Sweet white violet	*Viola blanda*	p. 219
Halberdleaf yellow violet	*Viola hastata*	p. 254
Yellow woodland violet	*Viola pubescens*	NI
Roundleaf yellow violet	*Viola rotundifolia*	NI
Common blue violet	*Viola sororia*	p. 247
Yellowroot	*Xanthorhiza simplicissima*	p. 240

Spring–Summer

Black cohosh	*Actaea racemosa*	p. 226
Pipsissewa, Striped wintergreen	*Chimaphila maculata*	p. 222
Whorled horsebalm	*Collinsonia verticillata*	NI
Wild hydrangea	*Hydrangea arborescens*	p. 225
Mountain laurel	*Kalmia latifolia*	p. 236
Whorled loosestrife	*Lysimachia quadrifolia*	p. 258
Indian cucumber root	*Medeola virginiana*	p. 264
Brook lettuce	*Micranthes micranthidifolia*	p. 217
Partridge berry	*Mitchella repens*	p. 223
Golden ragwort	*Packera aurea*	p. 257
Virginia creeper	*Parthenocissus quinquefolia*	NI
Rosebay rhododendron	*Rhododendron maximum*	p. 230
Fire pink	*Silene virginica*	p. 267
Poison ivy	*Toxicodendron radicans*	p. 223
Canada violet	*Viola canadensis*	p. 220

Summer

Poke milkweed	*Asclepias exaltata*	p. 228
Wood nettle	*Laportea canadensis*	p. 265

Summer–Fall

Hog peanut	*Amphicarpaea bracteata*	p. 238
Southern harebell	*Campanula divaricata*	p. 250
Canada horsebalm	*Collinsonia canadensis*	p. 261
White wood aster	*Eurybia divaricata*	p. 231
Joe Pye weed	*Eutrochium* species	NI
Roughleaf sunflower	*Helianthus strumosus*	NI
Rock alumroot	*Heuchera villosa*	p. 230
Orange jewelweed	*Impatiens capensis*	p. 268
Pokeweed	*Phytolacca americana*	p. 227
Jumpseed	*Polygonum virginianum*	NI
Heal all	*Prunella vulgaris*	p. 249
Cutleaf coneflower	*Rudbeckia laciniata*	p. 260
Goldenrod	*Solidago* species	NI

Fall

Witch hazel	*Hamamelis virginiana*	p. 262
Canada violet	*Viola canadensis*	p. 220

NI = species not included in the wildflower profiles (Part IV)

30 / Pocket Falls

CROCKFORD-PIGEON MOUNTAIN WILDLIFE MANAGEMENT AREA

Highlights	Exceptional spring wildflowers in a rich cove forest
Flowering season	Mid-February through June
Peak flowering	Mid-March to mid-April
Trail length	About 0.5 mile, partial loop
Trail rating	Easy
Elevation	1,080–1,100 feet
Nearest town	Lafayette, Walker County, Ga.
Contact	Georgia Department of Natural Resources; 706-295-6041; www.georgiawildlife.com
Directions	From Lafayette, take Ga. 193 west for 8 miles to Davis Crossroads. Turn left (south) onto Hog Jowl Road. At the fork just past a church (2.5 miles), continue left on Hog Jowl Road for another 0.2 mile (to the top of a hill) and turn left onto Pocket Road. Continue on this road (which becomes a gravel road) for 1.2 miles to the parking area at the end of the road. GPS: N34 42.75 W85 22.80

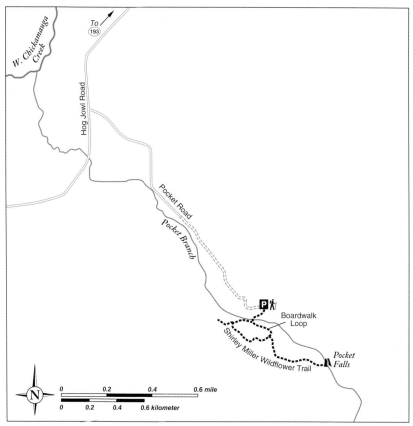

Pocket Falls, Crockford-Pigeon Mountain Wildlife Management Area

Overview   The spring wildflowers on this short easy trail (known as the
Shirley Miller Wildflower Trail) are wonderful. You'll hike through
a rich cove forest with a narrow valley and small creek surrounded
by steep slopes and limestone cliffs on either side. Water, nutrients
(including calcium from the limestone), and soil wash down the
slopes forming a nearly basic (rather than acidic) soil that is moist,
deep, and nutrient-rich. In early spring, the forest floor and lower
slopes are carpeted with an abundance of wildflowers that rivals any
hike described in this book. The first part of the trail is a wheelchair
accessible boardwalk; the second part is a narrow rocky trail that
follows a small creek to Pocket Falls. When the water levels are
up, a small double waterfall cascades down a limestone cliff at the
head of the cove. Because the trail is part of the Crockford-Pigeon
Mountain Wildlife Management Area, you'll need to purchase a
Georgia Outdoor Recreational Pass (GORP) before visiting the site
(see the website listed above for details, including how to purchase
an online pass). Because of the many songbirds that migrate
through this Wildlife Management Area in spring and fall, it has

been designated a Georgia Important Bird Area by the National Audubon Society. Pigeon Mountain was named for the now extinct passenger pigeon that once frequented this area.

The Hike

From the parking area, follow the gravel path (south) between the woods and a field where eastern redbud, flowering dogwood, and hawthorn bloom in spring. A small footbridge leads to a wide boardwalk that forms a loop trail within the narrow valley of this rich cove forest. The boardwalk protects the wildflowers, which in late winter and early spring cover the forest floor. Begin the boardwalk loop by going to the right.

If you're hiking in early March, look for early bloomers such as harbinger of spring (a diminutive plant with tiny white flowers), Carolina spring beauty, and acute-lobed hepatica, along with cutleaf toothwort, yellow trout lily, and bloodroot.

A common shrub along the boardwalk is spicebush—its dense clusters of tiny yellow flowers on leafless stems bloom in early March and its bright red high-fat-content fruits are an important food source for fall migrants, including gray catbird, eastern kingbird, and great crested flycatcher, which eat the pulp and disperse the seeds.

At the beginning of the boardwalk but a little later in the season (mid- to late March), look for the pale blue (to pinkish) tubular flowers of Virginia bluebells intermixed with the showy yellow flowers of celandine poppy and the nodding white flowers of shooting star. Locally common, these three wildflowers are relatively rare in the southern Appalachians.

Other showy wildflowers along the first part of the boardwalk include purple phacelia and woodland phlox, along with foamflower and wild geranium.

As your eyes feast on the wildflower displays, listen for the soothing sounds of the creek. You might also hear the drumming sound of woodpeckers in the distance. A woodpecker uses its bill to rap out a series of notes to attract a mate or to inform other woodpeckers "this is my territory." They also hammer away on dead or diseased trees to carve out nest cavities and to forage on insects beneath the bark.

As you head up the boardwalk, the north-facing slope to your right gets less sunlight and is cooler and moister than the south-facing slope on the left side of the cove. A dense carpet of wildflowers covers the north-facing slope, including larger plants such as blue cohosh, plumed Solomon's seal, and celandine poppy, as well as smaller plants such as rue anemone, Dutchman's britches, and Canada violet. Bright green mosses often cover the rocks and fallen logs at the base of the north-facing slope. The moist, nutrient-rich soil with lots of leaf litter coupled with the adjoining creek provide excellent habitat for salamanders. In fact, rich cove forests in the southern Appalachian mountains are among the world's richest habitats for salamanders.

As you continue up the boardwalk, see if you can spot three early spring-flowering trilliums. Trailing trillium, the most common species, has mottled leaves and purple flowers that lie flat on the ground. Sweet Betsy has similar leaves and flowers but has a more upright growth form. The third species, bent trillium, is readily distinguished by its solid green leaves and white flowers.

Look up into the canopy where trees such as American sycamore, yellow buckeye, sugar maple, white basswood, sweetgum, and tulip tree grow. Two rare trees along the trail are Ohio buckeye and yellowwood. Notice the rope-like stems of wild grape vines, some more than 6 inches across, reaching high into the canopy. Poison ivy also grows here, mainly as a groundcover, but also as a climbing vine.

When the wildflowers are at their peak in early spring and the forest floor is green and lush, the trees and shrubs above are leafless and drab. As the canopy trees and understory species leaf out and shade the forest floor (mid- to late April), many of the spring wildflowers die back and go dormant.

At the far end of the boardwalk, steps descend to a trail that follows the creek upstream to Pocket Falls. This part of the trail is a bit trickier as it's rocky and uneven and can be slippery in places, but it is also great for wildflowers (be sure to stay on the trail to avoid trampling the abundant wildflowers). Look for purple phacelia, yellow mandarin, doll's eyes, and Jack-in-the-pulpit, along with many of the species seen earlier. Closer to the waterfall, mountain stonecrop, red columbine, and purple phacelia grow in rocky areas with little soil, as does the rare walking fern.

A horseshoe-shaped limestone cliff with a steep rock face forms the head of the cove. When the water level is up, a double waterfall cascades down the cliff. In dry periods, the water slows to a trickle. The spray cliff zone is mostly bare rock with patches of moss and algae and flowering plants, including common alumroot.

After enjoying the waterfall, retrace your steps to the boardwalk and go right, keeping an eye out for the pale blue flowers and grass-like leaves of wild hyacinth, an uncommon species largely restricted to calcium-rich soils.

To fully experience the spring flora of this exceptional site, revisit the trail at 2–3 week intervals from late February through May.

Options. Good wildflower displays can be seen along the narrow trail north of the parking area immediately across the little creek and up and over the next couple of ridges toward Bird Gap. A second option—as you leave the parking area and head toward the Shirley Miller Wildflower Trail, take the horse trail that goes uphill to the left around the gate to see additional spring wildflowers.

30 / POCKET FALLS: WHAT TO LOOK FOR

Spring

Doll's eyes, White baneberry	*Actaea pachypoda*	p. 213
Acute-lobed hepatica	*Anemone acutiloba*	p. 207
Eastern columbine	*Aquilegia canadensis*	NI
Jack-in-the-pulpit	*Arisaema triphyllum*	p. 241
Wild hyacinth	*Camassia scilloides*	NI
Cutleaf toothwort	*Cardamine concatenata*	p. 210
Blue cohosh	*Caulophyllum thalictroides*	p. 242
Carolina spring beauty	*Claytonia caroliniana*	p. 234
Bearcorn, Squawroot	*Conopholis americana*	p. 255
Squirrel corn	*Dicentra canadensis*	NI
Dutchman's britches	*Dicentra cucullaria*	p. 208
Harbinger of spring	*Erigenia bulbosa*	NI
Yellow trout lily	*Erythronium americanum*	NI
Strawberry bush, Hearts-a-bustin'	*Euonymus americanus*	p. 264
Wild geranium	*Geranium maculatum*	p. 235
Broadleaf waterleaf	*Hydrophyllum canadense*	NI
Dwarf crested iris	*Iris cristata*	p. 247
Spicebush	*Lindera benzoin*	p. 263

Plumed Solomon's seal	*Maianthemum racemosum*	p. 216
Virginia bluebell	*Mertensia virginica*	NI
Bishop's cap	*Mitella diphylla*	NI
Pennywort	*Obolaria virginica*	NI
Sweet anise	*Osmorhiza longistylis*	NI
Violet wood sorrel	*Oxalis violacea*	NI
Lousewort, Wood betony	*Pedicularis canadensis*	p. 255
Purple phacelia	*Phacelia bipinnatifida*	p. 243
Mayapple	*Podophyllum peltatum*	p. 208
Solomon's seal	*Polygonatum biflorum*	p. 217
Eastern shooting star	*Primula meadia*	NI
Yellow mandarin	*Prosartes lanuginosa*	p. 263
Wild azalea, Pinxterflower	*Rhododendron periclymenoides*	NI
Dewberry	*Rubus flagellaris*	NI
Lyreleaf sage	*Salvia lyrata*	NI
Bloodroot	*Sanguinaria canadensis*	p. 209
Mountain stonecrop	*Sedum ternatum*	p. 218
Giant chickweed	*Stellaria pubera*	p. 214
Celandine poppy	*Stylophorum diphyllum*	NI
Rue anemone	*Thalictrum thalictroides*	p. 211
Foamflower	*Tiarella cordifolia*	p. 218
Sweet Betsy	*Trillium cuneatum*	p. 240
Trailing trillium	*Trillium decumbens*	NI
Bent trillium, White trillium	*Trillium flexipes*	NI
Large-flowered bellwort	*Uvularia grandiflora*	NI
Mapleleaf viburnum	*Viburnum acerifolium*	NI
Yellow woodland violet	*Viola pubescens*	NI
Common blue violet	*Viola sororia*	p. 247

Spring–Summer

Fourleaf milkweed	*Asclepias quadrifolia*	NI
Common alumroot	*Heuchera americana*	NI
Wild hydrangea	*Hydrangea arborescens*	p. 225
Roundleaf ragwort	*Packera obovata*	NI
Hairy beardtongue	*Penstemon canescens*	p. 245
Woodland phlox	*Phlox divaricata*	p. 248
Smooth phlox	*Phlox glaberrima*	NI
Blue-eyed grass	*Sisyrinchium angustifolium*	NI
Meadow parsnip	*Thaspium barbinode*	NI
Poison ivy	*Toxicodendron radicans*	p. 223
Canada violet	*Viola canadensis*	p. 220

NI = species not included in the wildflower profiles (Part IV)

WILDFLOWERING ALONG THE
LITTLE RIVER TRAIL
Names bloom around us,
singing the way through what's
    waiting
alongside the riverbank:
fairy wand, solomon's
seal, rue anemone,
snowy phacelia
and everywhere
trillium
trillium
trillium.

—Kathryn Stripling Byer
Cullowhee, North Carolina

PART IV
Wildflower
Profiles

The wildflowers profiled are arranged by flower color into seven groups: white, pink to lavender, purple to maroon, blue, yellow, yellowish-green, and orange to red. Within each flower color group, the species are listed sequentially by flowering time (for example, species that start flowering in February are listed before those that begin to flower in March). Of the 125 wildflowers profiled, 110 are herbaceous (nonwoody) and 15 are shrubs.

White Flowers

Epigaea repens
Trailing Arbutus
Ericaceae (Heath family)

Anemone acutiloba
Acute-Lobed Hepatica
Ranunculaceae (Buttercup family)

Early flowering evergreen herb 3–6 in. tall with a short underground stem (rhizome). *Leaves:* Clusters of basal *3-lobed leaves with sharply pointed tips*, hence the common name. *Flowers:* Nearly 1 in. wide; 5–12 petal-like sepals vary in color, white, pink, lavender, purple, or blue; numerous stamens and pistils; flowers solitary on elongate hairy stalks. Feb.–April. *Fruits:* Achenes. *Habitat/range:* Moist forests. Common. Widespread in eastern North America. *Hepatica acutiloba*.

Similar species: Round-lobed hepatica (*A. americana*) has *rounded* rather than pointed leaf lobes. Feb.–Apr. Moist forests. Common. *H. americana*.

Notes: Early European herbalists developed the "Doctrine of Signatures" believing herbs that resemble the shape of a human body part can be used to treat ailments of that body part (a similar belief was held by Native American and Asian cultures). Because the lobed leaves of hepatica resemble a human liver, it was traditionally used in the treatment of liver ailments. Hepaticas are one of our earliest blooming spring wildflowers.

Prostrate evergreen with reddish-brown stems rooting at intervals, forming *small dense patches. Leaves:* Leathery, ovate to oblong, 2–3 in. long, rounded or heart shaped at base. *Flowers:* Fragrant, white to pink, with 5 small petal lobes flaring abruptly from a short tube; in small clusters often hidden under thc leaves. Feb.–May. *Fruits:* Berry-like capsules. *Habitat/range:* Variety of dry to somewhat moist acidic forests. Common. Widespread in eastern North America.

Notes: Rarely exceeding 6 inches in height, this mat-forming evergreen occurs on acidic soils in woods and clearings, including road banks and trailside edges. Flowering occurs in early spring from buds produced the previous fall. Bumblebees pollinate the tubular white-to-pink flowers. The pea-sized fruits split at maturity, exposing tiny brown seeds embedded in a sticky white pulp that has a distinctly sweet taste. Ants actively harvest the sticky tissue and inadvertently disperse the seeds as they carry the pulp back to their nests. Also known as mayflower, trailing arbutus is said to be the first plant the Pilgrims saw in flower after enduring their very first winter in the New World.

Podophyllum peltatum
Mayapple
Berberidaceae (Barberry family)

Dicentra cucullaria
Dutchman's Britches
Fumariaceae (Fumitory family)

Early spring perennial 4–12 in. tall from a short rootstalk. *Leaves:* Long-stalked basal leaves deeply divided into *narrow leaf segments*. *Flowers:* Raceme of *dangling white flowers* with yellow petal tips extending above the leaves; each flower with 2 conspicuous, *upward-pointing nectar spurs*. Mar.–Apr. *Fruits:* Capsules. *Habitat/range:* Rich moist forests, especially in rich cove forests. Occasional. Primarily a northern species of the eastern and central United States, south in the mountains to Georgia and Arkansas.

Similar species: Squirrel corn (*D. canadensis*) has fragrant white flowers with 2 rounded nectar spurs that appear *heart shaped*. Mar.–Apr. Rich woods. Occasional.

Notes: A spring ephemeral, plants emerge and flower in early spring and then die back after the canopy trees leaf out. Long-tongued bumblebees pollinate the flowers and ants disperse the seeds. Alkaloids in the foliage deter most animals from feeding on the foliage. The upside-down flowers resemble a pair of old-fashioned knickers hanging out to dry, hence the common name.

Perennial herb up to 18 in. tall from a creeping rhizome that forms *large colonies*. *Leaves:* Newly emerged leaves look like *unfurling umbrellas*; expanded leaves are deeply lobed and up to 12 in. across, 1–2 per stem. *Flowers:* Solitary, nodding, about 2 in. across with *waxy white petals* and numerous yellow stamens, fragrant; often partially hidden under the leaves. Mar.–Apr. *Fruits:* Yellow, egg-shaped berry, 1–2 in. long. *Habitat/range:* Rich moist woods and meadows. Common. Widespread in eastern North America.

Notes: Pollinators (mainly bumblebees) infrequently visit mayapple's nectarless flowers. Mayapple plants growing near species with nectar-rich flowers, such as lousewort, are more likely to be visited by bumblebees, increasing pollination success and the number of flowers that produce fruit (demonstrating that the proximity of one plant species can promote the reproductive success of another). While ripe fruits are edible, all other parts of mayapple are highly poisonous to humans if ingested. Long known as a medicinal plant, compounds derived from mayapple have shown promise in treating certain types of cancer.

Sanguinaria canadensis
Bloodroot
Papaveraceae (Poppy family)

Early spring-flowering perennial herb to
6 in. tall from a short thick rhizome that
oozes a *bright orange-red juice* when cut.
Leaves: Solitary, long-petioled basal leaf
with a deeply lobed margin; the leaf continues to expand after flowering, reaching a width up to 8 in. *Flowers:* Showy,
1–2 in. across, with *8–24 white petals* and
numerous golden stamens; each flower
blooms on a separate leafless stalk partially enclosed by an upright expanding
blue-green leaf. Mar.–Apr. *Fruits:* Elongated green capsules *pointed at both
ends. Habitat/range:* Variety of moist
nutrient-rich forests. Common. Patchily
distributed in eastern and central North
America.

    Notes: Wildflower enthusiasts wel-
come bloodroot's showy white flowers
in early spring. In favorable sites, a single
plant can produce as many as 10 flowers
(and leaves). Native Americans used the
bright orange-red pigment (sanguinarine) from the rhizomes as face paint and
as a dye for baskets and clothing. Due to
its antibiotic properties, sanguinarine
is used as an antiplaque agent and as a
supplement in cattle feed.

Anemone quinquefolia
Wood Anemone
Ranunculaceae (Buttercup family)

Small (4–8 in. tall) perennial herb that
emerges from a slender rhizome in early
spring and then dies back and goes dormant by early summer. *Leaves:* A single
basal and several stem leaves are deeply
divided into 3 or 5 lobes, each lobe
deeply notched and sharply toothed.
Flowers: Solitary, white, about 1 in.
across with 5 or more *petal-like sepals.*
Mar.–May. *Fruits:* Small woolly achenes.
Habitat/range: Nutrient-rich, moist soil,
open woods, clearings, and streamsides.
Common. Widespread in eastern North
America.

    Notes: Spring ephemerals such as
wood anemone emerge in early spring
and then die back as the canopy trees leaf
out, leaving no sign of the plant until the
following spring. A recent study showed
that wood anemone flowers about 15
days earlier than it did in the early 1970s,
which apparently reflects warmer spring-
time temperatures associated with climate change. The light sensitive flowers
close in cloudy weather and at night, an
adaptation that protects the delicate reproductive parts when pollinators aren't
likely to be flying.

Cardamine concatenata
Cutleaf Toothwort
Brassicaceae (Mustard family)

Perennial herb 8–16 in. tall that spreads laterally via rhizomes forming small colonies. *Leaves: Single whorl of 3 stem leaves*, each deeply 3-parted into narrow segments which are further deeply lobed or toothed; similar basal leaves typically emerge after flowering. *Flowers:* Small white-to-pinkish cross-shaped flowers in terminal clusters. Mar.–May. *Fruits:* Elongated pods. *Habitat/range:* Rich moist woods. Common. Eastern North America. *C. laciniata, Dentaria laciniata.*

Similar species: Broadleaf toothwort (*C. diphylla*) has a *single pair of stem leaves* each divided into 3 broad ovate segments with *prominent veins*; basal leaves similar, *evergreen.* Apr.–May. Rich wooded slopes and ravines. Common. *D. diphylla.*

Notes: Like other spring ephemerals, cutleaf toothwort emerges, flowers, and fruits in early spring and then dies back just a few weeks later, as the canopy leafs out and the forest floor becomes shaded. The remaining 45–48 weeks of the year, the plant persists underground as a rhizome. Cutleaf toothwort was once a favorite spring herb of mountain folk because of the radish-like, peppery taste of the rhizome.

Chamaelirium luteum
Fairywand, Devil's Bit
Melanthiaceae (Bunchflower family)

Perennial herb with a basal rosette of evergreen leaves and a single flower stalk with either male or female flowers; male plants up to 2½ ft. tall, females to 4 ft. tall. *Leaves:* Large, spoon-shaped at base of plant, the stem leaves much smaller and fewer. *Flowers: A wand-like terminal cluster of small white flowers.* Mar.–May. *Fruits:* Capsules. *Habitat/range:* Moist-to-dry open woods. Common. Eastern North America.

Notes: Fairywand is dioecious (meaning male and female flowers occur on separate plants). Male flowering stalks are initially erect, but the tip usually droops with age. Female flowering stalks are erect with greenish-white flowers. Successful fruit set depends on insects moving pollen from male to female plants as they forage for nectar or pollen. Due to greater resource depletion associated with maturing fruits, female plants flower less frequently and have higher mortality rates than males. As a result, most populations have a skewed sex ratio with more males than females.

Phacelia fimbriata
Fringed Phacelia
Hydrophyllaceae (Waterleaf family)

Annual 4–16 in. tall, with weak hairy stems forming dense colonies. *Leaves:* Alternate, lower leaves with petioles, upper leaves sessile, *pinnately lobed*, up to 1½ in. long. *Flowers: White, bowl-shaped*, about ½ in. wide with 5 *deeply fringed petal lobes*. Mar.–May. *Fruits:* Capsules. *Habitat/range:* Moist forests, floodplains. Uncommon, but locally abundant. Southern Appalachian Mountains from Virginia south to Georgia.

Similar species: Miami mist (*P. purshii*) has deeply fringed *pale lavender or blue flowers* with a white center. Apr.–June. Moist woods, meadows, and roadsides. Occasional.

Notes: Numerous annuals grow in fields, roadsides, and other disturbed habitats but few occur in deciduous forests. An interesting exception is fringed phacelia, an annual that germinates in the fall, produces a rosette of overwintering leaves, and then flowers, fruits, and dies in the spring. Fall germination gives it a head start on vegetative growth, which enables it to complete its life cycle in the spring. Because dense patches of flowering fringed phacelia resemble light coverings of newly fallen snow, it's sometimes called snow phacelia.

Thalictrum thalictroides
Rue Anemone
Ranunculaceae (Buttercup family)

Slender perennial herb 3–8 in. tall from tuberous black roots. *Leaves:* Stem leaves opposite, with wiry stalks and 3 leaflets, each with 3 shallow, rounded lobes. *Flowers:* In umbels with 1 central and 1–4 lateral flowers; *5–10 showy white to pinkish petal-like sepals* surround a cluster of pistils and stamens. Mar.–May. *Fruits:* Achenes. *Habitat/range:* Moist forests, floodplains, and stream banks. Common. Widespread in eastern North America. *Anemonella thalictroides.*

Notes: Rue anemone may look delicate, but it's a tough plant that blooms through hard frosts in early spring and recovers readily after being stepped on by people and animals. One of the earliest blooming spring wildflowers, rue anemone's flowers are also long lasting, remaining open for up to 2 weeks, increasing the opportunity for successful pollination at a time of year when inclement weather often limits pollinator activity.

Trillium catesbaei
Catesby's Trillium
Trilliaceae (Trillium family)

Erect perennial herb 8–20 in. tall from a short, thick rhizome. *Leaves: Uniformly green*, ovate to widely elliptical, 3–6 in. long. *Flowers: 3 petals white to pinkish rose*, recurved, often with a wavy margin; prominent yellow anthers surround a *greenish-white ovary; flower stalk bent downward, usually below the leaves.* Mar.–May. *Fruits:* Berry-like capsules. *Habitat/range:* Moist to relatively dry forests. Common in the lower mountains. From North Carolina south to Georgia.

Notes: Trilliums are easily recognized by their single whorl of 3 leaves with a solitary terminal flower. Individual flowers remain open for up to 3 weeks, increasing the opportunity for successful pollination and subsequent fruit set. Queen bumblebees visit the nectarless flowers for pollen and are thought to be the primary pollinators. Following pollination, or perhaps simply with age, the flower color changes from white to pale pink or deep rose. Trilliums are a preferred food plant of white-tailed deer— a single bite can defoliate an entire plant. Areas with abundant deer typically have fewer trilliums.

Fragaria virginiana
Wild Strawberry
Rosaceae (Rose family)

Low-growing perennial that spreads by *runners. Leaves:* Long slender stalks with 3 coarsely toothed leaflets. *Flowers: White, with 5 petals*; in flat clusters of about 10 flowers, usually only one flower per inflorescence open at a time. Mar.–June. *Fruits:* Achenes in pits on the surface of a *roundish edible strawberry*, sweet and juicy. *Habitat/range:* Fields, roadsides, and woodland borders. Common. Eastern North America.

Notes: Wild strawberry spreads by seeds and above ground runners, often forming dense patches in open well-lit areas. In shaded areas, wild strawberry grows less vigorously and flowers infrequently. Stunted plants occur at high elevations, including grassy areas along the Blue Ridge Parkway. The open bowl-shaped flowers attract a variety of insects but bees are the primary pollinators. The fleshy red fruits are smaller but sweeter than the cultivated strawberry sold in stores. Numerous songbirds as well as small mammals consume the fleshy fruits and disperse the tiny seeds. The leaves can be brewed into a tea rich in vitamin C.

Actaea pachypoda
Doll's Eyes, White Baneberry
Ranunculaceae (Buttercup family)

Aromatic perennial herb to 3 ft. tall with smooth stems. *Leaves:* Large, 2–3 times compound with long petioles and numerous sharply toothed leaflets. *Flowers:* Small white in a single short compact raceme that extends above the leaves. Apr.–May. *Fruits: White berries* with a prominent *black spot* (the "doll's eye") born on *thick red stalks. Habitat/range:* Moist rich forests, ravines, and stream banks. Common. Widespread in eastern North America.

Notes: This is a plant that gets your attention twice–lacy clusters of white flowers open in spring, and white berries ripen on bright red stalks in late summer and fall. The numerous stamens give the flowers a distinctly feathery appearance. The nectarless flowers have a citrus-like fragrance that attracts bees, flies, and beetles that inadvertently pollinate the flowers as they forage for pollen. Birds and small mammals consume the berry-like fruits and disperse the seeds in their droppings, but the berries are toxic to humans, as indicated by the common name white baneberry.

Leucothoe fontanesiana
Mountain Doghobble
Ericaceae (Heath family)

Sprawling evergreen shrub 2–5 ft. tall, with *arching stems* forming dense thickets. *Leaves:* Alternate, shiny, and leathery, 3–6 in. long, elliptic, tapering to a long point, with sharply toothed margins. *Flowers:* White, *fragrant*, urn-shaped, in dense clusters (racemes) that *hang from the leaf axils.* Apr.–May. *Fruits:* Persistent capsules. *Habitat/range:* Moist acidic soils, often associated with streams and ravines. Common. Restricted to the southern Appalachian Mountains from Virginia south to Georgia.

Notes: Dense thickets "hobble" the progress of hunting dogs, hence the name doghobble. The shiny evergreen leaves have a waxy coating that reflects light and reduces water loss, a beneficial trait as doghobble is susceptible to drought stress. The dense clusters of small fragrant flowers vary in odor from cloyingly sweet to musky. The evergreen foliage, interesting flowers, and gracefully arching stems make it an attractive garden plant in moist areas. The Cherokee used the leaves to treat rheumatism.

Stellaria pubera
Giant Chickweed
Caryophyllaceae (Pink family)

An erect weak-stemmed perennial 4–16 in. tall, arising from a taproot. *Leaves:* Opposite, sessile, elliptic, up to 3 in. long. *Flowers:* Numerous *white* flowers up to ½ in. wide, *star-like*; the 5 petals cleft nearly to the base, making them appear to be 10; *sepals shorter than the petals.* Apr.–June. *Fruits:* Capsules. *Habitat/range:* Moist forests. Common. Eastern United States.

  Similar species: Tennessee chickweed (*S. corei*) has *sepals equal to or extending beyond the petals.* Apr.–June. Rich forests and seeps. Occasional. Common chickweed (*S. media*) is an introduced weedy species with smaller leaves and flowers and weaker stems. Flowers appear almost all months of the year. Lawns, gardens, and other *disturbed habitats.* Common.

  Notes: A poor competitor, giant chickweed typically occurs in relatively open areas on the forest floor. The short, relatively small-leaved flowering shoots of spring are replaced by taller, more vigorous, nonflowering shoots in summer. Small bees and flies pollinate the flowers and various songbirds eat the seeds, hence the common name "chickweed."

Trillium grandiflorum
Large-Flowered Trillium
Trilliaceae (Trillium family)

Upright perennial herb 6–20 in. tall. *Leaves: Uniformly green*, sessile, broadly ovate to rhombic, 3–6 in. long, in whorls of 3. *Flowers: Large (2–4 in. across)*, solitary, *funnel-shaped*, on an erect or gently arching stalk above the leaves; the 3 white petals with wavy margins *turn various shades of pink with age.* Apr.–May. *Fruits:* Pale green fleshy capsules. *Habitat/range:* Moist nutrient-rich woods, usually on nearly basic soils. Common. Eastern North America.

  Notes: One of our showiest and most common trilliums, large-flowered trillium forms large colonies that emerge from underground rhizomes in early spring and die back by late summer. The scentless flowers attract and reward insect pollinators (bees and flies) with both nectar and pollen. Trilliums develop slowly (it takes about 7 years for a young plant to produce its first flower), but individuals may persist for more than 40 years in favorable sites.

Diphylleia cymosa
Umbrella Leaf
Berberidaceae (Barberry family)

Perennial herb 1–3 ft. tall from a thick rhizome. *Leaves: Large* (12–24 in. wide) with a stout leaf stalk attached in the center (*peltate*); the lobes coarsely toothed and pointed; vegetative plants have a single leaf, flowering plants have two. *Flowers: White*, in a small cluster at the tip of a long stalk that extends above the leaves. Apr.–June. *Fruits: Dark blue berries on bright red fruiting stalks. Habitat/range:* Seepage areas and small streams, moist forested slopes. Occasional. Southern Appalachians from Virginia to Georgia.

Notes: The large surface area and horizontal orientation of the umbrella-like leaves make them particularly efficient at capturing the limited amount of light that reaches the forest floor in summer. The showy dark blue berries on red stalks attract birds and small mammals that eat the pulp and disperse the seeds. Alkaloids from umbrella leaf are used in the treatment of various kinds of cancer.

Cymophyllus fraseriana
Fraser's Sedge
Cyperaceae (Sedge family)

Perennial herb with distinctive *evergreen clumps of basal leaves* that arise from a short thick rhizome. *Leaves: Strap-like*, 1–2 in. wide and 8–20 in. long with wavy margins and prominent, parallel veins. *Flowers: Terminal spike, white and showy*, with clusters of male (pollen-bearing) flowers at the tip and female (pistil-bearing) flowers below. Apr.–June. *Fruits:* Single achenes enclosed in inflated sacs, about 20–30 sacs per spike. *Habitat/ range:* On cool moist slopes and stream banks. Rare. Appalachian Mountains from Pennsylvania south to Georgia.

Notes: Fraser's sedge is an unusual sedge with its showy white flowers that are insect pollinated. In contrast, almost all other sedges have nondescript wind-pollinated flowers. One typically encounters this rare species in mature or old-growth forests rather than in previously disturbed (younger) forests. White-tailed deer graze the foliage, flowers, and fruits, and disperse its seeds. Nonflowering plants are sometimes mistaken for lilies because of their broad, flat, strap-shaped leaves.

Erigeron pulchellus
Robin's Plantain
Asteraceae (Sunflower family)

Hairy perennial herb 8–24 in. tall with daisy-like flowers; spreads by runners, forming colonies. *Leaves: Basal rosette of spoon-shaped leaves* 1–5 in. long; stem leaves much smaller, progressively reduced upward. *Flowers:* Heads with 50–100 *white-to-lilac ray flowers* and *yellow disk flowers*; 2–5 flower heads at tip of a *hairy stem.* Apr.–early June. *Fruits:* Ribbed achenes. *Habitat/range:* Moist open woods, woodland borders, road banks, trailside margins. Common. Widespread in the eastern and central United States.

Notes: Unlike most members of the sunflower family, Robin's plantain flowers in spring rather than summer or fall. Its daisy-like flower heads consist of numerous tiny flowers with showy narrow white or lavender ray flowers on the outer rim and yellow disk flowers in the center. In a single visit, an insect visitor can pollinate dozens of flowers within a single head. Species of *Erigeron* are sometimes called fleabane because they help deter flies, gnats, and other insect pests. Dried plants were once used as stuffing material in mattresses to reduce the incidence of fleabites.

Maianthemum racemosum
Plumed Solomon's Seal
Ruscaceae (Ruscus family)

Perennial herb 1–3 ft. tall with erect unbranched *arching stems. Leaves:* Alternate, in two rows, sessile, elliptical, 3–6 in. long with conspicuous *parallel veins. Flowers:* Plumes of tiny white flowers in *dense terminal clusters,* 2–6 in. long. Apr.–June. *Fruits:* Berries green with coppery splotches ripening to a *deep translucent red. Habitat/range:* Moist, mostly deciduous forests. Common. Widespread in eastern North America. *Smilacina racemosa.*

Similar species: Solomon's seal (*Polygonatum biflorum*) has unbranched arching stems with two rows of leaves, but its flowers and fruits *hang beneath the stem.* May–June. Various dry to moist deciduous forests. Common.

Notes: Plumed Solomon's seal spreads by seed and branching rhizomes that give rise to multiple shoots that form discrete colonies. The flowers depend on insects moving pollen between colonies (cross-pollination) for successful seed production. The seeds take two years to complete germination—the seedling roots emerge in the first spring and in the second spring, the first leaf emerges, completing germination. The fruits are edible but mildly cathartic.

Polygonatum biflorum
Solomon's Seal
Ruscaceae (Ruscus family)

Micranthes micranthidifolia
Brook Lettuce
Saxifragaceae (Saxifrage family)

Perennial herb with leaves clustered near the base and upright flowering stems up to 30 in. tall. *Leaves:* 3–8 in. long, oblanceolate, with *sharply toothed margins.* *Flowers:* Flowering stalk branched above middle, forming a large open inflorescence of tiny (about ¼ in. wide) white flowers with a *yellow spot at the base of each petal.* Apr.–June. *Fruits:* Capsules about ¼ in. long. *Habitat/range:* Mountain brooks, seepage slopes, and spray cliffs. Occasional. Southern and central Appalachian Mountains, from Pennsylvania south to Georgia. *Saxifraga micranthidifolia.*

Similar species: Cliff saxifrage (*Hydatica petiolaris*) has *coarsely toothed* leaf margins, and white *irregular* flowers about ½ in. across; the 3 upper petals each have 2 spots of yellow whereas the 2 slightly smaller lower petals lack spots. Apr.–Aug. Rock outcrops and rocky seeps. Common. *S. michauxii, Micranthes petiolaris.*

Notes: The basal leaves can be used as a substitute for lettuce in salads.

Perennial herb with 1–6 ft. long smooth unbranched arching stems from a rhizome with knobby swellings. *Leaves:* Alternate, in 2 *rows*, elliptic to oval, with prominent parallel veins. *Flowers:* Tubular, greenish-white, *dangle beneath the stem.* May–June. *Fruits:* Blue-black berries hang below the stem. *Habitat/range:* Moist to dry woods. Common. Widespread in eastern and central North America.

Similar species: Plumed Solomon's seal (*Maianthemum racemosum*) has unbranched arching stems with two rows of leaves, but flowers and fruits are *clustered at the stem tip.* Apr.–June. Various moist deciduous forests. Common.

Notes: The long arching stems emerge in spring from a perennial rhizome running horizontally beneath the soil surface. The position of the narrow bell-shaped flowers beneath the leafy stem provides shelter from the damaging effects of wind, rain, and frost. Bumblebees pollinate the flowers in spring, birds consume the fruits and disperse the seeds in fall, and grazing by white-tailed deer reduces flower and fruit production. The graceful growth form of this plant adds interest to woodland gardens.

Sedum ternatum
Mountain Stonecrop
Crassulaceae (Stonecrop family)

Low mat-forming perennial with creeping stems and several erect vegetative shoots along with a single flowering shoot with a spreading inflorescence consisting of *3 distinct branches*. *Leaves:* Small rounded fleshy leaves in *whorls of 3*; the leaves of the erect flowering shoots are shorter, elliptic, and alternate; the lower larger whorled leaves are evergreen. *Flowers:* Small, with *4 narrow white petals* and *black tipped anthers* crowded on the upper side of the three-branched inflorescence. *Fruits:* Small pointed follicles. *Habitat/range:* Moist rocky slopes and bottomlands, shaded rock outcrops, fallen logs, and tree bases. Common. Most of the eastern United States.

Notes: Sedums have thick succulent leaves and star-like flowers with 5 (sometimes 4) narrow sharp-pointed petals. The water stored in the succulent leaves helps it survive periods of summer drought. Their generally small size and slow growth rate make sedums a poor competitor, so they typically grow in areas where the vegetation is relatively sparse. Sedums make an attractive groundcover in sunny gardens.

Tiarella cordifolia
Foamflower
Saxifragaceae (Saxifrage family)

Upright perennial herb 4–20 in. tall. *Leaves: Heart-shaped, basal leaves* with 3–5 lobes, unevenly toothed margins. *Flowers:* Numerous small white flowers with conspicuous *orange anthers* in a terminal raceme. Apr.–June. *Fruits:* Two-parted capsules. *Habitat/range:* Moist forests and stream banks. Common. Widespread in Eastern North America.

Notes: This spring-blooming wildflower is easily recognized by its open raceme of white flowers (with conspicuously orange pollen) at the tip of a hairy, leafless stalk. The leaves of foamflower have a relatively high photosynthetic rate in spring before the canopy trees leaf out and in fall after leaves drop. In contrast, photosynthesis and growth are very low in summer. Loss of the forest canopy (by logging or natural processes) adversely affects foamflower as shallow roots make plants susceptible to drought stress under an open canopy. Bitter-tasting tannins deter most animals from feeding on the leaves and stems. Foamflower is easily grown in moist woodland gardens.

Viola blanda
Sweet White Violet
Violaceae (Violet family)

Trillium undulatum
Painted Trillium
Trilliaceae (Trillium family)

Upright perennial herb 8–20 in. tall, often in small, scattered clumps. *Leaves:* A whorl of 3 ovate leaves, uniformly green, broadly rounded at the base, long-pointed at the tip; each with a distinct petiole. *Flowers:* Solitary, *stalked*, upright flower with 3 showy white petals with *wavy margins*; each petal with a *reddish V-shaped mark* near its base, hence the name painted trillium. Apr.–June. *Fruits:* Red berry-like capsules. *Habitat/range:* Cool, moist environments with acidic soils; mostly at high elevations. Common. Northeastern United States and Canada, south in the mountains to Georgia.

Notes: Painted trillium generally grows in partially shaded habitats, ben-efiting by cooler temperatures under a leafy canopy. Newly emerged shoots exposed to a warm spell in early spring expand so rapidly that plants not evident one day can be in flower the next. The showy flowers are largely self-pollinating, resulting in high fruit set. Painted trillium is best enjoyed in the wild, as it's difficult to grow in the garden.

Stemless perennial herb that spreads by stolons forming dense mats. *Leaves:* Basal, dark green with a satiny sheen, on long stalks; broadly heart shaped with small rounded teeth, short-pointed at apex. *Flowers:* White, mildly fragrant, 2 *upper petals twisted and bent backward*, 3 lower petals usually purple-veined near base, flower stalks typically reddish. Apr.–June. *Fruits:* Ovoid capsules. *Habitat/ range:* Moist woods. Frequent. Wide-spread in eastern North America.

Similar species: Northern White Violet (*V. macloskeyi* ssp. *pallens*) has smaller flowers (petals less than ½ in. long), with *upper petals not twisted*. The flower stalks green; leaves with a *blunt apex and lack-ing a satiny sheen*. Apr.–July. Moist habi-tats including streamsides, seeps, cool shaded woods. Occasional.

Notes: The emergence of leaves and flowers in early spring wildflowers is trig-gered by soil temperature. While the time of emergence varies from year to year, it always precedes when canopy trees leaf out. The latter is because the buds of woodland wildflowers are located close to the soil surface where temperatures are warmer than in the air above.

Viola canadensis
Canada Violet
Violaceae (Violet family)

Perennial herb with *erect leafy stems* 8–16 in. tall. *Leaves:* Narrowly to broadly heart shaped with long-pointed tips, 2–4 in. long. *Flowers: White with a yellow center*, purple-veined near base, fading to pink-purple with age; on long stalks from the leaf axils. Apr.–July (and sporadically in Aug.–Sept.). *Fruits:* Capsules. *Habitat/ range:* Moist woodlands, especially cove forests. Common. Widespread in eastern and central North America.

Notes: Canada violet commonly occurs in cove forests and other habitats with moist nutrient-rich soils. Like most violets, it produces open (chasmogamous) flowers that are potentially cross-pollinated and small bud-like (cleistogamous) flowers that never open and are self-pollinating. The chasmogamous flowers have white petals with a yellow center and purple veins (nectar guides) that attract sporadic visits by bees, hoverflies, and skipper butterflies. If cross-pollination fails to occur, delayed self-pollination can occur when stigmas curve down and contact pollen grains that have fallen from the anthers onto the lower petals. Wild turkeys, mourning doves, and white-footed mice eat the seeds.

Hydatica petiolaris
Cliff Saxifrage
Saxifragaceae (Saxifrage family)

Perennial herb with a *basal rosette* of greenish-red leaves and a *widely branched flower stalk* up to 20 in. tall. *Leaves:* 2–6 in. long, obovate with *coarsely toothed margins. Flowers:* An open inflorescence of white *irregular flowers* about ½ in. across with 5 petals (3 upper slightly larger petals each with 2 spots of yellow and 2 lower petals lacking spots); orange anthers. Apr.–Aug. *Fruits:* Capsules. *Habitat/range:* Rock outcrops and rocky seeps. Common. Southern Appalachian Mountains from Virginia south to Georgia. *Saxifraga michauxii, Micranthes petiolaris.*

Similar species: Brook Lettuce (*Micranthes micranthidifolia*) has regular flowers with *5 tiny white petals each spotted with yellow.* Apr.–June. Mountain brooks, seepage slopes, and spray cliffs. Infrequent. *S. micranthidifolia.*

Notes: This common high-elevation rock outcrop species often grows on dry rock surfaces where plants are exposed to intense sunlight and desiccating winds. The prostrate leaves provide protection from drying winds and the succulent leaves, with their waxy surfaces, provide moisture during periods of drought. Cliff saxifrage is a nice addition to rock gardens.

Sambucus canadensis
Common Elderberry
Adoxaceae (Moschatel family)

A deciduous multi-stemmed shrub with *smooth bark and warty lenticels*; twigs are brittle with a *white pith*. *Leaves:* Opposite, pinnately compound usually with 7–9 leaflets and fine toothed margins. *Flowers:* Numerous, small white flowers in *flat-topped to slightly convex terminal clusters*, 4–10 in. across. Apr.–July. *Fruits: Black or purple berries*; juicy, slightly sweet, and edible, in drooping clusters. *Habitat/range:* Moist forests, stream banks, roadsides, and clearings. Common. Eastern North America.

Similar species: Red elderberry (*S. racemosa* ssp. *pubens*) has a *pyramidal inflorescence and bright red berries*. Apr.– early June. Cool moist sites at higher elevations including wooded ravines, stream banks, and moist thickets in spruce-fir forests and northern hardwood forests. Occasional.

Notes: Elderberry grows best in open sunny areas where it spreads vegetatively by rhizomes, often forming dense thickets. The fruits are an important food source for numerous songbirds, including fall migrants. The fruits can also be used for making jelly, preserves, pie, and wine.

Achillea millefolium
Yarrow
Asteraceae (Sunflower family)

Aromatic herbaceous perennial with 1–3 ft. tall leafy stems arising from spreading rhizomes. *Leaves:* 1–6 in. long, *grayish green* and finely divided with a *feathery* appearance. *Flowers:* Numerous small white flower heads in flat-topped or rounded terminal clusters. Apr.–Nov. *Fruits:* Flattened achenes. *Habitat/range:* Fields, roadsides, and meadows. Common. Widely distributed in the Northern Hemisphere.

Notes: Yarrow includes both native and introduced (from Europe and Asia) populations that have hybridized, forming a single, highly variable species. This variability contributes to yarrow's ability to tolerate an unusually wide array of climates from mild coastal areas up to higher elevations and latitudes in both North America and Europe. Over the centuries, yarrow was best known as a plant that stops bleeding (in the American Civil War it was called "soldier's woundwort"). The genus name honors the Greek hero Achilles, whose use of the plant is said to have saved the lives of many soldiers in the Trojan War.

Chimaphila maculata
Pipsissewa, Striped Wintergreen
Ericaceae (Heath family)

A low-growing (4–8 in. tall) evergreen perennial arising from a creeping rhizome, often forming small colonies. *Leaves:* Thick, shiny dark green with sharp-toothed margins and a *broad white stripe along the midrib*; mostly crowded near the stem tip. *Flowers: Nodding,* white with a waxy appearance; occur in loose clusters above the leaves. May–June. *Fruits:* Spherical capsules. *Habitat/ range:* Forests and woodlands mostly on dry, acidic soils. Common. Throughout the eastern United States.

    Notes: Pipsissewa is a low-growing plant that grows and flowers in deep shade under deciduous forests as well as pines and other cone-bearing trees. The nodding flowers depend on insect pollinators (mainly bumblebees) for successful pollination and subsequent fruit and seed set. The large round green stigma in the center of the flower facilitates pollination success by increasing the likelihood of flower-visiting insects brushing against it, and the stigma's sticky aspect helps pollen grains adhere to its surface. Native Americans used pipsissewa to treat kidney stones.

Clintonia umbellulata
Speckled Wood Lily
Liliaceae (Lily family)

Erect perennial herb up to 15 in. tall. *Leaves:* 2–5 (usually 3) at base of plant, elliptic to ovate, 6–12 in. long with *long hairs on the margins. Flowers:* Similar petals and sepals (3 each), *white*, speckled with purple; in a terminal umbel at the end of a leafless stalk. May–June. *Fruits: Dark blue to black berries. Habitat/range:* Mesic to dry forests. Common. Appalachian Mountains from New York south to Georgia.

    Similar species: Bluebead lily (*C. borealis*) has *yellow flowers, bright blue fruits* and its *leaf margins lack long hairs.* May–June. Moist woods. Common at higher elevations.

    Notes: The genus *Clintonia* originated in eastern Asia and eventually migrated to North America across the Bering land bridge that joined Alaska and eastern Siberia at various times during the last Ice Age due to huge drops in sea level. The first humans to colonize America are thought to have migrated across this bridge, as did large numbers of plants and animals that originated in Asia.

Mitchella repens
Partridge Berry
Rubiaceae (Madder family)

Creeping evergreen with vine-like stems that form *large mats*. *Leaves:* Opposite, ovate, about ½ inch long, dark green with a *whitish midvein*. *Flowers:* Fragrant, white, trumpet-shaped, about ½ in. long; *occur in pairs* with fused ovaries that mature into a single berry that bears a mark where each of the two corollas was attached. May–June. *Fruits:* Red berries persist through winter. *Habitat/range:* Moist to dry forests, heath balds, stream banks, trailsides, typically on acidic soils. Common. Widespread in eastern North America.

Notes: Partridge berry has creeping stems that root at the nodes, forming dense patches on the forest floor. The flowers depend on insect pollinators (mainly bumblebees) to move pollen between plants. Because the flowers generally contain small amounts of nectar, bumblebees typically visit numerous flowers (and plants) to meet their energy demands. This, in turn, increases the likelihood that compatible pollen will reach a flower's stigmas. Various birds and small mammals eat the berries and disperse the small hard-coated seeds in their droppings. Partridge berry makes an attractive groundcover in woodland gardens.

Toxicodendron radicans
Poison Ivy
Anacardiaceae (Cashew family)

Poison ivy grows as a prostrate ground cover, low shrub, or high-climbing vine with *abundant hair-like rootlets attached to tree bark*. *Leaves:* Recognized by its *compound leaves with three (highly variable) leaflets*, the terminal leaflet long stalked, laterals nearly stalkless. *Flowers:* Small, whitish to cream colored in dense clusters, often partially hidden in the leaf axils. Late Apr.–May. *Fruits:* Small, whitish, berry-like, in loose clusters. *Habitat/range:* Occurs in a wide range of habitats including forests, open woods, fields, and roadsides. Common. Widespread in eastern North America. *Rhus radicans*.

Notes: All parts of the plant contain an oily resin known as urushiol that causes a highly irritating rash in most humans. Thorough lathering in soapy water shortly after exposure reduces the risk of reaction. Applying crushed leaves of jewelweed (*Impatiens*) to the rash helps alleviate the symptoms. Studies indicate that increasing atmospheric CO_2 associated with a warming climate promotes larger plants with higher urushiol concentrations. As such, we can expect poison ivy to increase in abundance and "itchiness" in the future.

Astilbe biternata
False Goatsbeard
Saxifragaceae (Saxifrage family)

Perennial herb with multiple stems 3–6
ft. tall, the *upper stems glandular hairy.*
Leaves: Up to 2 ft. long, 2–3 times pinnately compound, leaflets ovate, sharply
toothed, the *terminal leaflet usually
3-lobed. Flowers:* Small, white or yellowish; collectively form large, feathery,
terminal clusters. May–July. *Fruits:* Erect
follicles. *Habitat/range:* Rich wooded
slopes, shaded road banks, ditches, and
seeps. Occasional. Southern Appalachian Mountains from Virginia south
to Georgia.

   Similar species: Astilbe is often con-
fused with goatsbeard (*Aruncus dioicus*).
The two species grow in identical habitats, often side-by-side, and have large
compound leaves and terminal panicles
of numerous small, largely unisexual
flowers. *Aruncus* can be distinguished
from *Astilbe* by its *smooth upper stem,
unlobed terminal leaflet,* and by usually
having 3 (rather than 2) pistils per flower.

   Notes: False goatsbeard is the only
species of *Astilbe* in North America—the
other 23 species occur in eastern Asia.
Individuals along roadsides can become
quite large, producing multiple flowering stems in a given year. The numerous
small flowers attract a wide variety of
insects, some of which may function as
pollinators.

Galax urceolata
Galax, Skunkweed
Diapensiaceae (Diapensia family)

Low-growing evergreen perennial.
Leaves: Round shiny basal leaves with
toothed margins, heart shaped at base,
long petioles. *Flowers: Tiny, white, in
dense racemes* on slender stalks 18–24 in.
tall. May–July. *Fruits:* Capsules. *Habitat/
range:* Moist to dry open forests on
acidic soils. Widespread in the mountains. From Maryland south to Georgia.
G. aphylla.

   Notes: Galax thrives in various habitats but grows best in cool, moist sites
with acidic soils and partial shade. In
favorable sites, plants spread vegetatively
from rhizomes, forming a dense carpet
of shiny dark green leaves on the forest
floor. Numerous tall spike-like clusters of
tiny white flowers appear in late spring
through midsummer. The leaves turn
reddish bronze in autumn and persist
over winter. By spring, the reddish bronze
color dissipates and the leaves become
green again. The brightly colored autumn
leaves are highly prized in floral arrange-
ments (overcollecting can be a problem).
Strangely, the plant sometimes smells
like dog feces or skunk spray, hence the
common name skunkweed.

Hydrangea arborescens
Wild Hydrangea
Hydrangeaceae (Hydrangea family)

A deciduous shrub 3–10 ft. tall *with soft wood and peeling bark* on older stems. *Leaves:* Opposite, 2–7 in. long with a round or heart-shaped base, pointed tip, and coarsely toothed margins. *Flowers:* Small, white, in flat or rounded terminal clusters 2–4 in. wide. May–July. *Fruits:* Small dry capsules persist into winter. *Habitat/range:* Moist wooded cliffs and ravines, along streams, moist road banks, and forest edges. Common. Widely distributed in the eastern United States.

Similar species: Silverleaf hydrangea (*H. radiata*) and ashy hydrangea (*H. cinerea*) have a bright white or gray (rather than green) lower leaf surface.

Notes: Wild hydrangea is a rounded shrub that is often wider than it is tall due to new stems arising from lateral roots. The flowers in the center of the inflorescence are fertile, producing both pollen and seeds; in contrast, the larger showier flowers on the outer edge help attract pollinators but are sterile. The foliage is consumed by white-tailed deer but is toxic to humans if ingested in quantity.

Maianthemum canadense
Canada Mayflower
Ruscaceae (Ruscus family)

Low-growing (2–8 in. tall) herbaceous perennial that spreads via shallow creeping rhizomes forming a *lush green carpet*. *Leaves:* Alternate, smooth and shiny, sessile or short stalked, 1–3 in. long, with a *heart-shaped base*. *Flowers:* A short terminal raceme of tiny white flowers. May–July. *Fruits: Red translucent berries* persist into winter. *Habitat/range:* Moist forests especially at high elevations. Common. A northern species extending south in the mountains to Georgia.

Notes: Flowering shoots have 2–3 leaves; vegetative shoots have a single leaf. Because individuals are genetically self-incompatible, cross-pollination is necessary for fruits to mature. Bumblebees visit the tiny flowers for nectar and pollen and are the primary pollinator. Birds and small mammals (including ruffed grouse, eastern chipmunks, and white-footed mice) eat the berries and disperse the seeds in their droppings. Canada mayflower forms an attractive ground cover in moist woodland gardens.

Actaea racemosa
Black Cohosh
Ranunculaceae (Buttercup family)

Thalictrum clavatum
Mountain Meadowrue
Ranunculaceae (Buttercup family)

Smooth herbaceous perennial 6–24 in. tall. *Leaves:* Biternately compound (divided into 3 leaflets twice) with *rounded leaf lobes. Flowers: White petal-like sepals* and broad white stamens; the slender elongate flower stalks with few flowers. May–July. *Fruits: An upward curved achene. Habitat/range:* Rich moist forests, seepage slopes, mountain streams, and spray cliffs. Common. A southern Appalachian endemic.

Notes: Unlike many early emerging woodland wildflowers, mountain meadowrue has a long flowering period that extends from spring through midsummer. The flowers lack petals and nectar but have showy sepals and conspicuous white stamens that attract syrphid flies foraging for pollen. If insects fail to cross-pollinate the flowers, self-pollination readily occurs. Many different types of alkaloids have been identified in meadowrue, some of which deter herbivores; others have pharmacologic potential due to their ability to lower blood pressure and inhibit the growth of tumors.

Perennial herb with *3–9 ft. tall flower stalks. Leaves:* Large 2–3 times compound with 20 or more broad, coarsely toothed leaflets. *Flowers:* Small, white, foul smelling with numerous showy white stamens in long narrow terminal racemes; each flower has *1 ovary* (rarely 2) and lacks a stalk. May–Aug. *Fruits:* Follicles. *Habitat/range:* Moist fertile forests, ravines, creek margins. Common. Moderately widespread in eastern North America. *Cimicifuga racemosa.*

Similar species: Mountain black cohosh (*A. podocarpa*) grows to 5 ft. tall; each flower has *3–8 stalked ovaries.* July–Sept. Moist fertile woods. Occasional. *C. americana.*

Notes: The fetid-smelling flowers attract carrion flies and beetles that function as pollinators. In an emergency, one can rub the flowers on skin to repel mosquitoes (don't worry if a few carrion flies or beetles drop by—they'll quickly fly off once they discover you're not dead meat). Black cohosh has become a popular herbal remedy for treating menopausal symptoms, including hot flashes. Overcollecting is a potential threat.

Monarda clinopodia
Basil Bee Balm
Lamiaceae (Mint family)

Erect perennial herb up to 3 ft. tall. *Leaves:* Opposite, ovate, usually twice as long as wide with a pointed tip. *Flowers: White or cream*, about 1 in. long, fragrant; 2-lipped corolla, the upper lip narrow, erect, hairless; in a *solitary terminal head-like cluster*, subtended by *greenish or whitish bracts*. Late May–Sept. *Fruits:* Nutlets. *Habitat/range:* Moist forests. Common. Widespread in eastern United States.

Similar species: Wild bergamot (*M. fistulosa*) has *pink or lavender* 2-lipped flowers; the tip of the straight upper lip has a tuft of white hairs at the apex; the floral bracts are usually *pale green to lilac tinged*. June–Sept. Open woods and meadows.

Notes: Because the anthers shed their pollen before the stigmas are receptive, successful reproduction depends on pollinators (mainly bumblebees) transferring pollen from anthers to receptive stigmas on other flowers. Basil bee balm and other *Monardas* are susceptible to a powdery mildew that can completely defoliate the plant. *Monarda* leaves were used as a source of tea, most notably after the Boston Tea Party.

Phytolacca americana
Pokeweed
Phytolaccaceae (Pokeweed family)

Robust perennial herb 3–10 ft. tall with smooth stems that vary from *green to purplish red. Leaves:* Alternate, lanceolate to elliptic, 3–12 in. long. *Flowers:* Numerous small white flowers in 2–8 in. long racemes. May–frost. *Fruits:* Purplish-black berries. *Habitat/range:* Usually found in open disturbed sites such as fields, along fencerows, and forest openings. Common. Widespread in eastern North America.

Notes: One of our largest nonwoody plants, pokeweed emerges from a deep taproot or from newly germinated seeds in late spring. Flowers usually appear in May and continue to be produced until autumn frost. As the fruits ripen, the stems turn from green to purplish red. The contrasting colors of the purplish-black berries and reddish stems help attract fruit-eating birds, which benefit the plant by dispersing its seeds over a large area. Early colonists used the juicy berries to make ink. Young leaves and shoots are sometimes cooked and eaten as greens ("poke salad"), following careful leaching with hot water. Older parts of the plant (including the fruits) are poisonous and can be fatal if ingested.

Asclepias exaltata
Poke Milkweed
Apocynaceae (Dogbane family)

Erect mostly smooth perennial herb, 3–5 ft. tall from a taproot; foliage contains a milky sap. *Leaves:* Opposite, broadly elliptical, 3–8 in. long, pointed at each end. *Flowers: White, tinged with green or lavender;* several *loosely flowered drooping umbels,* 2–4 in. across, emerge from the upper leaf axils. June–July. *Fruits:* Smooth erect follicles 5–6 in. long. *Habitat/range:* Woodland borders, clearings. Occasional. Widespread in eastern North America.

Similar species: Common milkweed (*A. syriaca*) has *stout hairy stems,* grayish lavender or dull rose flowers with *spiny fruits.* June–Aug. Meadows, fields, and roadsides. Common.

Notes: Most animals avoid milkweeds because their milky sap contains bitter tasting toxic alkaloids. An interesting exception is the monarch butterfly, whose larvae (caterpillars) feed on milkweeds and in so doing accumulate the toxic alkaloids in their body tissue, which protects them (as caterpillars and as adult butterflies) from most predators (mainly birds). Milkweeds grown in gardens provide an important food source for migrating monarch butterflies—look for the conspicuously white, yellow, and black striped caterpillars on the leaves.

Trautvetteria caroliniensis
Tassel Rue
Ranunculaceae (Buttercup family)

Perennial herb 2–5 ft. tall, forming colonies from a spreading rhizome. *Leaves:* Basal, long stalked, up to 12 in. wide; stem leaves alternate, reduced upward on stem, palmately cleft into 5–11 wedge-shaped segments with sharply toothed margins. *Flowers:* White, about ½ in. wide; petals absent, the sepals fall off early; the showy part of the flower are the *numerous broad stamens;* clusters of flowers terminate the stem and branches, extending well above the foliage. June–July. *Fruits:* Utricles. *Habitat/range:* Stream banks, seepage slopes, and other moist areas. Occasional. Eastern United States.

Notes: A surprisingly large number of southern Appalachian plants have close relatives in eastern Asia. Examples include trees such as *Liriodendron* (tulip tree) and *Halesia* (Carolina silverbell), shrubs such as *Hamamelis* (witch hazel) and *Lindera* (spicebush), and herbs such as *Podophyllum* (mayapple) and *Trillium.* Typically a genus is represented by closely related, but different, species on each continent. Tassel rue is unusual in that the same species occurs in both the southern Appalachians and eastern Asia.

Gaultheria procumbens
Wintergreen
Ericaceae (Heath family)

Slightly woody perennial with *short erect stems* to 4 in. tall arising from a creeping rhizome. *Leaves:* A *few shiny evergreen leaves* crowded toward the stem tip. *Flowers: Small, white, waxy,* barrel-shaped with 5 tiny rounded lobes; flowers hang from the leaf axils. June–Aug. *Fruits: Bright red berries* often persist through winter. *Habitat/range:* Dry to moist acidic woodlands, heath balds, and openings. Common. Widespread in the northeastern United States and Canada, extending south in the Appalachian Mountains to Georgia.

Notes: Wintergreen spreads by seeds and creeping rhizomes that produce short (3–4 in. tall) upright leafy stems. Bumblebees pollinate the small dangling urn-shaped flowers. Birds and mammals (including ruffed grouse and chipmunks) consume its red berries and disperse the tiny seeds in their droppings. The leaves and berries contain oil of wintergreen which was once used to flavor gum, candy, and toothpaste. The shiny green leaves turn a bronzy red color in winter. Like other members of the heath family, wintergreen is a good indicator of acidic soils.

Goodyera pubescens
Rattlesnake Orchid
Orchidaceae (Orchid family)

Evergreen perennial herb with 4–8 leaves in a *basal rosette* arising from a creeping rhizome. *Leaves:* Ovate, bluish green, with a distinctive *network of white veins* and a *prominent white stripe down the midrib. Flowers:* Stout hairy flowering stalk up to 15 in. tall, the upper part densely packed with *small, downy, waxy white flowers*, each subtended by a small lanceolate bract. June–Aug. *Fruits:* Small erect capsules. *Habitat/range:* Dry to moist forests on acidic soils. Common. Eastern North America.

Similar species: Lesser rattlesnake orchid (*G. repens*) has a *basal rosette* of dark green variegated leaves that *lack a prominent white stripe along the midrib.* July. Moist forests. Infrequent.

Notes: Rattlesnake orchid is one of our most common and easily recognized orchids. The cluster of fruits at the stem tip resembles the "rattle" at the tail end of a rattlesnake, and the distinctive veins give the leaf a snakeskin look, hence the common name. Native Americans made a tea from the leaves to treat colds and kidney problems.

Rhododendron maximum
Rosebay Rhododendron
Ericaceae (Heath family)

Thicket-forming evergreen shrub or small tree, 6–20 ft. tall. *Leaves: Thick and leathery*, sharply pointed at tip, *wedge-shaped at base*, 4–10 in. long, 2–3 in. wide. *Flowers: White to pale pink* with 5 rounded petal lobes, the largest lobe with greenish-yellow or orange spots within; in showy rounded clusters at branch tips; June–Aug. *Fruits:* Elongate capsules with a persistent sticky style. *Habitat/range:* Moist to wet acidic slopes, stream banks, ravines, and coves. Common. From eastern Canada south to Georgia and Alabama, mostly in the Appalachian Mountains.

Notes: Often persisting for decades (in some cases, a century or more), rosebay rhododendron frequently forms dense thickets in the forest understory. In relatively sunny areas, individuals often produce dense clusters of white-to-pinkish flowers that blanket the plant in summer. Like our other evergreen rhododendrons, its leaves respond to drought in summer and freezing temperatures in winter by curling lengthwise (like a thick pencil) and drooping downward. The drier the soil or colder the temperature, the tighter the roll becomes.

Heuchera villosa
Rock Alumroot
Saxifragaceae (Saxifrage family)

Perennial herb with basal leaves and upright flowering stalks 8–36 in. tall. *Leaves:* 2–6 in. long and wide, *sharply lobed*, toothed, and hairy; resembling a maple leaf with a long hairy stalk. *Flowers:* Numerous, *tiny, white to pink*, with 5 long exserted stamens; born in clusters on a long leafless flowering stalk. June–Oct. *Fruits:* Capsules. *Habitat/range:* Moist shaded ledges and cliffs, often growing in crevices or in thin rocky soils. Common. Primarily in the Blue Ridge Mountains from Virginia south to Georgia.

Similar species: Common alumroot (*H. americana*) has *leaves with blunt lobes.* Apr.–June. Moist woods. Common. Cave alumroot (*H. parviflora*) has nearly circular leaves with *broadly rounded lobes.* July–Sept. Shaded rocks and ledges. Occasional.

Notes: Rock alumroot grows mostly on high-elevation cliffs and ledges on a variety of rock types, including granites, quartzites, schists, and gneisses. It spreads locally via underground stems (rhizomes) and colonizes more distant sites via seeds. Alumroots make attractive garden and container plants.

Monotropa uniflora
Indian Pipe, Ghost Flower
Ericaceae (Heath family)

One to several *translucent waxy-white* (rarely pink) *fleshy stems*, 2–8 in. tall, becoming black with age; a *parasitic flowering plant* sometimes mistaken for fungi. *Leaves:* Tiny, scale-like, lack chlorophyll (as does the whole plant). *Flowers: Solitary* at the stem tip; narrowly bell shaped, nodding, waxy white. June–Oct. *Fruits:* Capsules become erect as they mature. *Habitat/range:* Densely shaded coniferous and deciduous forests. Common. North, Central, and South America and eastern Asia.

Similar species: Pinesap (*Monotropa hypopitys*) has clusters of *yellow, pink, or red stems with multiple flowers at the stem tip*. May–Oct. Moist to dry woods. Uncommon.

Notes: This rather strange plant looks like a fungus but is actually a parasitic flowering plant. Because it obtains all its nutrients from other plants, Indian pipe lacks chlorophyll and the ability to manufacture its own food via photosynthesis. The albino shoots emerge suddenly, often after summer rains. The nodding flowers produce nectar and pollen and attract bumblebees as pollinators. This isn't a plant for bouquets as the stems turn black and ooze a clear gelatinous substance when picked.

Eurybia divaricata
White Wood Aster
Asteraceae (Sunflower family)

Perennial herb 1–3 ft. tall with *zigzag stems* and *daisy-like flower heads. Leaves:* Alternate with coarsely toothed margins; lower leaves conspicuously pointed at the tip and heart shaped at the base; upper leaves reduced in size and less heart shaped. *Flowers:* Heads composed of *5–10 white ray flowers* (outer petals) and yellow or red central disk flowers. July–Oct. *Fruits:* Achenes. *Habitat/range:* Moist to fairly dry forests and woodlands. Common. From Ontario south to Georgia and Alabama, mostly in the Appalachian Mountains. *Aster divaricatus.*

Similar species: Mountain wood aster (*E. chlorolepis*) has *10 or more* white ray flowers per head. Aug.–Oct. Common. Mostly above 4,000 ft. in spruce-fir forest and northern hardwood forest. *A. divaricatus var. chlorolepis.*

Notes: Wood asters spread by seeds and by rhizomes, forming dense colonies. Newly opened flower heads have yellow disk (central) flowers that turn reddish about a week after opening. The older reddish disk flowers have less nectar and pollen, making them less attractive to potential pollinators.

Cuscuta rostrata
Appalachian Dodder
Convolvulaceae (Morning glory family)

Ageratina altissima
White Snakeroot
Asteraceae (Sunflower family)

Parasitic twining vine with leafless, *bright orange-to-yellow slender stems*; a robust plant can form a tangled mat of intertwined stems that resemble orange (or yellow) cooked spaghetti noodles. *Leaves:* None. *Flowers: Tiny white flowers* in dense clusters. Aug.–Sept. *Fruits:* Small capsules. *Habitat/range:* High elevation forests and balds. Common. Appalachian Mountains from Maryland south to Georgia.

    Notes: Dodder is easily recognized by the mass of slender intertwined stems that look like orange or yellow twine tangled among the stems of a green plant. Appalachian dodder often parasitizes blackberries (*Rubus* spp.), but can also be found growing on wild hydrangea (*Hydrangea arborescens*), orange jewelweed (*Impatiens capensis*), and a few other species. Dodder seedlings use volatile cues (airborne chemicals) to locate a suitable host plant. When contact is made, dodder's slender stems coil around and penetrate the stems of the host plant (via specialized root-like structures called haustoria), from which the dodder plant derives all its water and nutrients. The host plant rarely dies, but it does lose vigor and appears unhealthy.

Perennial herb usually 3–4 ft. tall, often forming dense colonies. *Leaves:* Opposite, ovate to heart shaped with an acuminate tip; leaf margins *sharply serrate*, the petioles over 1 in. long. *Flowers:* Flat-topped or rounded clusters of *white disk flowers that look fuzzy* because the stamens project beyond the corolla tube. Aug.–Oct. *Fruits:* Achenes with a tuft of whitish bristles. *Habitat/range:* Moist forests and woodland borders. Common. Eastern North America. *Eupatorium rugosum.*

    Similar species: Aromatic snakeroot (*A. aromatica*) has thicker leaves with *rounded teeth* and *petioles less than 1 in. long.* Aug.–Oct. Dry, open woods. Common. *E. aromaticum.*

    Notes: The showy white flower heads of white snakeroot stand out along forest margins and clearings in late summer and fall. In overgrazed areas, cows sometimes eat the bitter-tasting toxic foliage; the toxins from this plant can pass to humans through milk, causing "milk sickness," a disease that killed thousands of pioneers that settled in the Appalachians. Today, the risk of milk sickness in humans is very low.

Epifagus virginiana
Beechdrops
Orobanchaceae (Broomrape family)

Root parasite with thin ascending *pale brown stems* 6–18 in. tall with *brownish-purple streaks. Leaves:* Tiny, scale-like; lack chlorophyll. *Flowers: Inconspicuous*, white with brown-purple stripes, 2-lipped; born singly in leaf axils. Sept.–Nov. *Fruits:* Tiny brown capsules. *Habitat/range:* Moist to somewhat dry forests *under or near American beech trees.* Common. Widespread in eastern North America.

Notes: This common but inconspicuous plant is easily overlooked because its brownish slender stems blend in with the forest floor. Occurring singly or in small colonies, it typically occurs wherever American beech trees grow. Lacking chlorophyll and therefore the ability to photosynthesize, beechdrops obtains nutrients by parasitizing the roots of American beech. Without its host plant, beechdrops can't survive. Its dust-sized seeds, carried down through soil by rainwater, detect an exudate produced by beech roots, which is apparently necessary to stimulate seed germination. When beechdrops roots make contact with a beech root, a haustorium forms through which nutrients flow from the host tree to the parasite.

Parnassia asarifolia
Kidneyleaf Grass of Parnassus
Parnassiaceae (Grass of Parnassus family)

Perennial herb 8–16 in. tall; not a grass nor does it resemble a grass, despite its common name. *Leaves:* Basal, *kidney shaped,* 1–2 in. wide on long stalks. *Flowers:* 5 white petals with *prominent green veins;* flowering stems with a single terminal flower and a single sessile leaf near the middle of the stem that is similar to the basal leaves but smaller. Aug.–Oct. *Fruits:* Capsules. *Habitat/range:* Swamps, bogs, stream banks, and seepage slopes. Occasional. Virginia south to Georgia and Texas, primarily in the Appalachian Mountains and Ozarks.

Similar species: Bigleaf grass of Parnassus (*P. grandifolia*) has *ovate leaves* and occurs mainly on nearly basic rather than acidic soils. Sept.–Oct. Wet, rocky habitats. Infrequent.

Notes: The delicate green lines on the white waxy petals make this one of our most beautiful wildflowers. The lines radiate toward the center of the flower, like spokes on a wheel, guiding potential pollinators (small bees and flies) to the nectar droplets at the base of each petal.

Pink to Lavender Flowers

Claytonia caroliniana
Carolina Spring Beauty
Portulacaceae (Purslane family)

Early spring perennial, 3–6 in. tall, arising from a corm. *Leaves:* Single pair of stem leaves 0.4–1.2 in. wide with *distinct petioles. Flowers:* White to pinkish petals (5) lined with *dark pink veins.* Mar.–May. *Fruits:* Ovoid capsules. *Habitat/range:* Moist, nutrient-rich forests at moderate to high elevations. Common. A mostly northern species extending south in the Appalachian Mountains to Tennessee and Georgia.

 Similar species: Virginia spring beauty (*C. virginica*) has similar flowers but much *narrower leaves* that *lack a distinct petiole*; occurs mostly at lower elevations than Carolina spring beauty. Feb.–Apr. Moist, nutrient-rich forests and clearings. Common.

 Notes: A spring ephemeral, spring beauty emerges and flowers in early spring while the canopy is still leafless. As the canopy leafs out and dense shade covers the forest floor, the aboveground parts of spring beauty wither and die, leaving only the underground corms to persist until the following spring. Native Americans dug up and ate the starchy corms, as do chipmunks, mice, wild hogs, and black bears.

Galearis spectabilis
Showy Orchis
Orchidaceae (Orchid family)

Showy, low-growing perennial herb. *Leaves: Basal*, 2 (sometimes 3), thick, *glossy*, widely elliptic, 4–8 in. long. *Flowers:* A single short stalk bears 2–12 flowers each about 1 in. long with a *pink or lavender hood* and a *white lip* with a prominent *nectar spur.* Apr.–May. *Fruits:* Erect capsules up to 1 in. long. *Habitat/ range:* Rich deciduous forests, especially near streams, at the base of slopes, and along trails. Occasional. Eastern North America. *Orchis spectabilis.*

 Notes: Showy orchis emerges and flowers in early spring, enabling it to take advantage of the high light levels reaching the forest floor before the canopy trees leaf out. Unlike spring ephemerals (such as trout lily and spring beauty), the green foliage of showy orchis remains throughout the summer and fall, continuing active growth before overwintering as a short tuber-like rootstalk. The showy nectar-rich flowers depend on long-tongued bees (mainly bumblebee queens) for successful pollination and fruit set. The genus *Galearis* has just two species—one in eastern North America, the other in eastern Asia.

Cypripedium acaule
Pink Lady's Slipper
Orchidaceae (Orchid family)

Showy perennial herb. *Leaves: 2, basal,* narrowly elliptical, 4–10 in. long, dark green with rib-like parallel veins. *Flowers:* Solitary with a distinctive *large pink pouch* (the "slipper") terminating a *leafless stalk* (scape) 6–18 in. tall. Apr.–June. *Fruits:* Elliptic capsules. *Habitat/range:* Dry to moist acidic forests, often under pines or other conifers. Common. Eastern North America.

Notes: Lady's slipper orchids depend on pollinators for successful pollination but lack a food reward. Instead, a form of deception is used as the large colorful flowers, nectar guides, and sweet fragrance falsely advertise the presence of food. Occasional visits by bumblebees seeking nectar or pollen result in infrequent pollination, with less than 5 percent of the flowers typically maturing fruit. When successful pollination occurs, the resulting fruit contains thousands of tiny wind-dispersed seeds. Very few of these seeds find the right combination of microclimate, soil, and symbiotic fungus to germinate and establish a new plant. The biggest threat to lady's slipper orchids is unscrupulous individuals digging them up.

Geranium maculatum
Wild Geranium
Geraniaceae (Geranium family)

Showy perennial herb 1–2 ft. tall arising from a fleshy rhizome. *Leaves:* Basal with long stalks; leaf blades 2–5 in. across with *3–5 narrow lobes*, toothed at the tips; stem leaves (one pair) smaller, short stalked. *Flowers: Bright pink to rose purple* about 1 in. across; in loose terminal clusters above the leaves. Apr.–June. *Fruits:* Capsules with a *slender beak. Habitat/range:* Moist open woodlands and stream banks. Common. Widespread in eastern North America.

Notes: The wild geranium described here is a true geranium, whereas the common ornamental geranium is in the same plant family but in a different genus (*Pelargonium*). After pollination, the petals of wild geranium fall off and a 5-parted capsule with beak-like projections develops. When ripe, each section curls up and twists as the humidity changes, eventually catapulting the seed up to 30 ft. away from the parent plant. Native Americans used an extract from the highly astringent roots to treat wounds (subsequent studies have shown that tannins in the roots promote blood clotting).

Kalmia latifolia
Mountain Laurel
Ericaceae (Heath family)

Thicket-forming evergreen shrub with a rounded crown and *crooked branches*, the thin reddish-brown bark divided into *long narrow ridges*. *Leaves:* Thick, leathery, 2–4 in. long, dark glossy green above, lighter green beneath, smooth with entire margins; crowded near ends of twigs. *Flowers: White to pink*, somewhat *bowl shaped*, in showy clusters 4–6 in. across. Apr.–June. *Fruits:* Rounded capsules in terminal clusters, persisting into winter. *Habitat/range:* Forests, dry rocky slopes, stream banks, bogs, and other habitats. Common. Widespread in the eastern United States.

Notes: The saucer-shaped flowers have ten tiny pouches each enclosing a single anther, their bent filaments held under tension. When touched by a large bee, the stamens spring forward showering the bee with pollen, which then may be deposited on another flower's stigma, resulting in cross-pollination. Try touching an anther filament with a pen tip or leaf stalk to cause the stamens to spring forward. Mountain laurel thickets make excellent cover for wildlife but provide little food as its tissues contain chemical compounds toxic to most animals.

Rhododendron catawbiense
Catawba Rhododendron
Ericaceae (Heath family)

Thicket-forming shrub, 3–10 ft. tall. *Leaves:* Evergreen, thick and leathery; narrowly to widely elliptical with a *rounded base* and blunt tip; upper surface shiny, dark green, the lower surface whitish. *Flowers: Deep pink to purple* in large dense clusters at branch tips. Apr.–June. *Fruits:* Elongate hairy capsules with a persistent style. *Habitat/range:* On ridges, health balds, forested slopes, and roadside embankments at high elevations. Common. Largely restricted to the southern Appalachians from Virginia to Georgia.

Notes: Catawba rhododendron's striking clusters of deep pink-to-purple flowers attract thousands of visitors to the mountains in spring. Individuals flower best in open sunny areas such as heath balds and roadside embankments; in the forest understory, plants grow taller but produce fewer flowers. Dense thickets of Catawba rhododendron provide excellent cover for a variety of birds and mammals, although the thick leathery leaves and tiny seeds provide little in the way of food. Catawba rhododendron is an attractive addition to mountain landscape plantings.

Rhododendron minus
Gorge Rhododendron, Punctatum
Ericaceae (Heath family)

An evergreen shrub, 3–10 ft. tall. *Leaves:* Thick and leathery, elliptical, sharply pointed at apex, wedge shaped at base, with *rusty scales on lower surface*; leaves curl up and hang down during times of drought and freezing temperatures. *Flowers:* Pink to white, mostly more than 1 in. long, often spotted with green, in terminal clusters. Apr.–June. *Fruits:* Elongate capsules with a persistent style. *Habitat/range:* Stream banks, rocky slopes, and high ridges. Common. From North Carolina south to Georgia and Alabama.

Similar species: Carolina rhododendron (*R. carolinianum*) has smaller flowers (mostly less than 1 in. long) than gorge rhododendron. Rocky summits, heath balds, and high elevation forests. Uncommon.

Notes: Rhododendron is a huge, nearly worldwide genus of more than 800 species with the largest number of species occurring in the Himalayas. About a dozen species occur in the southern Appalachians, representing a mix of evergreen and deciduous species. Many *Rhododendron* species are grown as ornamentals, including numerous cultivars of hybrid origin.

Oxalis montana
Mountain Wood Sorrel
Oxalidaceae (Wood sorrel family)

This perennial herb forms *prostrate mats* less than 4 in. tall. *Leaves:* Basal, long stalked with *3 clover-like leaflets. Flowers:* 5 white petals with *deep pink veins* and a yellow spot at the base; flowers born singly on stalks elevated slightly above the leaves. June–July. *Fruits:* Round capsules. *Habitat/range:* Cool moist forests on acidic soils at high elevations including spruce-fir forest, northern hardwood forest, and spray cliffs. Locally common. From southeastern Canada southward in the Appalachian Mountains to Georgia.

Notes: Mountain wood sorrel spreads vegetatively by slender creeping rhizomes that form dense patches that hug the ground. Deep pink veins on the white petals guide insects to the center of the flower where the nectar and pollen are located, increasing the efficiency of pollination. The fruits have a ballistic dispersal mechanism, flinging mature seeds up to 6 ft. from the parent plant. The sour-tasting leaves deter most herbivores from feeding on the plant.

Amphicarpaea bracteata
Hog Peanut
Fabaceae (Legume family)

Slender twining vine up to 5 ft. long.
Leaves: Divided into three ovate leaflets
with broadly rounded bases. *Flowers:*
Pale lilac to white, *pea-like*, in nodding
racemes on long stalks from the leaf axils.
July–Sept. *Fruits:* Flattened legumes.
Habitat/range: Dry to moist forests,
thickets, and stream banks. Common.
Eastern North America.

Desmodium nudiflorum
Beggar's Ticks
Fabaceae (Legume family)

Upright perennial herb with a *slender
arching flowering stem* up to 3 ft. tall with
separate leaf-bearing stems about 1 ft.
long. *Leaves: Trifoliate*, broadly ovate,
about 3 in. long, clustered at the tip.
Flowers: Whitish pink to rose purple, pea-
like, in a loose raceme. July–Aug. *Fruits:*
Flattened legumes (pods) with deeply
notched lower margins and covered with
hooked hairs that *adhere to clothes and
animal fur. Habitat/range:* Moist to dry
forests. Common. Throughout the eastern United States.

 Notes: The common name "beggar's
ticks" refers to the seedpods that attach
and cling like ticks to the fur of animals
(or the clothing of humans) dispersing seeds long distances from the parent plant. Like many members of the
legume (pea) family, *Desmodium* roots
form nodules in a mutualistic association
with nitrogen-fixing *Rhizobium* bacteria. Plants use the nitrogen; the bacteria
obtain food and shelter. Bumblebees
pollinate the flowers, birds consume the
seeds, and white-tailed deer feed on the
foliage.

 Notes: Hog peanut is a common, but
easily missed wildflower because of its
small size, inconspicuous flowers, and
habit of twining on other plants. It's
unusual because it produces both above-
and belowground flowers and fruits. The
aerial flowers open, can cross-pollinate,
and produce fruits with 1–3 small seeds
that are ballistically dispersed from the
parent plant. The subterranean flowers
self-pollinate without opening and produce fruits with a single large seed. The
larger subterranean seeds produce more
vigorous seedlings while the potential
for cross-pollination among the aerial
flowers results in more genetically variable offspring, facilitating adaptation to
a wider range of environments. Native
Americans boiled and ate the subterranean fruits.

Chelone lyonii
Pink Turtlehead
Plantaginaceae (Plantain family)

Perennial herb 15–40 in. tall. *Leaves:*
Opposite, 3–5 in. long, ovate to ovate-
lanceolate with serrate margins and
distinct petioles. *Flowers: Pink-to-purple
2-lipped corolla*, the lower lip with
prominent yellow hairs; in short terminal
spikes. July–Sept. *Fruits:* Broadly ovate
capsules. *Habitat/range:* Seeps, stream
banks, cove forests, and spruce-fir forests. Locally common at high elevations.
Restricted to the Blue Ridge Mountains
of North Carolina, South Carolina, and
Tennessee.

    Similar species: White turtlehead (*C.
glabra*) has *white flowers* and generally
occurs at lower elevations. Aug.–Oct.
Moist woods, seeps, and along streams.
Common.

    Notes: Bumblebees push their way be-
tween the closed lips into the flower and
crawl down the floral tube to obtain nectar at the base. In the process, the head
and thorax of the bumblebee becomes
dusted with pollen from the 4 fertile
stamens. When visiting other flowers, the
bee may inadvertently brush pollen from
its body surface onto a receptive stigma,
thereby pollinating the flower. Turtle-
heads spread by seeds and by rhizomes,
forming small colonies on moist sites.

Eutrochium fistulosum
Joe Pye Weed
Asteraceae (Sunflower family)

Multi-stemmed perennial herb 3–12 ft.
tall with *smooth, purplish-green, hollow
stems. Leaves: Whorls of 3–7*, lanceolate,
4–12 in. long. *Flowers: Pink-to-purplish*
flower heads in *round-topped clusters*,
3–12 in. across; *ray flowers absent*. July–
Oct. *Fruits:* Black achenes with a tuft of
purplish bristles. *Habitat/range:* Moist
to wet areas including rocky streamsides,
wet meadows, and roadside ditches.
Common. Widespread in the eastern
and central United States. *Eupatorium
fistulosum.*

    Similar species: Spotted Joe Pye weed
(*E. maculatum*) has *solid stems*, purple-
spotted or deep purple, and *flat-topped
inflorescences*. July–Oct. Common. Cove
forests and grassy balds. *Eupatorium
maculatum.*

    Notes: The dense flower heads at the
tips of tall stems provide abundant and
readily accessible nectar for a wide variety of potential pollinators including
butterflies, bees, flies, wasps, and beetles.
Among the many butterfly visitors are
tiger swallowtails, red admirals, painted
ladies, viceroys, and monarchs. Goldfinches and other birds glean ripe seeds
from the fruiting heads in autumn. Joe
Pye is an attractive garden plant in moist
open sunny areas.

Purple to Maroon Flowers

Trillium cuneatum
Sweet Betsy
Trilliaceae (Trillium family)

Erect perennial herb 6–15 in. tall from a stout rhizome. *Leaves:* In a whorl of 3, sessile, *mottled*, broadly ovate, 3–6 in. long. *Flowers:* Solitary, sessile, fragrant, *purple* (less often yellow or green) petals, erect, more than twice as long as the stamens, *stamens blunt at the tip.* Mar.–Apr. *Fruits:* Maroon red berries. *Habitat/range:* Moist woods, forests, and floodplains, often on less acidic soils. Common. From North Carolina and Kentucky south to Georgia and Alabama.

    Notes: On nutrient-rich sites with nearly basic soils, thousands of sweet Betsy plants can carpet the forest floor. In most populations, flowers have a faint spice-like odor that helps attract potential pollinators. Nonetheless, most flowers fail to set fruit and the aerial stems and leaves associated with each flower wither within a few weeks of flowering. In contrast, flowering shoots with a developing fruit persist until the seeds mature in late June or July. Once the above ground parts die back, trilliums persist as an underground rhizome until the following spring.

Xanthorhiza simplicissima
Yellowroot
Ranunculaceae (Buttercup family)

A low-growing deciduous shrub with *bright yellow rhizomes. Leaves:* Pinnately compound with sharply toothed leaflets and long petioles *clustered near the stem tips. Flowers:* Tiny *brownish-purple to yellowish–green, in long narrow drooping racemes.* Mar.–May. *Fruits:* Small 1–2 seeded follicles. *Habitat/range:* Shaded stream banks and wet rocky ledges. Common. Widely distributed in the eastern United States.

    Notes: Yellowroot grows best in cool moist areas along streams where it spreads laterally, forming dense thickets. It's rarely washed away during floods, as underground stems anchor the plant and its short stature and flexible stems bend with flowing water. The expansive root system also helps hold the soil in place when water levels rise, reducing stream bank erosion. The bitter bright yellow rhizomes yield a yellow dye and have been used to make a tea to treat various ailments.

Arisaema triphyllum
Jack-in-the-Pulpit
Araceae (Arum family)

Perennial herb 1–3 ft. tall whose distinctive hood makes it relatively easy to identify. *Leaves:* 1–2, each divided into *three leaflets*. *Flowers:* Tiny male or female flowers at the base of a *club-shaped spadix* ("Jack") surrounded by a *large purple- or green-striped spathe* that resembles a hooded pulpit. Mar.–June. *Fruits:* Cluster of *bright red berries*. *Habitat/range:* Moist woods and stream banks. Common. Widespread in eastern North America.

Notes: If you look at this unusual plant up close, you'll see the hooded pulpit and "Jack," the silent preacher, standing within it. The real flowers, tiny and clustered around the feet of "Jack" are typically all male (pollen producing) or all female (fruit producing). Female plants are larger in size and have larger corms (underground food storage organs) than males, reflecting the increased resources needed to mature fruits. Depending on resource availability (corm size), a male plant may change to a female; conversely, females may revert to being male (or nonreproductive) in successive years.

Calycanthus floridus
Sweet Shrub
Calycanthaceae (Sweet shrub family)

Deciduous aromatic shrub 3–6 ft. tall forms dense thickets from root sprouts; twigs *enlarged and flattened at nodes*. *Leaves:* Opposite, simple, 2–4 in. long, widest near middle with a pointed tip; turn bright yellow in autumn. *Flowers:* Solitary, showy, with *numerous maroon or brownish strap-shaped sepals and petals* with a *spicy fragrance*. Mar.–June. *Fruits: Pod-like*, up to 3 in. long, green in summer turning brown to black in winter. *Habitat/range:* Moist woods and stream banks. Common. Eastern United States.

Notes: The name sweet shrub refers to its fragrant flowers, leaves, and twigs. The strong fruity odor of the flowers attracts beetles, which function as pollinators. The flowers develop into large pods; mice and downy woodpeckers chew or drill a hole in the pod and feed on the seeds within. Because rodents often cache (bury) seeds, they play a role as both seed predators and dispersers. Easily grown from seed or cuttings, sweet shrub makes an attractive landscape plant, forming dense colonies via root sprouts.

Asarum canadense
Wild Ginger
Aristolochiaceae (Birthwort family)

Low-growing perennial herb with *paired leaves on long stalks* arising from a creeping rhizome. *Leaves:* Opposite, *heart shaped*, 3–5 in. wide, *winter deciduous.* *Flowers:* Solitary, at the base of plant, often hidden by the paired leaves; lacking petals, the flower consists of a *maroon urn-shaped calyx* about 1 in. long with *3 long-pointed lobes.* Apr.–May. *Fruits:* Fleshy capsules. *Habitat/range:* Moist fertile forests such as rich cove forests. Common. Widespread in eastern North America.

Notes: The urn-shaped, carrion-colored flowers at ground level attract flesh-eating flies seeking dead insects and other animals in early spring. Upon entering flowers, these flies often feed on pollen, some of which may inadvertently be transferred to a flower's stigma, resulting in pollination. A lipid-rich food body attached to the seed coat attracts ants, which function as dispersal agents. Wild ginger also spreads vegetatively by rhizomes, forming dense mats of leaves. Although not related to the tropical plant from which ginger is commercially produced, the rhizomes and leaves have a surprisingly similar ginger-like aroma when broken or crushed.

Caulophyllum thalictroides
Blue Cohosh
Berberidaceae (Barberry family)

Smooth perennial herb 1–3 ft. tall with a *bluish-white caste* early in the growing season. *Leaves:* One large compound leaf on the upper stem with a long stalk and many leaflets 1–3 in. long, irregularly lobed above the middle; above this leaf and just below the inflorescence is 1 (rarely 2) similar but smaller compound leaf. *Flowers:* From 1 to 3 loose clusters of *brownish-purple to yellowish-green flowers* terminate the stem. Apr.–May. *Fruits:* Berry-like *blue seeds*; poisonous if ingested. *Habitat/range:* Moist nutrient-rich forests. Common. Widespread in eastern North America.

Notes: The flowers attract nectar-foraging flies and bees that function as pollinators. If insects don't pollinate the flowers, the flowers can self-pollinate, an important backup since cool wet days in spring can limit pollinator activity. The bluish tinge of young leaves and the color of the seeds give blue cohosh its common name. Birds and small mammals that mistake the blue seeds for fleshy berries can function as seed dispersers. Blue cohosh makes a nice addition to woodland gardens.

Trillium erectum
Wake Robin, Stinking Willie
Trilliaceae (Trillium family)

Perennial herb 4–18 in. tall from a short thick rhizome; each stem with a whorl of 3 leaves and a single terminal flower on an erect stalk. *Leaves: Uniformly green,* sessile, about as long as wide. *Flowers: Maroon or white,* occasionally yellow or green with 3 widely spreading lance-shaped petals surrounding a *purple-black ovary;* a *"fishy"* odor at close range. Apr.–May. *Fruits:* Dark maroon berries. *Habitat/range:* Moist forests at mid to high elevations. Common. From Canada south in the mountains to Tennessee and Georgia.

    Notes: Most trillium populations include younger plants that are nonflowering (vegetative) as well as plants that have either single or multiple flowering stems. The number of flowering stems reflects the size of a plant's rhizome (larger plants can have 3–5 flowering stems, each of which has a single flower and three leaves). Ripe fruits drop to the ground and split open, exposing the seeds to ants, the primary disperser of trillium seeds.

Phacelia bipinnatifida
Purple Phacelia
Hydrophyllaceae (Waterleaf family)

An erect biennial to short-lived perennial 8–24 in. tall with spreading hairy stems. *Leaves:* Alternate, mottled, hairy, 2–4 in. long, pinnately divided, the *lobes coarsely toothed. Flowers: Purple with a white center,* bowl-shaped, about ½ in. wide with 5 rounded corolla lobes; hairy stamens extend beyond the corolla. Apr.–May. *Fruits:* Capsules. *Habitat/range:* Moist slopes and rocky woods, stream banks. Common. Widespread in the eastern United States.

    Notes: True biennials grow vegetatively their first year, overwinter (usually underground), and then flower, fruit, and die their second year. Studies indicate that most plants thought to be biennials are really short-lived perennials because they can take more than two years to produce flowers and fruits. Apparently, the driving force for flowering in most "biennials" is not reaching some minimum age (two years) but rather accumulating sufficient resources before flowering and producing fruits. Purple phacelia makes an attractive addition to woodland gardens, forming large showy colonies.

Aristolochia macrophylla
Pipevine, Dutchman's Pipe
Aristolochiaceae (Birthwort family)

Trillium vaseyi
Vasey's Trillium
Trilliaceae (Trillium family)

Upright perennial herb 12–24 in. tall from a short thick rhizome. *Leaves:* In whorls of 3, uniformly green, broadly elliptic, 4–8 in. long, tapered at base with a short stalk. *Flowers:* Solitary, *maroon*, occasionally white, *2–4 in. across* on a *long nodding stalk below the leaves*; the petals usually *strongly recurved.* Apr.–early June. *Fruits:* Dark maroon berry-like capsules. *Habitat/range:* Rich moist forests, ravines, stream banks. Uncommon. Restricted to the southern Appalachians.

Notes: Vasey's trillium usually occurs as scattered single-stemmed plants rather than growing in large clumps or dense stands like some trilliums. Up to 4 in. across, it has the largest flower of our native trilliums and is usually the last to bloom, flowering from April to early June, depending on elevation. The maroon flowers, with their sweet-sour fragrance, are often partially hidden under the whorled leaves. Trillium populations can decline dramatically in areas with abundant deer populations, while less palatable species such as hayscented fern increase in abundance.

High-climbing twining vine with woody stems. *Leaves:* Alternate, *heart shaped*, 4–12 in. wide. *Flowers:* Usually a dull purple-brown, about 1½ in. long, *strongly bent and pipe shaped*; born singly on long stalks, usually high above the ground. May–June. *Fruits:* 2–3 in. long pods. *Habitat/range:* Cove forests and other moist deciduous forests. Common. Appalachian Mountains from Pennsylvania south to Georgia. *Isotrema macrophyllum.*

Similar species: Woolly pipevine (*A. tomentosa*) has soft *hairy foliage* and *yellowish flowers. I. tomentosa.*

Notes: In woodland borders and other relatively open sunlit habitats, pipevines grow rapidly, reaching heights of 30 ft. or more with dense clusters of large heart-shaped leaves. The flowers are pollinated by flies attracted to fetid floral odors that mimic fungi, rotting flesh, or feces, depending on the particular species of pipevine. Toxins prevent most animals from feeding on pipevines. An exception is the pipevine swallowtail butterfly, whose caterpillars feed on the leaves, storing alkaloids in their tissues, thereby garnering protection from predators (especially birds).

Hexastylis shuttleworthii
Large Flower Heartleaf
Aristolochiaceae (Birthwort family)

Low-growing evergreen herb with several basal leaves arising from an underground stem. *Leaves:* Smooth, *heart-shaped to round leaf blades, 2–4 in. long,* usually with light green or white along the veins, on long petioles. *Flowers:* One to several at ground level, partially obscured by the leaves above; petals absent; flowers a fleshy *brown urn-shaped calyx* up to 1½ in. long, and 1 in. wide, constricted at tip with 3 large, spreading lobes mottled with purple. May–July. *Fruits:* Fleshy capsules. *Habitat/range:* Acidic soils, often along creeks, and under rosebay rhododendron. Common. Largely restricted to the southern Appalachians from Virginia south to Georgia.

Similar genera: Hexastylis and *Asarum* are closely related genera that have similar leaves and flowers and share the common name wild ginger. *Hexastylis* is evergreen; in contrast, *Asarum* is winter deciduous.

Notes: Small insects (flies and thrips) pollinate the unusual flowers, and ants disperse the seeds. Bitter-tasting compounds deter most animals from feeding on the foliage.

Penstemon canescens
Hairy Beardtongue
Plantaginaceae (Plantain family)

Erect perennial herb up to 30 in. tall, its stems and leaves *covered with short grayish hairs.* *Leaves:* Circular cluster of leaves at the base of the plant; the stem leaves opposite, 3–5 in. long with toothed margins. *Flowers:* Violet-purple to pinkish tubular flowers about 1 in. long, gradually expanding from the base into an *open-ridged throat* with *purple lines within;* 1 sterile (antherless) stamen covered with yellow hairs does not extend beyond the 2-lipped corolla; the bracts subtending the flowers are *much smaller* than the stem leaves. May–July. *Fruits:* Capsules. *Habitat/range:* Dry woods, rocky areas, roadsides. Common.

Similar species: Small's penstemon (*P. smallii*) has a tubular corolla up to 1¼ in. long, the bracts subtending the flower are leaf-like and *only slightly smaller* than the stem leaves. May–June. Woodlands, cliffs, roadsides. Common.

Notes: The lines of contrasting color on the petals help guide pollinators (bees) to nectar within the flower. Hairy beardtongue is a larval (caterpillar) host plant for the buckeye butterfly.

Tipularia discolor
Cranefly Orchid
Orchidaceae (Orchid family)

A perennial with basal leaves arising from small corms. *Leaves: Wintergreen, summer deciduous*; 3–4 in. long, elliptic, pleated, dark green above, *glossy purple below. Flowers:* Numerous small purplish green to bronze flowers in a loosely arranged raceme on a leafless stalk. July–Sept. *Fruits:* Capsules, each with thousands of dust-sized seeds. *Habitat/range:* Moist to dry forests, usually on acidic soils. Common. Eastern United States.

Notes: Cranefly orchid is unusual in that the leaves emerge in early fall and die back in spring. The only other wintergreen, summer-deciduous orchid in the region is puttyroot (*Aplectrum hyemale*). Both species flower when the plant is leafless. Night flying moths pollinate cranefly orchid's rather inconspicuous flowers. Nutrient limitations and insufficient pollen transfer often result in fewer than 25 percent of the flowers maturing fruit. Because the tiny seeds have few stored nutrients, they must partner with specific soil fungi for both seed germination and seedling growth. The genus *Tipularia* has just 3 species—one each in the eastern United States, Japan, and the Himalayas.

Vernonia noveboracensis
New York Ironweed
Asteraceae (Sunflower family)

Robust perennial herb 3–7 ft. tall. *Leaves:* Stems with numerous lanceolate leaves, 4–8 in. long, with toothed margins and dense woolly hairs on the lower surface. *Flowers:* A dozen or more deep purple-violet heads arranged in flat-topped clusters, each composed of *30–50 disk flowers*; ray flowers absent, *green leafy bracts with long, slender tips* enclose the base of each flower head. July–Sept. *Fruits:* Ribbed achenes. *Habitat/range:* Moist open areas including stream banks, meadows, roadsides, woodlands. Common. Widespread in the eastern United States.

Similar species: Tall Ironweed (*V. gigantea*) has *fewer than 30 disk flowers per head*; the green leafy bracts enclosing the base of the head are *rounded at the apex to a short tip*. Moist woods, meadows, and pastures. Common. *V. altissima.*

Notes: The showy flowers attract long-tongued bees and numerous butterflies. Where two or more species of *Vernonia* co-occur, hybrids often result, making species identification difficult. Robust plants with striking purple-violet flower heads make *Vernonia* a spectacular addition to moist sunny gardens.

Blue Flowers

Viola sororia
Common Blue Violet
Violaceae (Violet family)

Stemless perennial herb up to 6 in. tall from a stout rhizome. *Leaves:* Basal rosette of ovate to *broadly heart-shaped* leaves on long stalks. *Flowers:* Blue violet (less often white) with a whitish center, the 2 *lateral petals bearded*; about 1 in. across. Feb.–May. *Fruits:* Capsules. *Habitat/range:* Woodlands, meadows, fields, disturbed areas. Common. Widespread in the eastern United States.

    Notes: Considered to be the most common violet in the eastern United States, common blue violet forms large colonies in woodlands, fields, and disturbed areas. An early spring-flowering species, individuals die back in fall due to low temperatures, water stress, or both. White-tailed deer, rabbits, and other animals, including livestock, feed on the foliage. Giant slugs, a night-feeding mollusk, leave large raggedly holes and trails of slime on violet leaves. Dark spiny caterpillars (larvae) of fritillary butterflies feed on violet leaves at night, thereby reducing their risk of being eaten by birds. Rich in vitamin C, the leaves can be nibbled raw or made into a salad.

Iris cristata
Dwarf Crested Iris
Iridaceae (Iris family)

Low perennial herb, 4–6 in. tall, from shallow-rooted creeping rhizomes. *Leaves:* Broadly linear, 4–8 in. long, ½–1 in. wide. *Flowers: Showy*, 3 blue-purple petals above 3 petal-like sepals; each sepal has a small, *fluted yellow crest*, in the middle of a white or yellow central band. Apr.–May. *Fruits:* Three-lobed capsules. *Habitat/range:* Rich moist open woods, trailsides, usually on nearly basic soils. Common. Maryland south to Georgia.

    Similar species: Dwarf iris (*I. verna*) has *narrower leaves* (less than ½ in. wide); the 3 drooping sepals have a yellowish-orange stripe, bordered with white, but *lack a crest*. May. Open woods. Occasional.

    Notes: Dwarf crested iris spreads vegetatively via thick creeping rhizomes, forming dense colonies on favorable sites. Bees push their way into the flower in search of nectar and, in the process, function as pollinators. White-tailed deer eat the flowers, fruits, and foliage but may occasionally benefit the plant by dispersing its seeds. Like many ornamental irises, dwarf crested iris is an easily grown and attractive garden plant.

Houstonia serpyllifolia
Appalachian Bluet
Rubiaceae (Madder family)

Small mat-forming perennial, 4–8 in.
tall, with creeping multi-branched leaf-
bearing stems. *Leaves:* Numerous, opposite, roundish leaves less than ¼ in.
long with *short petioles. Flowers:* Tiny,
blue violet with a *yellow center* and 4
petal lobes, the *narrow tube hairy within*;
solitary on long erect stalks. Apr.–June.
Fruits: Flattened capsules. *Habitat/
range:* Cool moist areas including stream
banks, seepage areas, spray cliffs, moist
disturbed areas. Common. Restricted to
the southern Appalachians from Pennsylvania to Georgia. *Hedyotis michauxii.*

 Similar species: Quaker ladies (*H.
caerulea*) *lacks prostrate runners*, the
stem leaves *without a distinct petiole*,
and the *corolla tube is smooth within.*
Apr.–May. Open woodlands and meadows. Common. *Hedyotis caerulea.*

 Notes: The delicate prostrate stems
of Appalachian bluet root at the nodes,
sometimes forming large colonies with a
dense array of blue-violet flowers, which
are attractive to bees, butterflies, and
hover flies that function as pollinators.
Bluets can be used as a groundcover in
cool moist gardens to create a pleasing
moss-like effect.

Phlox divaricata
Woodland Phlox
Polemoniaceae (Phlox family)

Herbaceous perennial up to 20 in. tall
with both erect and basal shoots. *Leaves:
In widely spaced pairs*, lanceolate to elliptic, 1–2 in. long. *Flowers:* Slightly fragrant,
light blue violet to lavender (rarely white),
about 1-in. across, in loose clusters at
shoot tips; the *5 notched petal lobes* radiate from a very narrow tube; anthers
remain inside the flower tube. Apr.–June.
Fruits: 3-valved capsules. *Habitat/range:*
Moist woods including rich cove forests
and alluvial forests, occasionally growing in drier calcium-rich soils. Common.
Widely distributed in the eastern United
States.

 Notes: Long-tongued bees (especially
bumblebees), bee flies, butterflies, skip-
pers, and moths visit the narrow tubular
flowers for nectar and function as pollinators. The foliage is browsed by various
mammalian herbivores including rab-
bits, deer, and livestock. Woodland phlox
spreads by stolons forming small colonies, making it an attractive garden plant.

Commelina communis
Asiatic Dayflower
Commelinaceae (Spiderwort family)

Prunella vulgaris
Heal All
Lamiaceae (Mint family)

Erect to reclining perennial herb 6–20 in. tall with square stems, often forming large colonies. *Leaves:* Opposite, lanceolate or elliptical, 1–3 in. long. *Flowers: Blue violet or purplish*; 2 lipped, the hooded upper lip covers the 4 stamens, the lower lip shorter, with 3 lobes; in a *dense terminal spike* 1–2 in. long with *fringed bracts.* Apr.–Oct. *Fruits:* Nutlets. *Habitat/range:* Woodland borders, fields, meadows, and roadsides. Common. Widespread in North America.

Notes: Both native and introduced varieties of this highly variable species have been described. Under favorable conditions, individuals grow up to 20 in. tall. With repeated mowing or grazing, heal all exhibits a sprawling growth form with short stems (only 2–3 in. tall). Bees visit the small, densely packed flowers for nectar, pollen, or both. A sticky mucilage on the seed coat adheres to leaves, which, when blown by the wind, disperses the seeds. Most herbivores avoid this plant due to its bitter taste. Heal all has long been used by herbalists to treat a wide variety of ailments.

Annual herb with branched stems 8–30 in. long, initially upright, later reclining and rooting at the lower nodes. *Leaves:* Alternate, lanceolate to ovate, 2–5 in. long, with parallel veins and basal sheaths. *Flowers:* A showy *pair of dark blue upper petals* with a much *smaller white, lower petal* subtended by a folded *spathe (leaf-like bract) with edges open to the base*; flowers typically open at sunrise and close by midday, hence the name dayflower. May–frost. *Fruits:* Capsules. *Habitat/range:* Moist shaded areas, including roadsides and other disturbed sites. Common. Introduced from eastern Asia and naturalized throughout the eastern United States.

Similar species: Erect Dayflower (*C. erecta*) has linear-lanceolate leaves and the *spathe edges are fused for about the lower third.* June–frost. Dry openings and woodlands, especially in thin soil around rock outcrops. Occasional. Dayflowers and spiderworts (*Tradescantia*) are quite similar, except that spiderwort flowers lack spathes and their 3 petals are uniform in size and color.

Notes: A tea from dayflowers is used to treat sore throats, colds, and urinary infections.

Tradescantia subaspera
Wideleaf Spiderwort
Commelinaceae (Spiderwort family)

Stout perennial herb 12–36 in. tall.
Leaves: Alternate, lanceolate, up to 8 in.
long, usually *wider than 0.8 in.*, dark
green with long parallel veins. *Flowers:*
Purplish-blue, 3 ovate petals, *3 hairy
sepals*, and 6 large yellow anthers (pollen
sacs) with bearded stalks; flowers about
1 in. across. June–August. *Fruits:* 3-cham-
bered capsules. *Habitat/range:* Moist,
nutrient-rich woods and clearings. Common. Widespread in the eastern United
States.

    Similar species: Ohio spiderwort
(*T. ohiensis*) has *smooth stems*, leaves
that are usually *less than 0.8 in. wide*,
and *smooth sepals*. Apr.–July. Woods,
meadows, and roadsides. Occasional.

    Notes: Individual flowers last just
a single day, but flowers are produced
throughout the summer. The purplish-
blue flowers depend on large bees
(mainly bumblebees) for successful pollination and subsequent seed production.
Pollen is the sole food reward as the flowers lack nectar. Because significant exposure causes the petals and staminal hairs
to change from blue to pink, spiderworts
have been used as a natural barometer
for air pollution and radiation.

Campanula divaricata
Southern Harebell
Campanulaceae (Bellflower family)

Multi-branched, somewhat weak-
stemmed perennial herb, 1–3 ft. tall.
Leaves: Elliptic to lanceolate, 1–3 in. long,
with coarsely toothed margins. *Flowers:*
Pale blue, bell shaped, about ¼ in. long, in
loose clusters; a straight style protrudes
well beyond the corolla. July–frost. *Fruits:*
Tiny capsules. *Habitat/range:* Rocky
woods, cliffs, unstable soil on steep
slopes. Occasional. From western Maryland south to Georgia and Alabama.

    Similar species: Tall bellflower (*Cam-
panulastrum americanum*) is *2–6 ft. tall*
with a loose spike of pale blue flowers
with a *flat (rather than bell-shaped) corolla* and a long curved style. Late June–
frost. Moist nutrient-rich forests and
stream banks. *Campanula americana.*

    Notes: Bees use the elongated style
as a walkway to reach the nectar secreted
at the top of the flower's ovary. As bees
move up and down the style, they pick up
pollen on their abdomen, some of which
may be deposited on subsequently visited flowers. *Campanula* seeds derived
from cross-pollination generally give rise
to more vigorous offspring than seeds
derived from self-fertilization.

Lobelia siphilitica
Great Blue Lobelia
Campanulaceae (Bellflower family)

Robust erect perennial herb up to 4 ft. tall. *Leaves:* Alternate, lanceolate to elliptic, up to 5 in. long with toothed margins. *Flowers: Lavender-blue* (rarely white) tubular corolla up to 1 in. long, 2 lipped, the *tube striped beneath and slightly inflated*; flowers crowded together on the upper stem forming a long slender terminal raceme. Aug.–Sept. *Fruits:* Capsules. *Habitat/range:* Moist to wet sites including stream banks, wet meadows, low woods, roadside ditches. Common. Widespread in eastern North America.

Notes: The inflorescence develops from the base upward, with the oldest flowers at the bottom of the inflorescence and the youngest at the tip. By late summer, a typical inflorescence will have a mix of developing fruits, open flowers, and flower buds. New flowers usually continue to be produced until the first frost of autumn. Bumblebees are the primary pollinators, but hummingbirds, butterflies, and small bees also visit the flowers. Lobelias are toxic if ingested.

Symphyotrichum cordifolium
Heartleaf Aster
Asteraceae (Sunflower family)

A leafy herbaceous perennial with *smooth* branched stems 1–4 ft. tall and numerous daisy-like flower heads. *Leaves:* Alternate, relatively thin with *toothed margins*; lower leaves *heart shaped* with a deep cleft at base; upper stem leaves somewhat heart shaped, lack a deep cleft. *Flowers:* Clusters of small heads up to 0.7 in. diameter in a dense rounded panicle with blue-to-violet (rarely white) rays and yellow-to-purplish disk (central) flowers; the bracts surrounding the base of each head are green and purple tinged. Aug.–Oct. *Fruits:* Achenes. *Habitat/range:* Moist open woods, woodland borders, meadows, stream banks, roadsides and ditches, sometimes weedy in urban areas. Common. Widespread in eastern North America. *Aster cordifolius.*

Notes: Formerly placed in a single genus (*Aster*), researchers have now split asters into several genera. Most of the North American asters are currently in the genera *Eurybia* and *Symphyotrichum*. Heartleaf aster is a tough plant that provides late-season color in home landscapes.

Gentiana saponaria
Soapwort Gentian
Gentianaceae (Gentian family)

Clump-forming perennial herb 8–24 in. tall with smooth stems and leaves. *Leaves:* Opposite, fleshy, widest near middle, pointed at both ends, 2–4 in. long. *Flowers:* Tubular corolla, 1–2 in. long, bluish purple, the *lobes usually closed at the tips*; in clusters at the stem tip and leaf axils. *Late Sept.–Nov. Fruits:* Elongate capsules. *Habitat/range:* Bogs, marshes, moist hardwood slopes, and roadside areas. Occasional. Eastern United States.

Similar species: Striped gentian (*G. decora*) has minutely hairy stems and somewhat open tubular flowers that are *white with dark blue or violet stripes.* Sept.–Nov. Moist woods. Occasional.

Notes: Gentians typically grow in moist habitats, flower in late summer and fall, and are pollinated by bumblebees. Individuals spread vegetatively via underground stems (rhizomes) as well as by producing numerous tiny winged seeds dispersed by the wind. While deer sometimes browse the tops of gentians, most herbivores avoid the bitter-tasting foliage. Reflecting on gentians' beauty, Thoreau wrote that gentians are "too remarkable a flower not to be sought out and admired each year."

Yellow Flowers

Erythronium umbilicatum
Dimpled Trout Lily
Liliaceae (Lily family)

Low-growing early spring perennial that arises from a bulb, sometimes forming a dense ground cover. *Leaves: Paired, elongated, fleshy; purplish markings on the leaf surface* loosely resemble the splotches on a rainbow trout, hence the common name. *Flowers: A single nodding yellow flower with strongly recurved sepals and petals* rising above the paired leaves. Feb.–May. *Fruits:* Mature capsules are *indented at the top* and *lie flat on the ground. Habitat/range:* Rich moist woods to somewhat dry habitats. Common. Virginia south to northern Florida.

Similar species: Yellow trout lily (*E. americanum*) flowers have a *small auricle ("ear") just above the base of the petals;* the fruits (capsules) are *not indented at the top* and are *held above the ground.* Mar.–May. Moist forests. Occasional.

Notes: A spring ephemeral, trout lily blooms in early spring and then dies back and goes dormant as the canopy leafs out and the forest floor becomes shaded. Some populations form a nearly continuous ground cover with few plants flowering in any one year.

Potentilla canadensis
Dwarf Cinquefoil
Rosaceae (Rose family)

Low-growing perennial to 4 in. tall with long slender hairy runners that root at the nodes, forming dense mats. *Leaves:* Palmately compound with 5 *leaflets,* rounded and toothed on the upper half, wedge shaped and smooth margined on the lower half. *Flowers:* Solitary, with 5 yellow rounded petals; the *first flower typically arises from the axil of the first well-developed stem leaf.* Mar.–May. *Fruits:* Aggregate of achenes. *Habitat/range:* Dry open woods, fields, roadsides, and trail margins. Common. Throughout eastern North America.

Similar species: Common cinquefoil (*P. simplex*) is a larger plant (up to 12 in. tall); leaves toothed ⅔ of the way from the tip; the *first flower usually arises from the axil of the second well-developed stem leaf.* Apr.–June. Dry woods, fields, and other disturbed areas. Common.

Notes: Dwarf cinquefoil forms a dense ground cover in relatively open habitats including trailside margins. Bitter-tasting tannins deter most herbivores from eating the plant. Native Americans made a tea from the roots as an astringent to treat diarrhea.

Trillium luteum
Yellow Trillium
Trilliaceae (Trillium family)

Upright perennial herb 6–15 in. tall. *Leaves:* A single whorl of 3 sessile, variably shaped leaves 3–6 in. long, *mottled* with 2–3 shades of green, the mottling fading with time. *Flowers:* Solitary, *sessile,* with 3 long-lasting *yellow petals, widest near base,* tapering to a long-pointed tip; a *green ovary* and *strong lemony fragrance.* Mar.–early May. *Fruits:* Greenish berry-like capsules. *Habitat/range:* Moist nutrient-rich forests, stream banks and flats, often on nearly basic soils. Uncommon (but locally abundant, especially in the Great Smoky Mountains). Mainly in the southern Appalachians from North Carolina and Kentucky south to Georgia and Alabama.

Similar species: Pale yellow trillium (*T. discolor*) has similar flowers but with *spoon-shaped petals widest at the tip* and a *purple ovary.* Late Mar.–early May. Moist forests with nearly basic soils. Rare (restricted to the Savannah River Drainage).

Notes: Trilliums occur naturally across North America and eastern Asia. Of the 50 species in the genus, nearly half occur in the southern Appalachian mountains and adjoining piedmont.

Viola hastata
Halberdleaf Yellow Violet
Violaceae (Violet family)

Perennial herb 2–10 in. tall from a white fleshy rhizome. *Leaves:* Alternate, usually 2–4 *triangular shaped* leaves clustered near the stem tip; upper leaf surfaces often *mottled with silvery gray blotches.* *Flowers:* Bright yellow; borne on slender stalks just above the leaves. Mar.–May. *Fruits:* Elliptic capsules. *Habitat/range:* Moist forests. Common. Eastern United States.

Similar species: Roundleaf yellow violet (*V. rotundifolia*) has *broadly ovate or rounded basal leaves* and bright yellow flowers, with *two bearded lateral petals.* Mar.–Apr. Moist forests. Common.

Notes: More than 80 species of violets (*Viola*) occur in North America, most of which are native. Hybridization between violet species results in intermediate forms that make species identification difficult. Many violets have ballistic seed dispersal; mature seeds are explosively flung 3–15 feet from the parent plant. A lipid-rich food body attached to the seed coat attracts ants, which also disperse the seeds. Violets have a rich folklore; for example, Shakespeare wrote that violets represent humility and loyalty paired with love.

Pedicularis canadensis
Lousewort, Wood Betony
Orobanchaceae (Broomrape family)

Upright, *hairy* perennial herb 6–16 in. tall forms dense colonies from short rhizomes. *Leaves:* In basal clusters and alternate on stems, the latter reduced in size upward; blades *deeply divided* into toothed segments, *fern-like. Flowers:* In dense terminal heads with small leaf-like bracts; with a *2-lipped corolla*, the hood-like upper lip arching over a 3-lobed lower lip, forming a tube-like corolla, *pale yellow to reddish brown.* Apr.–May. *Fruits:* Flattened capsules. *Habitat/range:* Moist to dry forests, woodlands, and meadows. Common. Widespread in eastern North America.

Notes: Lousewort is considered to be a hemiparasite because it produces sugars via photosynthesis and obtains additional water, mineral elements, and nutrients by tapping into the roots of nearby plants. Because this interaction can be detrimental to the host plant (e.g., reducing its growth), lousewort can gain a competitive advantage over its neighbors for various resources including light and space. Herbalists use *Pedicularis* as a muscle relaxant for treating back, neck, and shoulder pain.

Conopholis americana
Bearcorn, Squawroot
Orobanchaceae (Broomrape family)

Yellowish brown *root parasite* with erect stems, 2–8 in. tall and about 1 in. thick, *resemble small ears of corn* popping up through the leaf litter. *Leaves:* The usually clumped stems are covered with numerous brown, fleshy, scale-like leaves that lack chlorophyll. *Flowers:* Yellowish 2-lipped tubular corolla with leaf-like bracts in a dense terminal spike that forms half or more of the stem. Mar.–June. *Fruits:* Ovoid capsules. *Habitat/range: Under or near oaks* in moist to dry forests. Common. Eastern North America.

Notes: Seedlings of this unusual root parasite form a parasitic connection to small oak roots, resulting in the formation of a gall-like mass called a tubercle. From this underground structure, up to a dozen fleshy shoots arise in spring, each densely covered with small tubular flowers that produce grape-sized fruits, each containing about 5,000 tiny seeds. Black bears actively feed on bearcorn in spring and summer and disperse the tiny seeds in their droppings.

Uvularia perfoliata
Perfoliate Bellwort
Colchicaceae (Meadow saffron family)

Hieracium venosum
Rattlesnake Hawkweed
Asteraceae (Sunflower family)

Upright perennial herb 8–16 in. tall that spreads vegetatively via rhizomes forming small colonies. *Leaves:* Alternate, blue green, perfoliate (*stem pierces the leaf*). *Flowers: Lemon yellow* narrowly bell-shaped flowers with look-alike petals and sepals (3 each); nodding singly from the upper leaf axils. Apr.–May. *Fruits:* 3-chambered green capsules. *Habitat/range:* Moist to fairly dry deciduous forests. Common. Eastern North America.

Similar species: Large-flowered bellwort (*U. grandiflora*) has *twisted look-alike sepals and petals* (3 each) that *appear limp*, even when fresh. Apr.–May. Moist nutrient-rich forests. Common. Sessileleaf bellwort (*U. sessilifolia*) has *sessile leaves* that are *not perfoliate*. Mar.–May. Moist deciduous forests. Common.

Notes: Perfoliate bellwort grows under a leafy canopy as well as in forest openings (gaps) where light levels are considerably higher. Bellwort individuals growing in gaps are generally larger and produce more flowers and fruits than individuals growing in the shade. Bumblebees pollinate the flowers, ants disperse the seeds, and deer browse the foliage.

Perennial herb up to 2 ft. tall with 1 to several smooth, mostly leafless stems. *Leaves:* Basal, 2–6 in. long, elliptical to oblanceolate with *distinct purple veins*. *Flowers: Dandelion-like heads* with golden yellow ray petals, each fringed at the tip; disk flowers absent. Apr.–July. *Fruits:* Achenes. *Habitat/range:* Dry open woodlands and forest edges. Common. Throughout the eastern United States.

Notes: Rattlesnake hawkweed occurs as scattered plants or in loose groupings in relatively open areas. A benefit of having a basal rosette of leaves is that it's difficult for grazing animals such as white-tailed deer to eat the leaves. On the other hand, it's easily outcompeted for light by taller plants. The network of purple veins on the leaves has a snakeskin pattern, hence the common name. The plant was also thought to be a cure for rattlesnake bites as the leaves were chewed and applied directly to the wound.

Packera aurea
Golden Ragwort
Asteraceae (Sunflower family)

Smooth-stemmed perennial 1–3 ft. tall with numerous stolons *often forming dense colonies. Leaves: Basal leaves heart shaped at base* with a rounded tip and blunt toothed margins, up to 5 in. long and wide, the *undersides purplish*, on long thin stalks; stem leaves reduced in size, mostly pinnatifid, becoming sessile upward. *Flowers:* Several to many *golden yellow flower heads*, up to 1 in. wide, daisy-like, showy. Apr.–Aug. *Fruits:* Achenes. *Habitat/range:* Moist woods and fields. Common. Widespread in eastern North America. *Senecio aureus.*

Similar species: Roundleaf Ragwort (*P. obovata*) has obovate or nearly round leaves *tapered at the base*. Apr.–June. Common. Wooded slopes, rocky bluffs, often on calcium rich soil. *S. obovatus.*

Notes: Bees and other insects visit the small yellow flower heads of golden ragwort for nectar or pollen. Because species of *Packera* are generally interfertile, hybrid plants often occur where two or more species occur in close proximity. Golden ragwort was used as a "female remedy," including reducing the pain of childbirth.

Oenothera fruticosa
Sundrops
Onagraceae (Evening primrose family)

Perennial herb *1–3 ft. tall. Leaves:* Alternate, lanceolate, 2–3 in. long. *Flowers:* In terminal clusters; each flower includes 4 bright yellow petals up to 1 in. long notched at the tips, a 4-lobed (cross-shaped) stigma, and 8 stamens. Apr.–Sept. *Fruits: Ribbed capsules. Habitat/ range:* Moist to dry woodlands, forest edges, rock outcrops, fields, roadsides, seepage slopes, and spray cliffs. Common. Widespread in eastern North America.

Similar species: Common evening primrose (*O. biennis*) is a short-lived perennial with an erect stem *up to 6 ft. tall*, with stem leaves reduced in size up the stalk. The *flowers open in the evening* (and close the next day), developing into *cylindrical capsules*. June–Oct. Fields, roadsides, and other disturbed sites. Common.

Notes: Most species in the genus *Oenothera* flower in the evening and are pollinated primarily by hawkmoths. Other species, including sundrops, bloom in the morning and are typically pollinated by bees. Sundrops make a great addition to gardens, as it's a hardy plant with showy yellow flowers and a long blooming season.

Lysimachia quadrifolia
Whorled Loosestrife
Myrsinaceae (Myrsine family)

Upright perennial herb 1–3 ft. tall with a smooth to slightly hairy rarely branched stem. *Leaves:* Lanceolate, 2–4 in. long, in widely spreading *whorls of 4–6. Flowers:* Solitary, *yellow, star-shaped corolla,* about ½ in. across with a *reddish center;* on long stalks arising from the leaf axils of upper 2–6 whorls. May–Aug. *Fruits:* Round capsules. *Habitat/range:* Variety of moist to dry forests and openings, usually in full sun. Common. Eastern United States.

Notes: Flowering plants generally attract pollinators with showy flowers, enticing odors, and by offering a food reward in the form of nectar and pollen. Unusually, loosestrife flowers have specialized glands that secrete glistening droplets of oil instead of nectar. Female bees in the genus *Macropsis* function as pollinators as they collect oil and pollen from the flowers, which they mix together into a moistened pollen ball, which becomes food for their developing larvae. Dried loosestrife plants were burned in pioneer houses to produce smoke to drive away gnats, flies, and snakes.

Krigia montana
Mountain Dwarf Dandelion
Asteraceae (Sunflower family)

Herbaceous perennial with *mostly basal leaves,* the individual shoots bearing a single flowering head. *Leaves:* Vary in shape from linear, lance-shaped, or lobed and toothed like a dandelion leaf. *Flowers:* The heads consist solely of ray (no disk) flowers, *bright yellow orange with fringed tips;* the leafy green bracts at the base of the flower head are about the same length as the rays. May–Sept. *Fruits:* Achenes. *Habitat/range:* Moist cliffs, granitic domes, and rocky streamsides. Rare. A southern Appalachian endemic.

Notes: The foliage of mountain dwarf dandelion releases a milky sap in response to injury. Toxins in the sap deter most herbivores from feeding on the plant. Individuals spread vegetatively via root buds, forming colonies. The genus name honors David Krig, a physician and early plant collector.

Coreopsis major
Whorled Coreopsis
Asteraceae (Sunflower family)

Clusters of upright *hairy stems,* 20–40 in. tall, from a long slender rhizome. *Leaves:* Opposite, sessile, *compound leaves, each divided into three narrow leaflets,* giving the appearance of a *whorl of six leaves. Flowers:* Flat-topped heads 1–2 in. across with 7 or more bright yellow ray flowers (outer petals) surrounding yellow (purplish with age) disk flowers. June–Aug. *Fruits:* Black narrowly winged achenes. *Habitat/range:* Dry open woods, fields, and roadsides. Common. Eastern North America.

Notes: Whorled coreopsis grows best in open sunny areas where its showy yellow flower heads attract bees, butterflies, and other insects that sip nectar or harvest pollen from the many tiny flowers within each head. White-tailed deer browse the foliage, and finches, sparrows, and other songbirds feed on the seeds. The first frost of fall turns the entire plant black but new shoots arise the following spring from dormant buds on long slender rhizomes. Whorled coreopsis makes an attractive garden plant due to its showy flowers, long blooming season, and ability to tolerate drought.

Pityopsis graminifolia
Grassleaf Golden Aster
Asteraceae (Sunflower family)

Grass-like perennial herb, 12–36 in. tall, whose leaves and flowering stalks *appear silvery* due to a dense cover of long silky hairs. *Leaves:* Linear with parallel veins, *mostly basal,* up to 12 in. long, reduced upward on stem. *Flowers:* Small heads of *bright yellow ray* and *disk flowers,* several to many, terminating the branches. June–Oct. *Fruits:* Achenes. *Habitat/range:* Dry woodlands and open forests, road banks. Common. Eastern United States, south to Mexico and Central America. *Heterotheca nervosa.*

Notes: By reflecting sunlight, the dense silky hairs moderate leaf temperature and evaporative water loss, a beneficial trait given the dry habitats this aster occupies. Individuals spread vegetatively by underground stems (rhizomes) and by seeds, often forming dense colonies. Vegetative growth and flowering typically increase after fires because a more open canopy increases the amount of light reaching the ground. This low-maintenance, drought-tolerant plant with silvery gray foliage and bright yellow flowers makes a great addition to sunny wildflower gardens.

Smallanthus uvedalius
Bearsfoot, Yellow Leafcup
Asteraceae (Sunflower family)

Coarse perennial herb 3–10 ft. tall; forms dense colonies. *Leaves:* Opposite, triangular to ovate, up to 12 in. long, the *lobes mostly palmate* with winged petioles, upper leaves smaller, lack petioles. *Flowers:* Large, showy flower *heads about 2–3 in. across*, in branching clusters near the stem tip; ray flowers yellow, fertile; disk flowers bright yellow, sterile. July–Sept. *Fruits:* Achenes. *Habitat/range:* Woodland borders and meadows. Common. Widespread in the eastern United States. *Polymnia uvedalia.*

 Notes: This robust plant with numerous large yellow flower heads provides a splash of color in meadows, woodland borders, and other open sunny areas in summer-fall. The flower heads function as a landing platform for bees, butterflies, and other insects that sip nectar or harvest pollen from the numerous flowers within each head. Goldfinches and other birds actively harvest the ripe seeds in fall. The large lobed leaves are said to resemble a bear's paw, hence the common name bearsfoot. Cherokee people used the roots to relieve back pain and rheumatism.

Rudbeckia laciniata
Cutleaf Coneflower
Asteraceae (Sunflower family)

Highly branched perennial 3–8 ft. tall with *smooth stems* arising from slender spreading rhizomes. *Leaves:* Alternate, *deeply cut, 3–5 lobed* lower leaves up to 8 in. long, the upper leaves reduced in size and less dissected. *Flowers:* Showy heads, the *central disk flowers greenish yellow* with drooping yellow ray flowers about 2 in. long. July–Oct. *Fruits:* Achenes. *Habitat/range:* Moist woodlands, stream banks, meadows, forest edges. Common. Widely distributed in North America.

 Notes: This robust plant with multiple stems and showy flowers is a conspicuous component of moist woodland borders and stream banks from late summer to fall. Like many wildflowers, it shows visible signs of damage from exposure to the high ozone levels that frequently characterize the southern Appalachians. Exposure symptoms in cutleaf coneflower include dull red mottled areas between the veins on the upper leaf surface. Goldfinches and other birds glean seeds from the fruiting heads in late summer to fall. Various cultivars are grown as ornamentals and the young leaves can be cooked as greens and are a traditional Cherokee potherb.

Collinsonia canadensis
Canada Horsebalm
Lamiaceae (Mint family)

Solidago curtisii
Curtis's Goldenrod
Asteraceae (Sunflower family)

Robust, aromatic perennial herb 2–4 ft. tall. *Leaves:* 3 or more pairs of large (greater than 4 in. long) coarsely toothed opposite leaves more or less evenly spaced on the stem. *Flowers: Tubular yellow flowers,* about ½ in. long, with a 2-lipped corolla, the lower lip conspicuously fringed with 2 protruding stamens; in terminal branched clusters. July–Oct. *Fruits:* Nutlets. *Habitat/range:* Rich moist woods. Common. Widespread in eastern North America.

Perennial herb 2–3 ft. tall with *angled, finely grooved stems. Leaves:* Alternate, mostly 3–10 times as long as wide, sharply toothed, tapering to an elongated tip and a broader base; the lower stem and basal leaves smaller than the upper leaves and deciduous by flowering time. *Flowers: Yellow,* 5–10 per head; *heads in clusters of 3–15 from the axils of the upper leaves.* Aug.–Oct. *Fruits:* Hairy achenes. *Habitat/ range:* Moist forested slopes. Common. Appalachian Mountains from Pennsylvania south to Georgia.

Similar species: Whorled horsebalm (*C. verticillata*) is less than 2 ft. tall with 2–3 pairs of leaves crowded together on the upper stem, giving a whorled appearance; the pink-tinged flowers have 4 stamens and bloom in late spring to early summer (May–June). Rich moist woods. Occasional.

Similar species: Bluestem Goldenrod (*S. caesia*) has a *round stem, without grooves.* Aug.–Oct. Woodlands. Common. Zigzag Goldenrod (*S. flexicaulis*) has a *conspicuously zigzag stem;* its leaves are ovate, usually less than twice as long as wide, with a *distinct winged petiole.* July–Oct. Woodlands. Common.

Notes: The seeds mature in autumn but don't germinate until spring, as they require an overwintering period prior to germination. The roots have been used as a diuretic. The leaves are thought to improve circulation in the capillaries, which in turn facilitates the healing of wounds. Overharvesting of this medicinal herb is a concern.

Notes: Curtis's goldenrod occurs in the forest understory rather than in open sunny habitats such as roadsides and fields where most goldenrods are found. Species of *Solidago* can be difficult to identify because hybridization is common and plant characteristics within a species can be quite variable.

Verbesina alternifolia
Common Wingstem
Asteraceae (Sunflower family)

Perennial herb 4–10 ft. tall with leafy stems; forms dense colonies via offshoots from underground stems (rhizomes). *Leaves: Alternate, lanceolate*, 4–10 in. long and up to 2½ in. wide with a rough texture; *winged stalks extend down the stem*, hence the common name. *Flowers:* Numerous daisy-like yellow flower heads have a raggedy appearance; each head 1–2 in. across with *2–10 irregularly spaced ray flowers* that droop downward; greenish-yellow disk flowers project outward from the center of the head forming a sphere. Aug.–Oct. *Fruits:* Achenes with broad wings. *Habitat/range:* Floodplain forests, woodland borders, moist thickets. Common. Widespread in eastern North America.

Similar species: Yellow crownbeard (*V. occidentalis*) has *opposite, ovate leaves* with winged stalks that extend down the stem, and numerous large yellow flower heads. Aug.–Oct. Floodplain forests, thickets, fields. Common.

Notes: This tall weedy plant is conspicuous in late summer when its numerous yellow flower heads are in bloom. Various bees and butterflies visit the flowers for nectar or pollen. Adult checkerspot butterflies sip nectar from the flowers, and their larvae (caterpillars) feed on the leaves.

Hamamelis virginiana
Witch Hazel
Hamamelidaceae (Witch hazel family)

A deciduous shrub or small tree with a short trunk and numerous spreading branches. *Leaves:* Alternate, 2–6 in. long, oval to nearly round with *scalloped margins* and an *asymmetrical leaf base*; the cone-shaped galls on the upper leaf surface resemble a witch's hat, hence the common name. *Flowers:* In small, showy axillary clusters with 4 twisted strap-shaped yellow petals. Oct.–Dec. *Fruits:* Two-beaked woody capsules. *Habitat/ range:* Moist woods including stream banks, ravines, and forest openings. Common. Widespread in eastern North America.

Notes: Witch hazel blooms in mid- to late fall, a time when most other plants are dropping their leaves and going dormant. When the temperature and humidity are just right, ripe fruits split open with an audible pop, flinging small black seeds up to 15 feet from the parent plant. Native Americans made bows from the stems. An extract from the bark is used as a lotion for treating muscle aches and bruises. Dowsers locate groundwater using the forked twigs of witch hazel.

Yellowish-Green Flowers

Prosartes lanuginosa
Yellow Mandarin
Liliaceae (Lily family)

Lindera benzoin
Spicebush
Lauraceae (Laurel family)

A multi-stemmed *aromatic* shrub 6–9 ft. tall. *Leaves:* Alternate, pointed at tip, wedge shaped at base; emit a *lemony odor* when crushed; leaves *decrease in size* toward the base of twigs. *Flowers:* Tiny, fragrant yellow-green flowers in axillary clusters appear before the leaves emerge. Mar.–Apr. *Fruits:* Bright red drupes with a spicy odor. *Habitat/range:* Along streams and in moist forests. Common. Widespread in eastern North America.

   Notes: Spicebush is one of the first woody plants to bloom in early spring. The leaves, twigs, and red fruits exude a pleasantly spicy fragrance when crushed. White-tailed deer readily browse the foliage and numerous birds consume the high-energy (lipid-rich) fruits and disperse the seeds. Spicebush is an important larval (caterpillar) food plant for the spicebush swallowtail butterfly. Look for the smooth green caterpillars with 4 eyespots hiding under curled leaves. The bark, leaves, and twigs can be used to make a spicy tea. Spicebush is a great landscape plant on moist nutrient-rich soils.

Upright perennial herb 1–3 ft. tall with branched stems. *Leaves:* Alternate, sessile, ovate to lanceolate, with *prominent veins. Flowers:* Nodding, *yellowish green*, bell shaped, partially hidden under the foliage; similar sepals and petals (3 each) *lack spots.* Apr.–May. *Fruits: Orange-to-reddish* berries. *Habitat/range:* Moist, nutrient-rich deciduous woods, especially cove forests. Common. From Ontario south to Georgia and Alabama, mostly in the Appalachian Mountains. *Disporum lanuginosum.*

   Similar species: Spotted mandarin (*P. maculata*) has *cream-to-white flowers*, speckled with tiny *purplish spots*; its fruits are *3 lobed, white-to-yellowish berries.* Apr.–May. Moist, nutrient-rich deciduous forests, especially cove forests. Occasional. *D. maculatum.*

   Notes: The orange-red fruits really stand out in late summer to fall. Birds and small mammals feed on the fruits and disperse the seeds in their droppings. Fruits not removed by animals fall to the ground, usually directly beneath the parent plant. Seeds in undispersed fruits are unlikely to successfully establish new plants, since the parent plant already occupies the site and seedlings are inferior competitors.

Medeola virginiana
Indian Cucumber Root
Liliaceae (Lily family)

Erect perennial herb, 12–30 in. tall, with tufts of woolly hairs on the stem. *Leaves: 1–2 whorls*; lower whorl of 5–11 leaves, the upper usually with 3 smaller leaves (only flowering plants have an upper whorl). *Flowers:* 1 to several on slender stalks that hang beneath the upper whorl of leaves; flowers *greenish yellow* with 3 long brown thread-like stigmas. Apr.–June. *Fruits:* Dark purplish-black berries on erect stalks above the leaves. *Habitat/range:* Moist forests. Common. Throughout eastern North America.

Notes: Indian cucumber root has small inconspicuous flowers for a species that depends on pollinators for successful fruit and seed set. In this regard, it's not surprising that low flower visitation rates result in pollination failure, which in turn limits seed production. As fruits ripen, the basal portion of their associated leaves turns scarlet. The contrasting colors of the scarlet leaves and the purplish-black fruits in autumn attract fruit-eating birds and mammals that eat the pulp and disperse the seeds in their droppings.

Euonymus americanus
Strawberry Bush, Hearts-a-Bustin'
Celastraceae (Bittersweet family)

A mostly erect deciduous shrub 2–6 (12) ft. tall with smooth *four-angled green stems. Leaves:* Opposite, lanceolate to narrowly ovate, 2–4 in. long, with finely toothed margins and a very short leaf stalk. *Flowers:* Small and inconspicuous with 5 light green petals. May–June. *Fruits: Warty reddish capsules* containing *orange-red seeds. Habitat/range:* Woods, bottomlands, and along streams. Common. Widespread in the eastern United States.

Similar species: Running strawberry bush (*E. obovatus*) is a *low-trailing shrub* with a few ascending branches up to 1 ft. tall. May–June. Moist forests and stream banks. Occasional.

Notes: Strawberry bush often goes unnoticed until fall when the showy reddish capsules split open revealing the orange-red seeds within. Various songbirds, wild turkeys, and white-tailed deer eat the fruits and disperse the seeds. Deer frequently browse the slender green stems and leafy twigs, reducing plant size. Strawberry bush is an interesting addition to woodland gardens.

Aralia racemosa
Spikenard
Araliaceae (Ginseng family)

Widely branched smooth-stemmed perennial herb 3–5 ft. tall from a large aromatic root. *Leaves:* Several, *alternate, pinnately compound* leaves up to 2 ft. long with 9–21 coarse, heart-shaped leaflets 2–6 in. long with sharp tips. *Flowers: Tiny, greenish white* in numerous small umbels arranged in *long terminal panicles.* June–Aug. *Fruits:* Dark purple berries in large clusters. *Habitat/range:* Nutrient-rich moist woods. Common. Widespread in eastern North America.

Similar species: Wild sarsaparilla (*A. nudicaulis*) is a smaller plant (about 2 ft. tall) with a *single basal compound leaf* with 3 primary forks; greenish flowers usually in 3 small umbels on a *separate stalk* about 8 in. tall. May–July. Nutrient-rich woods. Infrequent.

Notes: Bees and wasps visit the tiny greenish-white flowers for nectar or pollen and function as pollinators. Various songbirds as well as mammals such as red fox, striped skunk, and eastern chipmunk eat the purple berries and disperse the seeds in their droppings. White-tailed deer browse the foliage. The fragrant roots have been used to flavor teas and root beer.

Laportea canadensis
Wood Nettle
Urticaceae (Nettle family)

Multi-stemmed perennial herb to 3 ft. tall; stems and leaves covered with *stinging hairs. Leaves:* Alternate, broadly ovate, 3–6 in. long with coarsely toothed margins. *Flowers: Greenish or greenish white*; female flowers at the base of the upper leaves and on top of the plant; male flowers in clusters at the base of the leaves lower on the stem. June–Aug. *Fruits:* Achenes. *Habitat/range:* Nutrient-rich moist woods, stream banks, floodplains. Common. Widespread in eastern North America.

Similar species: False nettle (*Boehmeria cylindrica*) *lacks stinging hairs,* has *opposite* rather than alternate leaves, and forms dense clusters of tiny greenish flowers in arching spikes. June–Aug. Moist woodlands and streams. Common.

Notes: Stinging hairs on the stems and leaves of wood nettle penetrate bare skin (and thin pants) on contact, causing a painful stinging sensation that lasts several minutes. Crushed leaves of jewelweed (*Impatiens)* or dock (*Rumex)* relieve the nettle's sting. Dense patches of wood nettle overtop other wildflowers in rich moist forests by midsummer.

Ambrosia artemisiifolia
Common Ragweed
Asteraceae (Sunflower family)

Angelica triquinata
Mountain Angelica
Apiaceae (Carrot family)

Perennial herb 2–5 ft. tall with a *smooth and rather stout purplish stem. Leaves:* Pinnately or bipinnately divided with coarsely serrate leaflets; the leaves progressively smaller toward the shoot tip. *Flowers:* Tiny, greenish yellow and densely packed in large terminal compound umbels about 3–6 in. across. July–Sept. *Fruits:* Flattened capsules (schizocarps) with 2 lateral wings. *Habitat/ range:* Mesic forests, grassy balds, open rocky slopes, and stream banks at higher elevations. Common. Appalachian Mountains from Pennsylvania south to Georgia.

Similar species: Hairy angelica (*A. venenosa*) has downy stems, inflorescences, and fruits. June-Aug. Woodland borders and roadsides. Common.

Notes: Various insects visit the flowers for nectar or pollen, while others seek a mate, or simply a resting place to bask in the sun. Based on their erratic behavior, bees appear to get intoxicated while foraging for nectar from the flowers. For example, it's not uncommon to see a dozen or more bees bumbling into each other while crawling about the flowers.

Weedy annual with branched stems up to 6 ft. tall. *Leaves:* Opposite on lower stem, *alternate on upper stem;* 2–4 in. long, *deeply dissected,* fragrant when crushed. *Flowers: Greenish male flowers with yellow pollen sacs in spike-like clusters that* terminate the stem and upper branches; female flower heads single or in small clusters in upper leaf axils below the more conspicuous male flowers. Aug.-frost. *Fruits:* Beaked achenes. *Habitat/ range:* Disturbed areas, including fields, roadsides, and gardens. Common. Widespread in North America and much of the world.

Similar species: Giant ragweed (*A. trifida*) has *all opposite leaves* with *3–5 large, pointed, palmate lobes.* Sept.-frost. Disturbed areas near rivers. Common.

Notes: Ragweed is a bane of late summer-fall hay fever sufferers. Ragweed produces enormous amounts of airborne pollen whose surfaces contain proteins that cause sneezing, watery eyes, and breathing difficulties for people sensitive to it. Unfortunately, there is little relief in sight as widespread disturbance continually creates favorable habitat for ragweed. In addition, increasing atmospheric CO_2 levels, a longer growing season, and warmer temperatures cause increased pollen production in ragweed.

Orange to Red Flowers

Silene virginica
Fire Pink
Caryophyllaceae (Pink family)

Upright perennial herb 12–30 in. tall with *sticky stems. Leaves:* Basal 3–5 in. long on stalks; 2–4 pairs of stem leaves that are opposite, sessile, and narrow. *Flowers: Scarlet red*, 1–2 in. wide; *5 petals deeply notched at the tip.* Apr.–July. *Fruits:* Elliptic capsules that tip downward at maturity to release the seeds. *Habitat/range:* Woodlands, rocky slopes, crevices in cliffs, road banks. Common. Widely distributed in eastern North America.

Notes: A poor competitor, fire pink typically grows in areas where the ground-layer vegetation is relatively sparse. It's a classic hummingbird pollinated plant with tubular red flowers producing abundant nectar, without fragrance, nectar guides, or a landing platform. The long corolla tube generally limits flower visitors to those with long tongues. The sticky hairs on the tubular calyx also deter nonpollinating crawling insects from obtaining nectar. However, bees sometimes chew holes at the bases of flowers and rob them of nectar. Its long flowering season and spectacular scarlet red flowers add color to wildflower gardens.

Rhododendron calendulaceum
Flame Azalea
Ericaceae (Heath family)

Deciduous shrub up to 10 ft. tall and 15 ft. wide that flowers *before the leaves are fully expanded. Leaves:* Alternate but mostly *crowded toward stem tips,* 2–4 in. long, pointed at apex, wedge-shaped at base, woolly hairy beneath. *Flowers:* Terminal clusters of slightly fragrant *bright orange, yellow, or red tubular corollas* with 5 spreading lobes; 5 long reddish stamens and a solitary stigma extending well beyond the petals. Late Apr.–July. *Fruits:* Persistent hairy capsules. *Habitat/range:* Dry to moist open woods. Common. Mostly Appalachian Mountains, from Pennsylvania south to Georgia.

Similar species: Cumberland azalea (*R. cumberlandense*) has bright orange-red *flowers that open after the leaves have fully expanded* and the *sepals lack glandular hairs.* June. Mountain slopes and ridgetops. Occasional.

Notes: Flame azalea is one of our most beautiful and widely cultivated native azaleas. Its dense clusters of bright orange-to-red flowers create the impression of fire in the forest understory, hence the common name. The various flower color morphs partially reflect past hybridization with other native azaleas.

Impatiens capensis
Orange Jewelweed
Balsaminaceae (Touch-me-not family)

Fleshy annual 2–5 ft. tall with *smooth hollow stems*, often forming dense colonies in moist open areas. *Leaves:* Alternate, ovate to elliptic, 1–4 in. long with gently scalloped margins. *Flowers: Orange yellow* with reddish-brown spots, about 1 in. long, forming a funnel-shaped sac that ends in a *curled spur*; May–frost. *Fruits:* Elongate, narrow green capsules. *Habitat/range:* Moist forests, stream banks, roadsides. Common. Widespread in eastern and central North America.

Similar species: Yellow jewelweed (*I. pallida*) has bright *yellow flowers*. July–Oct. Moist forests, stream banks, and forest edges. Common.

Notes: The common name jewelweed refers to droplets from rain and dew, which bead up on the leaves and sparkle in the sun, producing jewel-like reflections. Hummingbirds and bumblebees actively visit the nectar-rich flowers. Ripe seeds occur within a tightly coiled capsule that bursts open when touched, scattering seeds up to 9 ft. away (try touching a mature fruit to elicit this response!). Freshly crushed leaf stalks soothe the itch and rash caused by poison ivy.

Lilium superbum
Turk's Cap Lily
Liliaceae (Lily family)

Perennial herb *4–8 ft. tall* with stout erect stems often bearing *numerous nodding flowers*. *Leaves:* Mostly in *whorls* of 5 to 20 lance-shaped leaves up to 7 in. long, tapering at both ends, becoming alternate on the upper stem. *Flowers:* Large (3–4 in. across), showy, *orange to red* and densely *spotted with purple*; a distinguishing *green "star" inside the flower tube*; the sepals and petals flare outward and then *recurve strongly*. July–Aug. *Fruits:* Angular capsules up to 2 in. long. *Habitat/range:* Moist open woods, meadows, trailside thickets. Common. Eastern North America.

Notes: One of our most spectacular wildflowers, Turk's cap lily can reach heights of 8 ft. and bear a dozen or more large, showy flowers that attract numerous swallowtail butterflies that sip nectar and function as pollinators. Without these butterflies, there would probably be no Turk's cap lily, as cross-pollination is necessary for seed production. White-tailed deer browse the shoot tips, hindering plant growth and preventing flower and fruit production for that year.

Lobelia cardinalis
Cardinal Flower
Campanulaceae (Bellflower family)

Upright perennial herb with 1 to several unbranched stems 2–4 ft. tall. *Leaves:* Alternate, lanceolate, 2–6 in. long with coarsely toothed margins; a rosette of basal leaves persists over winter. *Flowers:* Intensely *red or scarlet tubular flowers* with a 2-lipped corolla in a *showy terminal raceme*; it's the only red-flowered *Lobelia* in the southern Appalachians. July–Oct. *Fruits:* Roundish capsules. *Habitat/range:* Stream banks, wet meadows, bogs, roadside ditches. Common. Widely distributed in eastern North America.

    Notes: The brilliant red-to-scarlet flowers attract numerous hummingbirds whose long tongues extend well past their bills, giving them access to nectar at the base of the tubular flowers. Long-tongued butterflies, especially swallowtails, also sip nectar from the flowers and function as pollinators. White-tailed deer and other mammals usually don't eat the foliage because of toxic white latex in the sap. Native Americans used this plant to treat various ailments, including stomachache, colds, and syphilis. The deep red flowers make a spectacular addition to gardens.

Monarda didyma
Crimson Bee Balm
Lamiaceae (Mint family)

Perennial herb 2½–5 ft. tall; like most members of the mint family, it has a square stem, opposite leaves, and pungent foliage. *Leaves:* Lanceolate to ovate, 3–6 in. long with serrate margins; the leaves on the upper stem often tinged with red. *Flowers:* Terminal whorl of showy 2-lipped, *scarlet-to-crimson flowers*, 1–1½ in. long, subtended by *showy, reddish bracts*. July–Oct. *Fruits:* Nutlets. *Habitat/range:* Seepage slopes, stream banks, boggy places, and roadside ditches. Common. A mostly northeastern species, south in the Appalachian Mountains to North Carolina and Georgia.

    Notes: Hummingbirds are the most common and probably most effective pollinator of this plant. As they move from flower to flower harvesting nectar, yellow pollen accumulates on their foreheads. When a flower's stigma brushes against the pollen mass, successful pollination typically occurs. Other native plants that attract hummingbirds include cardinal flower, orange jewelweed, crossvine, trumpet vine, and coral honeysuckle.

Glossary

Terms marked with an asterisk (*) are illustrated at the back of the book, after the index.

Achene: A small dry single-seeded fruit.

Acidic soil: A soil with a pH less than 7.0.

Acuminate: Tapering to a point, as the tip of a leaf.

Aerial rootlets: Small roots produced on stems, as in English ivy.

Alluvial soil: A fertile soil deposited by water flowing over floodplains.

*Alternate leaves: Leaves arranged singly along the stem.

Annual: A plant that germinates, flowers, sets seed, and dies in one year or less.

*Anther: The pollen-bearing part of a stamen.

Basic soil: A soil with a pH greater than 7.0; an alkaline soil.

Berry: A fleshy or pulpy fruit with several to many seeds within, as in a tomato.

Biennial: A plant that lives two years, generally producing a basal rosette of leaves the first year, and flowers and fruits the second.

Bottomland: Low-lying land along streams and rivers, in contrast to upland.

Bract: A leaf-like structure usually near the base of a flower or an inflorescence.

Browse: Leaves, twigs, and young shoots of woody plants used as food by deer and other animals.

Bulb: An underground food-storage organ composed of overlapping fleshy scales, such as an onion.

Cache: Seeds and other food items stored by certain animals for later consumption.

Calcareous: Soils that contain large amounts of calcium carbonate, usually from limestone.

*Calyx: The outermost whorl of a flower consisting of sepals; usually green.

Canopy: The uppermost layer of a forest, consisting of the branches and leaves of the taller trees.

Capsule: A dry fruit that splits open at maturity into two or more sections, as in azaleas.

Cascade: A small waterfall or series of waterfalls.

Cathartic: A natural laxative, as found in some fruits.

Catkin: An inflorescence consisting of a dense spike of apetalous unisexual flowers, as in willows and birches.

Chestnut blight: The widespread loss of American chestnut as a dominant canopy tree in the first half of the twentieth century due to a pathogenic fungus.

Circumneutral: A soil that is neither strongly acidic nor basic, as the soil pH is near 7.0; such soils are usually relatively high in calcium, magnesium, or both.

Cleistogamous species: Plants that produce two types of flowers—small self-pollinating flowers that don't open (cleistogamous flowers) and larger flowers that open and are potentially cross-pollinated (chasmogamous flowers).

Climax community: A stable mature community that persists until natural or human-caused disturbance significantly alters it.

Clone: A genetically identical individual resulting from vegetative reproduction.

Closed cone: A long-lived cone that remains closed until the heat of fire causes the cone to open and release the seeds, as in table mountain pine.

Cobbles: Small, stream-rounded rocks.

Community: An assemblage of species that occur together.

Compound leaf: A leaf divided into two or more leaflets.

Conifer: A cone-bearing (rather than flowering) tree or shrub such as pine, spruce, and fir.

*Cordate: Heart-shaped.

Corm: A short vertical underground stem.

*Corolla: Collective name for the petals of a flower.

Cross-pollination: The transfer of pollen from the anthers of one plant to a stigma of another plant.

Crown: The top part of a tree.

Crown fire: A fire that burns the treetops, jumping from one tree to another.

Cuticle: The waxy layer on the surface of a leaf or stem.

Deciduous: Plants that shed their leaves at the end of the growing season.

Defoliation: The shedding or loss of leaves due to herbivory, drought, or other factors.

Dioecious: Refers to species that have male and female flowers on separate plants.

Diploid: Plants that have two sets of chromosomes.

Disjunct: Refers to populations of the same species occurring in widely separated geographic areas.

*Disk flower: A tubular flower in sunflower heads.

*Elliptic: Broadest near the middle, tapering at both ends.

Endemic: Restricted to a relatively small geographic area.

Ephemeral: Lasting a short time.

Epiphyte: A plant that grows upon another plant but doesn't derive water or nutrients from it, as in a moss growing on a tree trunk.

Evergreen: Having green leaves throughout the year, not deciduous.

Exotic: A nonnative species introduced from elsewhere.

Extra-floral nectary: A nectar-producing gland that isn't associated with a flower.

Floodplain: Low-lying land along streams and rivers that is periodically flooded.

Flora: The plant species that occur in a particular place.

Follicle: A dry fruit that splits down one side when ripe, like a milkweed pod.

Frond: A fern leaf.

Frugivore: An animal that eats fruits.

Fruit set: The transition of flower to fruit.

Gall: An abnormal growth caused by an insect, as often occurs on oak leaves.

Gap: A small to large opening in the vegetation.

Genus: A group of related species (plural: genera).

Glabrous: Smooth, without hairs.

Glade: A relatively open grassy area within a woodland or forest.

Graze: Animal feeding on grass and other low-growing plants.

Habitat: The environment where an organism lives.

Hardwood: A general term that refers to broad-leaved flowering trees.

Haustorium: A specialized structure by which a parasite penetrates and draws nutrients from a host plant.

*Head: A dense cluster of sessile or nearly sessile flowers, as in sunflowers.

Heath shrub: Shrubs in the heath family (Ericaceae) such as rhododendron and blueberry.

Hemiparasite: A parasitic plant that produces sugars via photosynthesis and which obtains water and nutrients from a host plant.

Herb: A plant that lacks a persistent aboveground woody stem.

Herbaceous: Refers to nonwoody plants.

Herbivore: An animal that feeds on plants.

Host: A plant that provides nourishment to a parasite.

Hybrid: The offspring from a cross between parent plants of different species.

Inflorescence: A cluster of flowers.

Introduced: A species that occurs in a geographic area outside its native range; also known as a nonindigenous, alien, or exotic species.

*Lanceolate: Lance-shaped, several times longer than wide, broadest at base, tapering to apex.

Leaf axil: The upper angle between a leaf and a stem.

Leaf blade: The wide flat portion of a leaf.

Leaflet: A single segment of a compound leaf.

Legume: A dry fruit that splits along two sutures, characteristic of plants in the legume or bean (Fabaceae) family.

Lichen: A composite organism consisting of a fungus and either a green alga or cyanobacterium.

Masting: Refers to trees that produce large seed crops in some years interspersed with years in which relatively few seeds are produced, as in oaks and hickories.

Mesic: Habitats of moderate moisture as opposed to xeric (dry) or hydric (wet).

Mesophyte: A plant that lives in moderately moist soils.

Microclimate: The climate of a small localized area which may be different from that of the general area.

Midrib: The main rib or vein of a leaf or other organ.

Monoecious: Refers to species that have separate male and female flowers on the same plant.

Mycorrhiza: A mutualistic relationship between certain soil fungi and the roots of a plant.

Nectar: The sugary liquid produced in flowers that attracts insects and other potential pollinators.

Nectar guide: Lines, spots, or odors that help direct potential pollinators to where the nectar is located within a flower.

Nectar spur: A slender tubular or sac-like extension of the flower that bears nectar.

Nectary: A nectar-secreting gland.

Nitrogen fixation: The conversion of atmospheric nitrogen into a compound that can be used by plants, usually either ammonium or nitrate.

Node: The point on the stem where leaves and branches emerge.

Nutlet: A small nut or nut-like fruit.

Oblanceolate: Lance or spear-shaped with the broadest part above the middle.

Old-growth forest: Forests that have reached sufficient age to resemble the composition and structure of native forests prior to European settlement. They vary by forest type but generally include more large trees, canopy layers, standing snags, and native species than do young or intensively managed forests.

*Opposite leaves: A pair of leaves that grow directly across from each other on the stem.

Outcrop: Bedrock that is exposed and protruding through the soil.

*Ovary: The expanded basal portion of the pistil that contains the ovules (potential seeds).

*Ovate: Egg-shaped in outline with the widest point at the base.

*Palmately compound: A compound leaf in which the leaflets radiate out from a single point.

Parasitic plant: A plant that obtains part or all of its nutrients from another living organism to which it's attached.

Pendant: Hanging or drooping downward.

Perennial: A plant that lives three or more years.

*Petal: An individual segment of a corolla.

Petiole: The stalk of a leaf.

*Pinnately compound: A compound leaf in which the leaflets are arranged along a common axis.

Pinnatifid: A leaf that is divided or cleft in a pinnate fashion but not separated into leaflets.

Pioneer species: Refers to plants that often colonize newly disturbed areas.

Pistil: The female part of a flower consisting of a stigma, style, and ovary.

Plant community: A group of plants within a particular area that form a relatively uniform patch that is distinguishable from neighboring patches of different vegetation types.

Pollination: The transfer of pollen from the anther to the stigma of a flower.

Prescribed burn: The controlled use of fire by land managers to maintain the health of forests and other naturally occurring vegetation types that benefit from periodic fire.

Pubescent: Covered with hairs.

*Raceme: An unbranched elongate inflorescence with flowers on stalks.

Rachis: The central axis of an inflorescence or compound leaf.

*Ray flower: A strap-shaped flower in sunflower heads.

Rhizome: A horizontal underground stem from which shoots and roots emerge.

Riffle: A rocky or shallow part of a stream with rough water.

Rosette: A circular cluster of leaves usually at or near ground level.

Sapling: A small tree.

Self-pollination: The transfer of pollen from the anthers to a stigma on the same plant.

*Sepal: A segment of the calyx, usually green.

*Serrate: A saw-like margin, with the teeth directed forward.

Shade intolerant: A species that grows well in the open or as a member of the forest canopy, but which dies out in densely shaded habitats.

Shade tolerant: A species that can survive and reproduce in shaded habitats such as in the forest understory.

Shrub: A woody plant usually with multiple stems that is shorter than a typical tree.

*Simple leaf: A single leaf not divided into leaflets.

Spadix: A spike with small flowers on a fleshy axis.

Spathe: A large bract subtending or partially enclosing an inflorescence, as in Jack-in-the-pulpit.

Species richness: Refers to the number of species in a given area or community.

*Spike: An unbranched elongate inflorescence with sessile flowers.

Spring ephemerals: Wildflowers with a short growing season that emerge in late winter or early spring and then die back after the canopy trees leaf out, persisting underground the rest of the year.

*Stamen: The pollen-bearing organ of a flower, consisting of an anther and a filament.

*Stigma: The pollen-receptive tip of the pistil.

Stolon: A horizontal aboveground stem that roots at the nodes.

Subshrub: A low-growing shrub, slightly woody at the base.

Succulent: A plant with thick water-storing stems or leaves.

Taproot: A main root from which smaller root branches arise.

Tendril: A slender twining structure used for climbing or support, as in greenbriers.

Tetraploid: A plant with four sets of chromosomes.

Topkill: When the above ground parts of a plant die back due to fire, wind, logging, or other factors.

Trailing: A plant that runs along the soil or leaf litter surface, such as some vines.

Transpiration: The loss of water (in vapor form) from plants mostly through stomatal pores on the leaves.

Tree: A large woody plant usually with a single main stem or trunk.

Trifoliate: A compound leaf with three leaflets.

*Umbel: A flat-topped or rounded inflorescence in which the flower stalks arise from a common point, as in members of the carrot family.

Understory: Refers to the plants growing under the forest canopy, including smaller trees, shrubs, and herbs.

Unisexual: A flower (or plant) that has either male or female reproductive parts but not both.

Vine: A weak-stemmed climbing or trailing plant that uses other plants (or structures) for support.

Waterfall: A place where flowing water rapidly drops in elevation as it flows over a steep region or cliff.

*Whorled: Refers to three or more structures (e.g., leaves, flowers, or fruits) that arise from a common point.

Wildflower: Can refer to any flowering plant that occurs in the wild, but is often applied to herbaceous (nonwoody) flowering plants.

Windthrow: Refers to trees knocked down by high winds.

Xeric: Refers to dry environments.

Index of Wildflowers Profiled

Basic Plant Structures

INFLORESCENCE TYPE

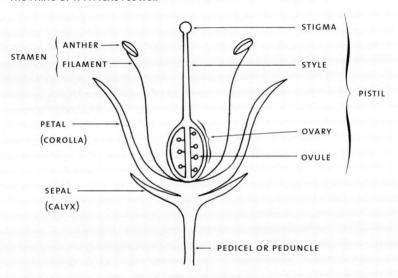

FLOWER SOLITARY   SPIKE   RACEME   UMBEL

THE PARTS OF A TYPICAL FLOWER

STIGMA

STAMEN

ANTHER

FILAMENT

STYLE

PISTIL

PETAL
(COROLLA)

OVARY

OVULE

SEPAL
(CALYX)

← PEDICEL OR PEDUNCLE

INFLORESCENCE OF A COMPOSITE (DAISY HEAD)

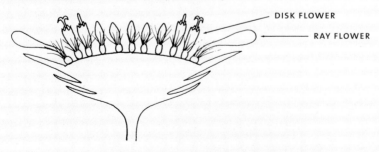

DISK FLOWER

RAY FLOWER

LEAF TYPE

| SIMPLE | PINNATELY COMPOUND | BIPINNATELY COMPOUND | PALMATELY COMPOUND |

LEAF ARRANGEMENT

| OPPOSITE | ALTERNATE | WHORLED | BASAL |

LEAF SHAPE

| LANCEOLATE | ELLIPTIC | OVATE | CORDATE |

LEAF MARGIN

| ENTIRE | SERRATE | DENTATE | LOBED |

About the Author

Lisa K. Wagner

Tim Spira's love for nature began in the mountains of California, where he studied alpine gentians as a graduate student and did rare plant surveys for the U.S. Forest Service. Since completing a Ph.D. in botany at the University of California, Berkeley, Tim has shared his passion for plants with students and colleagues for nearly 30 years, including 10 years as a faculty member at Georgia Southern University and 20 years at Clemson University, where he's taught a variety of courses, including field botany, plant ecology, and natural history. Tim enjoys hiking, bicycling, gardening, and traveling to natural areas throughout the world, as well as exploring wildflowers and waterfalls in the southern Appalachian Mountains. He's published numerous papers in scientific journals and his photographs have appeared in books, scientific journals, and magazines. Most recently, he's the author of the award-winning book *Wildflowers and Plant Communities of the Southern Appalachian Mountains and Piedmont: A Naturalist's Guide to the Carolinas, Virginia, Tennessee, and Georgia*. Tim and his wife, Lisa Wagner, (along with their dog Woody) live in Asheville, North Carolina.

Other **Southern Gateways Guides** you might enjoy

Exploring Southern Appalachian Forests

An Ecological Guide to 30 Great Hikes in the Carolinas, Georgia, Tennessee, and Virginia

STEPHANIE B. JEFFRIES AND
THOMAS R. WENTWORTH

Seeing the forest as well as the trees

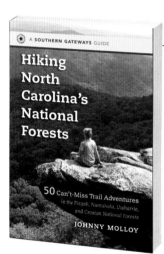

Hiking North Carolina's National Forests

50 Can't-Miss Trail Adventures in the Pisgah, Nantahala, Uwharrie, and Croatan National Forests

JOHNNY MOLLOY

Hiking all four national forests in North Carolina, from the mountains to the sea

Wildflowers and Plant Communities of the Southern Appalachian Mountains and Piedmont

A Naturalist's Guide to the Carolinas, Virginia, Tennessee, and Georgia

TIMOTHY P. SPIRA

A habitat approach to identifying plants and interpreting nature